Jason O'Hare.
25-12·95

D0306001

THE NEMESIS FILE

PAUL BRUCE

BLAKE

Published by Blake Publishing Ltd,
98-100 Great North Road,
London, N2 0NL, England

First published in Great Britain in 1995

ISBN 1 85782 135 1

All rights reserved. No part of this publication may be
reproduced, stored in a retrieval system, or in any form or
by any means, without the prior permission in writing of the
publisher, nor be otherwise circulated in any form of binding
or cover other than that in which it is published and without
a similar condition including this condition being imposed
on the subsequent purchaser.

British Library Cataloguing-in-Publication Data:
A catalogue record for this book is available
from the British Library.

Typeset by Pearl Graphics

Printed by England by Clays Ltd, St Ives plc

1 3 5 7 9 10 8 6 4 2

© Text Bruce/Davies 1995

© Back cover definition of nemesis reproduced by kind permission of
Oxford University Press from *The Shorter Oxford English Dictionary*,
edited by C. T. Onions, 1964

Maps reproduced from the 1989 Ordnance Survey Sheet 14/Sheet 20
with the permission of the Controller of Her Majesty's Stationery Office
© Crown Copyright

This book is dedicated to lasting peace
in Ireland

CONTENTS

GLOSSARY

APC	Armoured Personnel Carrier
ASM	Articifer Sergeant-Major
BBC	British Broadcasting Corporation
CO	Commanding Officer
CS Gas	tear gas
CSM	Company Sergeant-Major
HGV	heavy goods vehicle
HQ	Headquarters
JCB	mechanical digger
KF shirt	Khaki coloured army shirt
GOC	General Officer Commanding
LMG	light machine gun
Millies	9 mm pistols
MI5	British Intelligence (domestic)
MI6	British Intelligence (overseas)
MRF	Military Reconnaissance Force (see Smerfs)
NAAFI	army canteen
NCO	Non-Commissioned Officer

PE	physical education
PT	physical training
RCT	Royal Corps of Transport
RUC	Royal Ulster Constabulary
REME	Royal Electrical and Mechanical Engineers
RP NCO	Regimental Police Non-Commissioned Officer
SD (caps)	Service Drill caps
SLR	self-loading rifle
Smerfs	IRA informants known formally as MRFs (Military Reconnaissance Force)
SMG	sub-machine gun
Special Branch	Police Intelligence
UDR	Ulster Defence Regiment
WO	Warrant Officer

CHAPTER ONE

A LOVE OF soldiering must run in our family. After the Second World War my father would talk to me about his exploits as a member of the famous Long Range Desert Group, those legendary heroes who patrolled North Africa harassing German supply lines. His stories always excited me and made me yearn for the day when I would be old enough to join the army too.

My first recollection of my father is of a big, powerful man, a stranger in army uniform, walking into our house and taking command of the place, ordering my mother, sister and me about. I was frightened of him from the start – and would soon have reason to be.

My father never seemed to like me and for no reason at all would hit me, frequently and hard. Even today, 40-odd years later, my recollections are of waiting for him to come home, waiting for him to slap me and knock me off a chair or into a corner. He never seemed to want me around and I would spend most of the time when he was at home in my room, alone.

My mother never seemed to have time for me either. She was always busy; always rushing about. She would spend time laughing with my elder sister but never with me. She did not abuse me but just didn't seem to want me around, as though I was surplus to requirements. However, times were hard and life would have been difficult for my mother who had had to take care of everything because my father was away in the army for most of those early years.

After the war, when the Long Range Desert Group was disbanded, my father was retained by the army and served in the Far East, in Borneo and Malaysia. It wasn't until I was five years old that he was demobbed and came home for good, back to his old job of driving lorries.

With my father back home, the family grew as my mother bore two more daughters and two more sons. No wonder she felt she had had enough of having kids — her first had been born when she was only sixteen, the last when she was 36! She had only ever wanted two!

I loved listening to stories of my father's time in the army. One of my favourites was of the days when he was in the Long Range Desert Group. They would drive hundreds of miles, searching out German positions, before attempting to blow up the enemy oil and arms dumps and supply routes. As he explained to me, they could not cope with prisoners and would do all in their power to avoid finding themselves in a position where they might have to take any.

On one occasion, however, they were driving their Jeeps in convoy when they came over the brow of a hill and into a wadi. There, in front of them, was the enemy — about forty infantry troops who had spent the night resting in the river bed. There was no way to escape and my father thought that this was the end, that they would be captured and probably killed. There were only twelve men in their unit. The odds were enormous.

To my father's amazement, however, the German troops immediately raised their hands, eager to surrender. They were calling out 'Tommy, Tommy, comrade' before the British Jeeps had come to a halt in their midst.

The Germans seemed desperate to surrender but my father's group could not take them prisoner. They had no food for hungry men, little water and the idea of marching forty enemy troops perhaps hundreds of miles through the desert was unthinkable. Besides, they were under orders never to take any prisoners; it wasn't their function.

My father and the other sergeants had no idea what to do. If they left the Germans in the river bed and drove off, their position and direction would be known, their mission ruined. There could be only one answer. They told the Germans that they would have to surrender their weapons and made them leave their rifles and revolvers in a pile and then walk to the other side of the wadi with their hands on top of their heads. Then they told them to face the rising sun. Four of my father's group picked up machine guns, inserted the magazines and then shot every single one of them. Dad told me that he could never forget it; that he hated doing it but they were in the middle of a war, they had no option. That story, which I am sure was true, instilled in me a profound and lasting respect for my father and not a little fear.

Another story was of another occasion during the war when Dad was convinced he would die. His group was about to blow up a large German petrol store. They had laid the explosives and were leaving the barbed wire enclave when a German sentry, on his inspection round, stopped for a cigarette immediately in front of my father and two of his mates. He could have been only a few feet from them; they could even hear him breathing in the stillness of the desert night. For three minutes he stood there smoking while they tried desperately to hold their breath, fearful of betraying their position. If that sentry had turned to face them, he could not have failed to see them. They were ready to shoot if necessary but that was the last thing they wanted to do as they knew there were at least twenty more German soldiers on the site, but they could not get close enough to him to take him out silently. Finally, after what my father said seemed like a lifetime, the sentry threw away his cigarette butt and continued on his way.

Despite the bad times, he obviously missed the excitement of the Desert Group. He would speak with pride about their exploits in blowing up dumps and ammunition supplies, engaging in the occasional gun battle with pursuing German troops, the narrow escapes and the life they had led in the desert. I would plead with him to repeat these *ad infinitum* and their effect was to make me long to grow up and join the army myself. I couldn't wait to be old enough to sign on and experience the excitement and adventures that he had known. For me, however, it wouldn't be like that but I wasn't to know.

After the war ended, my father discovered that he could never rekindle that wartime sense of commitment, coupled with the belief that he was helping, in his small way, to win the war. He never liked the jungles of the Far East the way he had developed an affection for the open desert, despite the scorching sun and the terrible sandstorms from which there was no real protection. He would hardly ever talk about his active service in Malaysia, as though he wanted to forget that period of his life. There was nothing of the pride he always showed when talking of the men he had served with in the desert. That was his war, his manhood, his life. Nothing could, or would, ever equal that.

As a result, he found life in civvy street very difficult and it became all but impossible for him to hold down a job. He thought all his work boring and tiresome and found driving an overladen lorry along the crowded North Circular road a poor comparison to the freedom of those war years spent driving hundreds of miles through empty desert. Every few months he would quit his job in anger, the frustration tearing him apart. Then he would go on a drinking bout and become a different man. It was on those occasions that I feared him most for he would be unable to control himself and would take it out on me, his eldest son. Now, after my own experiences in the army, I can understand the pressures that he fought against, the reasons why he drank and why he would inevitably end up hitting me. But I didn't understand then, and my memories are of being afraid.

One day, when I was about nine years old, I learned about the other side of war – death.

I remember coming down to breakfast one day and seeing my father sitting in a chair with his head in his hands. He was making a groaning noise and his shoulders were hunched up and shaking. I had no idea what was happening. He didn't look at me and he didn't say anything. I stared at him for a minute or so and then I realised that he was crying and the emotion was shaking his body. However, my father's tears and sobbing seemed very different from the tears I had seen my mother shed. There was anger in him, a frustration which he could not control and which I could not then understand.

It transpired that his younger brother, my Uncle Stanley, had died in North Korea, shot out of the sky while parachuting behind enemy lines. The house was silent; no one uttered a sound; we just watched

Dad crying, furious, his eyes violent and a single word coming from his lips over and over again, 'Why, why, why?'

At lunch time he went out and I did not see him again for a day and a half. I think he went on a bender but I remember my mother saying it was best for him to get it out of his system. She knew it was better for him to bury his anger and his violence in drink than try to bottle it up and then take it out on us.

This episode left me in no doubt about what I wanted to do with my life. From that moment I just wanted to grow up, join the army, become a parachutist and kill as many Koreans as possible.

I don't really remember having a close relationship with my mother. She would simply give me my food, tell me what to wear, tell me what to do and tell me to behave myself. I can, however, remember her saying at least five or six times a day, 'Wait till your father gets home. He'll give you a good hiding.' What seems odd, though, is that I can't really remember ever doing much wrong because most of the time I kept myself very much to myself and away from my mother and brothers and sisters. I became a bit of a loner.

There were some incidents from my childhood that I have always remembered. I smile about them now, although I didn't smile at the time.

My first vivid memory of excitement tinged with fear dates from when I was only two years old. My sister Jan, who was seven years older than me, would be told to take me with her down to the shops whenever my mother asked her to do some shopping. I would be put in the pushchair and my sister, under duress, would have to take me with her.

Just for sport, she would always let go of the pushchair when we came to the brow of a hill, about 50 yards from the shops. She would run beside the pushchair as I screamed at her, not knowing what would happen next. Of course, when the pushchair began picking up speed she would take hold of it and roar with laughter at my terrified face.

One day, however, she failed to catch hold of the pushchair as it careered down the hill, gathering speed. I can remember seeing the road at the bottom of the hill, with vehicles moving along it, and being convinced that I would end up under one of those cars or lorries. I can remember screaming and looking back at my sister as she ran vainly down the hill, desperately trying to catch me. The pushchair bounced off the kerb but, thank God, there were no vehicles coming. I held on grimly as the pushchair sped across the road, smashing into the opposite kerb and throwing me out on to the pavement. I was distraught, screaming and crying, and she tried to comfort and quieten me, knowing that she would get a good hiding from my mother when she discovered how my bloody face had become so covered in cuts and bruises.

My sister would always take the opportunity to have as much fun as possible at my expense. Another favourite trick was to encourage me to walk under her big overcoat whenever we went to the shops. Hidden under the coat, I could see nothing and she would walk quickly along, with me running to keep up. Then, suddenly, there would be a crash as I smashed into a lamppost or pillar box and I would hear Jan roaring with laughter as I cried in pain. It was months before I realised she was walking me into these objects on purpose. I assumed, all along, that they were mere accidents.

My first memory of real pain, however, was not the result of a beating from my father but an argument I had with an old-fashioned, stand-up mangle that my mother kept in the kitchen which led through to the hall. I loved to slide up and down the linoleum in the hall, especially after my mother had spent time polishing it. One day I ran along the hall, landed on my backside and slid into the kitchen, crashing headlong into the mangle, my face hitting the iron stand on which it rested.

I screamed in pain and cried even louder when I realised that blood was pouring from my mouth and three teeth had fallen out. My mother, however, left me in no doubt as to who was to blame for the accident while she propelled me down the road to the doctor's surgery to check precisely what damage I had done to myself. Even today I can still recall the pain.

I had a rather ambivalent attitude towards my elder sister for she had a knack of blaming me for everything that went wrong, usually when she had done something naughty herself and didn't want to accept responsibility. As a result, I later became more and more wary of her and her motives but in those early childhood days I didn't realise why I was always getting into trouble when I had done nothing bad.

On one occasion we were sent to the shops to buy something for supper. I was about six and my sister was thirteen. Unfortunately, the shop was out of stock of the item we had been sent to buy so my sister spent the money on sweets. When we returned home my mother could see that we had been eating chocolate and quickly realised that we had spent the money on sweets rather than on what we had been told to buy. My sister told her that it was totally my fault and that I had forced her to buy them. As a result, I received a good hiding and my sister was simply given a caution to take more control of me! In retrospect, of course, it was wonderful training for army life but I didn't appreciate that at the time.

On another occasion, when I was about seven, my father had been tiling the living room fireplace and, having finished the job, went out to the shops. While he was out, my sister decided the top row of tiles was not correctly matched and took all of them off. When my father returned, an hour later, all the tiles were on the floor and the fireplace looked a mess. In a fury, he asked what the hell had happened and my dear sister told him that I had taken them off while she was out of the room. I protested my innocence and told him I had not touched them, which was true. On that occasion he not only gave me a good thrashing for removing the tiles but also for telling lies.

After that episode I really hated my sister. However, revenge is sweet. A couple of years later she began dating a boy who my mother didn't like at all. She forbade my sister to see him. Of course, she continued to do so but needed my co-operation. I seized my chance. At that time I loved Airfix aeroplane models and for three months I made her buy me a model plane every Saturday to ensure my silence. She hated it but had to go along with it.

In many respects, I suppose my mother was quite Victorian in the way she brought up her children. She undoubtedly had high standards. She would never give us pocket money and made us work around the house and run errands. We were never allowed to go out and play with other children without her express permission which, quite frequently, she wouldn't give. She wanted us to mix with children whose parents she respected, which were not the ones we wanted to play with. She was particularly tough with my sisters. The last thing Mother wanted was one of her daughters coming home pregnant.

However, like mother, like daughter. A year after she banned my sister from seeing her boyfriend, Jan did, indeed, come home and announce that she was having a baby. She, too, was only sixteen. When she told my parents there was an almighty row so I went to my bedroom to keep out of trouble while their voices reached screaming pitch. They quietened down, however, when she told them that the boy had offered to marry her and they stood by her although my mother never forgave my sister or forgot the shame.

Another traumatic event also occurred when I was nine years old. My school friends and I had started playing a stupid game of 'chicken' on the railway line that we passed each day on the way to and from school. The game began as a dare. It was only a bit of bravado but it would end in tragedy.

Four or five of us would stand on the railway line used by the steam engines because we all realised that the other line, being electric, would kill us instantly if we ever stepped on it. When a train approached we would leap from the line, landing on the grass embankment. The first to jump was chicken, the last to jump the winner.

One evening, as a steam train sped towards us, we all jumped as usual, but, for some reason, two jumped towards the electric rail instead of to the embankment. I shall never know why. When the train had passed we looked for them. One, a boy called Roy, was lying on the live electric rail with smoke rising from him. He was motionless. I knew at once that he was dead and felt panic. We didn't know what to do, but worse would follow.

We suddenly saw that an electric underground train was rocking along the line towards where Roy lay. We waved our arms at the driver, trying to attract his attention, to make him stop. I saw his face as he looked at us and then at the rail, suddenly realising that someone was lying on the live wire only a matter of yards ahead of him. We heard the screech of the brakes and saw the train lurch violently as he tried to prevent it hitting the boy but he couldn't stop. We watched helplessly as the train went over Roy. It was awful. I don't know if I panicked or fainted. Suddenly there were police and ambulance men all over the place and I began running around, obviously in a state of shock. A policeman caught hold of me and slapped me across the face, trying to calm me, to bring me to my senses. I couldn't stop shaking; I couldn't control my body. Then I saw the remains of poor Roy, the blood, the mess, the gore. It was horrific.

We were taken to hospital and checked over to see if we were all right to be sent home. We were all in shock. Dad collected me from the hospital. He, too, was shaken by what had happened. When we returned home, he sat me down and lectured me. He went on and on and on, telling me of the dangers, the stupidity of playing on the railway lines. All I could do was think of poor Roy, of the mess, of the police picking up bits of his bloodied body and putting them in plastic sacks. For two days I couldn't eat a thing.

I never went near the railway line again and never again did I play 'chicken'. Roy's death made me feel guilty, as though I had killed him myself. For weeks I had nightmares, not only about Roy dying but in the realisation that I, too, could have been killed. I would wake up screaming, believing I was about to die under a train. Even today, I never go near the edge of a station platform for every time I do I still see poor Roy's body.

However, there were also happy childhood memories. I always looked forward to visits from my Aunty Marje. When I was seven and eight, she would come to visit regularly, bringing with her sweets and a bag of broken biscuits. She was a good-looking woman, with dark brown hair and dark brown eyes and she exuded warmth. She was the epitome of everyone's ideal mother. I loved her. She always wanted me to sit on her lap, something I can never remember doing with my own mother. She seemed to love me and I, of course, loved the fuss, the affection and the warmth she showed me.

Another happy childhood memory was visiting my grandad, my mother's father. A Yorkshireman, an ex-miner and a keen pigeon fancier, he would take me to see his prize pigeons in a shed in his back-garden. He, too, was warm and showed me affection. From him I would learn things that were much more interesting than what was taught at school. He would chat to me and explain things and I found I could ask him questions without risking a cuff round the ear. More than anything, however, the pigeons fascinated me.

Sometimes he would allow me into the pigeon loft where he kept perhaps twenty to 25 birds. He bred them. They always seemed to be hatching eggs and he took great pride in breeding pigeons which went on to win races. He would follow the careers of the more successful pigeons that he bred and would tell me how they were doing. He would allow me to stroke them, to feed them and would point out to me the particular attributes of each and every bird. He had his favourites and I had mine.

I would visit him once a week or so, although it was a long bus ride away, taking about twenty minutes. When I was very young it seemed that he lived really far away. On my tenth birthday Grandad gave me a set of three bird books as a special present. The books were written by T. H. Coward, who, I later learned, was a noted ornithologist. This gift seemed to signal that I was becoming an adult, finally growing up. I treasured those books and would spend days reading them, memorising them, trying to learn as much as I could so that I could become a pigeon breeder just like my Grandad. I still have them, I still prize them and still read them.

It was that introduction to bird life that sparked an interest in birds that I have retained all my life. When I was around eleven years old, I began going to nearby woods to look for birds' nests. It didn't matter what type of birds they were. When I found a nest I would watch it for hours, usually hiding in a nearby bush from where I could see the birds' 'toings and froings' while they reared their chicks. To this day, watching the simple act of birds feeding their young gives me a feeling of inner warmth.

Birdwatching did, however, interrupt my school life. In junior school the teachers had managed to instil in me a desire to learn and I enjoyed it. However, once I found my hobby school work never seemed as important as birdwatching and when I was eleven years old I decided to leave home and go and live in a den on the Thames marshes about two miles from home.

I bunked off from school and went off to the marshes, to an area where builders had dumped their refuse. From the discarded planks, bricks and pieces of masonry I made a den where I intended to live. I hadn't thought about food or washing or clean clothes. I was happy just to watch the birds over the marshes.

Later on that first day I met another boy of about my age. I can't remember his name because we never met again. He immediately agreed to join me. By evening, of course, we became hungry and went off in search of food. We found some large bottles of sweets that a shopkeeper had left out at the back of his premises and took one each. We returned to our hideout and began eating our way through the sickly stuff. After an hour or so, I had had enough of sweets; I wanted something proper to eat. It was becoming cold. I didn't know what to do. I didn't want to go home because I knew my father would give me a good thrashing.

As night fell, we saw torch lights coming towards us in a great arc across the marshes. Then we saw police cars driving slowly along the surrounding roads. We realised that they must be searching for us so we left the den and began walking towards the line of torches. Someone shouted, 'There they are' and some police officers came running towards us. It was after one a.m. before the police took us home and, unbelievably, I wasn't given a good smacking. I think my parents were too overcome with relief to hit me. However, I had learned my lesson. I would never run away from home again.

When I moved on to secondary school, all my good intentions about working hard went out of the window. I was far more interested in birdwatching and playing football. I just didn't bother with school work. I would bunk off from school and go to the marshes off the main Southend Road, where I would spend the whole day birdwatching. Of course, I would always be back in school in time for football training. I loved football. I played inside right and played for the school from the age of thirteen right through until I left at fifteen. The teachers said I showed real aggression.

To improve my soccer I decided to start weight training. I was just thirteen! My parents used to kid me along and take the mickey out of me but, as far as I was concerned, my weight training was deadly serious. I believed it would help me to gain strength in my legs and upper body and improve my football. I would work out really seriously three times a week in the school youth club. I doubt if it helped me at all but it did at least keep me out of trouble – for most of the time anyway.

My second brush with the police occurred when I was thirteen and this also resulted from innocent behaviour. Accompanied by my best pal Phil, I was travelling by train to watch Tottenham Hotspur play a match on a November evening. We had bought some fireworks, bangers of course, and were throwing them harmlessly out of the train window. Suddenly the guard appeared, demanding to know who was firing a gun out of the window. The train stopped at the next station and the police were called. They didn't believe our story about the bangers and preferred to believe the guard. As a result, we were taken home by the police and never saw the match.

That episode made me think hard about telling the truth. My mother had told me that I must always tell the truth, never tell lies, and all would be well. It seemed to me, however, that every time I told the truth I was not believed and that some other person, who I knew to be lying, was accepted as telling the truth and I was branded a liar. It seemed terribly unfair at the time and it worried me throughout my teenage years.

Problems with my father were becoming more frequent. He was forever telling me what to do, criticising me, ordering me about and, whenever he felt justified, he would whack me, slapping me on the side of the head, punching me in the arm or chest and throwing me to the ground. I was beginning to feel humiliated and angry and the weight training at the youth club had given me some confidence in my own strength.

One evening he came home from work and my mother told him that I had again been playing truant from school. He turned on me, hitting me around the face and sending me across the room. Something snapped inside me; I had had enough and I went for him. I punched him straight in the face, a real hard punch, hitting him the way I had been taught to use the punch bag. I had never even attempted to hit my father before. He was taken aback by the ferocity of my attack.

'You little bastard,' he said grimly, 'I'll teach you to hit your father, come here.' He hit me back, hard, and we traded punches. He probably hit me more than I hit him but I didn't feel any of his punches because of my fury. I kept hitting him as hard as I could wherever I saw an opening – on his face, his chest, his stomach, his arms, anywhere. My mother came into the room and screamed at us to stop. We both stopped and looked at each other. Then I walked straight out of the house. However, my anger had done the trick; never again would my father attempt to hit me. I was fourteen.

My faith in adults was shaken again during the following year. My pal Phil and I would hang around outside the Thatched House pub in Dagenham, listening to the music. We couldn't go in, of course, but we could hear the music if we stood by the window. We enjoyed listening to pop music as we drank a bottle of lemonade and ate crisps.

One evening a man in a big, two-tone maroon Humber Super Snipe came to the pub and, while we were admiring the car, he asked Phil and me whether we wanted to earn a few pounds in pocket money. At that age, a few pounds seemed like riches and we readily agreed. He told us to go to a nearby factory which manufactured car batteries and explained that he wanted us to load some lead ingots into the car. We climbed over the fence and he broke open the gates with a crow bar. We must have loaded 40 or more ingots into the car, some in the boot and others in the front to level the weight. 'I'll be back in a couple of hours', he said, 'to give you the money.' We waited and waited but he never came. We kept an eye open for his car because it was quite unusual, but we never saw him again. That adventure made me realise that there was no easy way to make money. It also taught me not to trust people.

Despite our repeated pleading, neither of my parents ever gave any of us any pocket money. All my mates at school received pocket money every week and I felt ashamed that I never had any. Never having money to buy sweets or comics made me feel inadequate. I knew I had to do something to rectify the situation but there weren't many options.

Phil also came from a large family and although he was given a little pocket money it was never enough. We thought of doing a paper round but that meant waking at six a.m. It seemed too much like hard work, especially in the cold winter months. Phil and I would talk about ways of making money and then we hit on the idea of stealing things people wanted so that we could sell them easily. We knew that all our friends at school loved having new fountain pens so we decided that they would be the easiest to sell. Being small, they were also the easiest things to steal and conceal. We decided on Woolworths because it was so easy to nick things from the counters.

My life of crime began one Saturday morning when the store was crowded. I was about thirteen. We decided to steal two pens each. We went up to the counter and pretended to find a pen that we particularly liked. Then, when the assistant's back was turned, we put two in our trouser pockets and walked slowly away from the counter. I think we sold them for a shilling each.

Our shoplifting career went on for several months. We won such a reputation at our school, a secondary modern in Dagenham, Essex, that the boys and girls began giving us orders for items they wanted. The principal items ordered were pens, Dinky Toys, Airfix ships and planes for the boys and combs, make-up, compacts and lipsticks for the girls. On most Saturday mornings we would visit a Woolworth store, mainly the branches in Dagenham and Barking, and take what we wanted. Sometimes we earned as much as five pounds a week each – a small fortune!

I knew we were doing wrong. I knew it was theft. I also knew that we would get into enormous trouble if we were ever found out. And yet those Saturday morning escapades became a drug to me, a thrill, a challenge to see if I could pit my wits against the Woolworth counter assistants and any store detectives who might be around. I came to look forward to Saturday mornings and, somehow, we were never caught.

Only once did we nearly came to grief. One Saturday Phil and I were standing in front of the pen counter and suddenly I felt a hand grab my shoulder. I looked round, at the same time shouting to Phil to run. I broke free from the man and darted out of the shop. Neither of us looked back, we just ran like hell until we were half a mile or more away. It scared the hell out of us and cured us of shop lifting. We never tried it again.

Around then I also had a stroke of luck. My uncle, who owned a greengrocer's shop in Manor Park, offered me a Saturday job, working in the back of the shop for the princely sum of £2.10s. for the entire shift. He really made me earn the money. I had to work from eight in the morning to six at night. He did feed me, though, with a couple of cheese rolls in the morning, fish and chips for lunch and as much fruit as I wanted. It was hard graft but I enjoyed it. I was beginning to feel like a man even though I was just fourteen.

However, I still wasn't bothering to study at school. I had failed my eleven plus miserably and had been allowed to drift along, hardly paying attention in class, concentrating on my football and dreaming of birdwatching. When I was fourteen, however, my form teacher asked me to stay behind one day and we sat and talked. He told me, quietly and patiently, that I was wasting my potential. He knew I was keen on football and sport but pointed out that the chances of ever being a professional footballer, or a professional sportsman of any kind, were probably negligible.

He asked why I was wasting my time, not bothering to study when the whole of my future life depended on getting good exam results and being able to hold down a good job with decent pay. He made me see how stupid I had been in neglecting my school work. He also made me determined to rectify the situation in the three months I had left at school. I hadn't passed any of the mock exams so I would not be staying on to take the GEC O level exams. I was about to leave.

For those not staying on there was a school leaving exam which was intended to show any potential employer whether an applicant had any intelligence. For those last three months I worked really hard, studying at home and paying attention one hundred per cent of the time during classes, something I had never done before. I was determined to prove to the teacher and myself that I could do the work, that I did have real intelligence. The work paid off when I came tenth out of the 90 who were leaving. For the first time I felt a sense of achievement. I had proved myself.

Armed with my school leaving certificate, I knew I would get a job. Round the corner from my home in Dagenham was a fur factory where pelts were cured, prepared and graded before being despatched to the furriers. Two days after leaving school I went round to the facory and asked to see the foreman.

'Any vacancies?' I asked with some degree of confidence.

'Is this your first job?' he asked.

'Well, I've worked in my uncle's shop,' I explained, 'but this is my first real job.'

'We might have something for you,' he replied. 'Come on in.'

I sat and waited while he went off to talk to someone. Then he returned, offered me a job as an engineer's apprentice and added, 'You'll get £7.10s a week. You can start tomorrow.'

I left the works elated and happy with the world. I was just fifteen, I had a job and I was about to make my way in the world. It also meant that I would now be independent.

Despite the fact that I had a job, I knew in my heart that this would only be a stop-gap until I was old enough to join the army. I had set my heart on becoming a Paratrooper like my uncle; that would be my real career. There was no question that I wouldn't be accepted, that I wouldn't pass the fitness test, the medical or any other exam they might ask me to take. I knew that one day I would become a Para like my Uncle Stan.

A month later, however, the teenager whose job I had been given suddenly returned to the works and was given his old job back. I was offered the alternative job of hanging the pelts in the drying rooms. Within hours of starting this new job I was bored. I would spend all day, every day, looking at the large clock that hung in the works, hardly able to wait until five o'clock and freedom. The job was so boring and monotonous that I felt I could not wait until I was old enough to join the army.

I managed to stick with the job for a few months but finally I knew I had to leave or I would go mad. I kept popping into the Labour Exchange and looking at the jobs on offer. One day I saw an ad for a tea boy on a building site and decided to go after that. I reckoned that it could never be so boring as working in the pelt factory.

This time I was working out in the open, helping to build a factory about twelve miles from home in the Essex countryside. It seemed like freedom to be out in the open air. During lunch breaks I could even do a spot of birdwatching. Every day I would clamber into the back of the van with other building workers to be driven to the site. I didn't like being the tea boy, though. I wanted to work on the site as a proper labourer and was pleased when, after a couple of months, another youngster joined the firm and took my job. Now I was a proper labourer, earning very good pay at £35 a week. I felt really wealthy.

It was about this time that I met Ann, the love of my young life. She was a good-looking, dark-haired, dark-eyed girl and not too tall. She had a lovely figure and looked about eighteen, three years older than her real age. I was just sixteen and smitten. We met in the cafe where my pals and I drank coffee after weight training at the youth club.

I would spend two or three hours every night, just looking at her, too shy to talk, and hoping that she would speak to me. One night she did and my heart leapt.

After a month we began dating every night. This would be the real thing. I would arrive home at six p.m., filthy after a day's hard work on the site. After a quick dinner, a bath, clean clothes and five minutes spent on my hair, I would meet her at the cafe by 7.15. If the weather was fine we would stroll over to Mayes Brook Park and find a secluded spot in a copse at the edge of the park. We couldn't get enough of each other. We would make love until dark. She was fantastic. I was in love.

Six months later Ann became pregnant. We had been taking precautions but not all the time. My parents were livid; her parents were even angrier. At first they demanded that she should have an abortion but she refused. Instead, I was banned from her house and her parents refused to let her out after six o'clock at night, the time I arrived back from work. Neither of us was on the telephone and, as a result, we virtually never saw each other. Her parents must have known that such a strict regime would result in killing our love for each other. Finally, it did.

Then, one day, ten months since I had last seen her, we bumped into each other in the road. She had

had the baby, a little boy, but her parents had persuaded her – ordered would be more accurate – to have the child adopted. She had wanted to keep him but her parents had so knocked the spirit out of her that she finally, reluctantly, agreed to give up the baby. When we met, we looked at each other but the passion we had once felt had gone. We never saw each other again and perhaps that was for the best. I felt very sad. I also felt a terrible sense of guilt.

I needed a change. I was still only sixteen but reckoned that I had been on the building site long enough. I applied to Redbridge Council for a job and ended up working in the Maintenance Department, helping to laying new drains and repair council property. I can still remember the first time I had to fill in my weekly time sheet. I worked out exactly how many hours I had done and wrote them down correctly. The chargehand came along and asked to look at my time sheet.

He looked aghast when he saw what I had written. 'Do you want to get us all hanged?' he protested. 'That's no bloody good, lad. Give me another time sheet.' As I watched, he rewrote another time sheet with my name on the top. 'That's better,' he said as he handed it over to me.

I looked at what he had written with astonishment. By his reckoning I had worked twenty hours' overtime! In reality it had been only four. I didn't know what to do. Then he said, 'And don't put in another time sheet until I've checked it. Do you understand?' I just looked at him and said nothing.

Throughout the following week I worried about what he had done; worried that I might be found out; worried that I might end up in court. Then when I received my pay packet and realised how much extra money I had made, I decided to stay quiet and keep the money. However, the chargehand still wasn't confident that I would keep up the pretence and checked my time sheet every week.

With good money in my pocket, a good job and the thought that I had only another year to go before joining the army, I decided to enjoy myself. Every Saturday was party night at someone's house. After a few drinks down at the local, we would descend on some poor person's house and rock'n'roll the night away.

At one of these parties I met Jennifer, a well-built, good-looking blonde – and a true blonde – with beautiful hair and bright blue eyes. She was only sixteen but I thought she was great and I found her very sexy.

It really was a case of love at first sight. Our eyes met as everyone danced and I walked over to her. Immediately we began talking to each other, we both realised that we were attracted. We danced and smooched and danced and smooched. Within an hour we had made our way upstairs to one of the bedrooms. We started to undress each other as we kissed. Within ten minutes we were making love. Three times that night we went upstairs to the bedroom to make love. I walked her home at three in the morning. When we were saying good night at her front door and I was about to leave I suddenly realised that I didn't know her name!

We dated for the next year, until after I joined the army. We had a wonderful time together, dancing, having a drink or going to parties. Whenever possible, which was virtually every time we dated, we found somewhere to make love. However, I had learned my lesson. I never went anywhere without a packet of three. The last thing I wanted to do was make another girl pregnant.

The early sixties was the time of the height of Mods and Rockers' rivalry and Southend was one of their principal battle grounds. Jennifer and I would often visit Southend with our friends, most of whom had motorbikes. As a result, I would sometimes find myself in the middle of a pitched battle. My main objective was to protect Jennifer and myself but, on occasions, when my mates were being beaten up, I would wade in, throwing fists and putting in the boot. I can remember ending up with the odd black eye and bruised ribs but nothing more. I was learning to look after myself.

On one occasion during a Southend battle a Mod hit Jennifer in the face. He was wearing a knuckle-duster when he smashed her in the eye. I went berserk. Jennifer had simply been standing with me watching what was going on, not interfering at all. I chased the bastard, threw him to the ground and gave him a bloody good kicking. I was livid.

We would often visit Southend in the summer months because Jennifer adored making love in the open air and we would usually find some semi-secluded place to get it together. I would also take her birdwatching. She wasn't that interested in birds but, of course, we would always end up naked and she seemed to love that more than anything.

In my heart, however, I knew that I was just playing for time. My real life was about to begin.

CHAPTER TWO

FOR TWO FULL months Jennifer and my mates tried to talk me out of joining the army. Jennifer would kiss me all over my body as we lay in bed, reminding me of what I would miss if I joined up. Sometimes, as we were making love, she would even tell me that there would be no sex for me in the army. My mates just thought I was a bloody fool throwing in a good job, good pay, a great girlfriend and great parties for what – square-bashing, spit and polish and bullshit! But I would not be deterred. I would lie awake at night thinking over what I should do but I knew in my heart that my destiny lay in the army.

One morning in September 1966, aged eighteen, I took the train from Dagenham to Romford, intent on visiting the Army Recruiting Office. On the way there, however, I got cold feet. I wasn't sure. I kept thinking of Jennifer and our relationship; I kept hearing my mates' words in my mind, telling me how stupid it would be to throw away my life and join the army. For more than 30 minutes I walked around Romford trying to decide what to do. Then, like a flash, I knew I had to join up, forget about the past, forget the good times, the good pay and Jennifer, and find the career I had longed for all my life. I took a deep breath and pushed open the door of the recruiting office. There would be no turning back.

An army sergeant sat behind one desk, a corporal behind another. Along the walls were recruiting posters showing squaddies in exotic overseas locations. It looked more like a holiday travel bureau than an Army Recruitment Office.

'Right, young man, what can I do you for?' said the sergeant.

'I want to join the Parachute Regiment,' I replied confidently.

'Right then, you've come to the right place. Come and sit down.'

We chatted for a while. His corporal made me a cup of coffee and he gave me the forms to fill in. An hour later I walked out, having abandoned the idea of joining the Paras and having agreed, for some extraordinary reason, to signing on with the REME to train as a mechanic. As I took the train back home I wasn't at all sure I had done the right thing.

Two days later I returned to the recruiting office for my medical. Ninety minutes later I left the office, having been passed A1 fit and with a railway warrant to Arborfield in Berkshire. There was no going back. I was now a member of Her Majesty's armed forces.

My mates threw a party for me on the Saturday night, determined to get me blind drunk. Jennifer had other ideas. We spent half the night drinking and dancing and the other half in bed, making love. I saw Jennifer again on the Sunday night but she could not be consoled; the tears flowed down her face as we kissed goodbye.

I had no real idea what to expect at Arborfield. As

I stepped off the bus and walked along the road to the main gates I could see squads of soldiers marching about to the accompaniment of lots of shouting and swearing and I wondered in my naivety what was going on. I would soon learn.

The next six weeks were a blur of marching, shouting, drilling, more shouting, spit and polish, cleaning and bedmaking and, of course, weapons training. I slept like a child and always seemed to be hungry. I never had time to think of Jennifer or my mates for there was so much to do and so little time in which to do it. I enjoyed the PE and the cross-country runs; I hated the drill.

My mother and elder sister Jan came to see my passing out parade and I loved the 72-hour leave which followed, enjoying a few pints with my mates and spending as much time as possible with Jennifer. Back at camp we only had time to pack before being bussed down to Borden in Hampshire to start training as mechanics.

During the next twelve months the army instructors taught us everything there was to know about army three-tonners and the ubiquitous Land-Rover. By the time I took the REME exam I could change the clutch on a three-ton truck in 40 minutes. I had not only learned everything there was to know about vehicle maintenance but I was now the proud possessor of an HGV licence.

I was posted to a place I had never heard of before in my life — Bielefeld, near Dortmund in north Germany. I had reservations about the place even before I arrived for the weather conspired to keep me away. The original flight from Heathrow was cancelled because of fog; other flights from other airports were also cancelled and I ended up taking a train from London to Harwich and had a dreadful Channel crossing followed by a long, weary rail journey to Bielefeld. I arrived three days late, exhausted.

I was assigned to 9 Squadron, Royal Corps of Transport, and sent to work in a small light aid detachment workshop in the camp. Most of the time I seemed to do nothing except drink tea and play darts. This wasn't the army life I had envisaged. It was a far cry from the life I had dreamed of enjoying as I listened to my father's desert adventures.

To make life more interesting, I persuaded the others in the workshop to keep more of the heavy work that we should have sent to the main workshop. So, for example, when a three-tonner came in for inspection and we found it needed a new engine fitted, we would carry out the work ourselves rather than sending it to the main workshop five miles away.

I still found life boring so I volunteered to join the REME recovery unit, going out in all weathers to recover broken down vehicles within a 60-mile radius of the camp. I finally felt as though I was earning my keep as well as leading a more interesting life. Deep down, however, I still felt frustrated.

My mind kept wandering to the life I wanted to lead, where there would be some real action. One day, these thoughts nearly cost me my life. I was day-dreaming as I drove a Land-Rover along a country lane, having collected some spares from the main depot. I forgot I was in Germany, where I should have been driving on the right side of the road. Suddenly, I realised that a huge truck was coming straight towards me. Inadvertently, I had drifted over to the left side of the road but it took me vital seconds to realise that I was the one in the wrong. If I had braked and come to a halt, the huge truck would have smashed into me and I would probably have been a goner. So, instead, I drove straight off the road and into the hedge at the side. The truck must have missed me by a matter of inches. As the Land-Rover came to a halt, half-buried in the hedge, my heart started thumping as I realised just how close I had come to a very serious accident. 'Stupid bastard,' I kept mouthing to myself, about myself, as I drove back to camp.

Bielefeld did have some compensations, however. My footballing ability came in useful. After a trial I was selected to play for the squadron football team. We would play teams from around the area and those were always great days, finishing with a few beers and a singsong. There was also an army gymnasium where I was encouraged by the PT instructors to continue my weight training.

It was in that gymnasium that I met the man who would change the course of my life. One day I noticed a powerfully built, tough-looking geezer, aged about 30, who concentrated on weights to increase his stamina. I had seen him around the camp but had no idea of his rank or his job.

When he dressed at the end of his training session, I realised he was a provo sergeant. However, sewn on the upper right arm of his shirt I noticed a navy blue set of wings which I had never seen before. I knew the emblem did not represent the Paras because their wings are a lighter blue. The next time we met I plucked up courage to ask him what the wings represented. 'SAS, son,' came the reply. I looked at him somewhat bewildered for I had never before met anyone who had been a member of the SAS. To me they had always seemed more like ghosts than real army personnel.

Occasionally our paths would cross outside the gym and the sergeant would nod or wink. I took it for granted that he wouldn't speak to me but I was determined to find an opportunity to ask him how he came to wear SAS wings. I was fascinated and wanted to know more. One day the opportunity arose as we trained in the gym together. I summed up the courage to ask him: 'I suppose you must be really fit to get into the SAS?' The question sounded a little pathetic but it was all I could think of.

My simple question began a series of conversations that we would have during the next few weeks whenever we trained together. Outside the gym we never spoke but the more we talked during training, the more he realised he had found someone who was genuinely interested in the Special Air Service.

He told me that he had served with the SAS in Aden and had seen action there. He confessed that he missed the SAS lifestyle and the mates he had made during his time with the regiment and that he desperately wanted to get back into it but he couldn't. Since serving in Aden he had married. He now had a couple of kids and his wife was absolutely against him risking his life by rejoining the regiment. So now he was a provo sergeant back with his parent unit, the Royal Corps of Transport.

He told me of occasions in Aden when he had had to kill people in cold blood. I looked at him, not knowing whether to believe what he was saying or take it all with a pinch of salt. I couldn't believe that a British Army sergeant would actually kill someone except in wartime. Everything I had heard about the British Army I had taken as gospel – that the Brits always fought clean, that the British Army wasn't like other armies, that the rules of combat were never flouted. Nevertheless, everything he told me made my blood race. I was hooked.

I asked the sergeant how I could go about applying to join the SAS and he told me. He even picked up an application form for me from corps headquarters. It is, in fact, a simple, straightforward form. I only had to write my name, rank and number to apply to attend an SAS selection course. He took the signed form and sent it to Hereford, the SAS headquarters. I never heard another word.

I could not believe that the SAS had turned me

down without even seeing me or giving me an interview so I tried to forget about joining and concentrated instead on enjoying myself in Germany and
keeping fit.

Only an hour's drive from Bielefeld was the city of
Dortmund and I listened to the tales of other RCT
soldiers about weekends of drinking and the sex on
offer to British squaddies. About three months after
arriving in Germany, four of us hired a car and went
to Dortmund for the weekend. I was nineteen and a
man of the world, or so I thought, but the sights that
greeted me as we walked around the red light district
of Dortmund made me realise I hadn't started to live.
I could not believe that the Germans were so totally
open about sex and prostitution – so very different to
the British attitude.

The first pub we walked into, The Blue Lamp, was
an eye-opener. I could hardly believe what I saw. On
one wall a huge screen showed hard-core porn films.
Everything that I had ever heard about went on, from
group sex to bondage to sado-masochism, and every
detail was filmed in close up in full colour. As I looked
around the pub, I realised that some couples were
openly having sex and some of the tarts were playing
with blokes under the table.

I watched with my mouth open as a barmaid came
over to one table and plonked down a couple of large
steiners of beer while the couple sitting there carried
on playing with each other. It was later that I discovered that the cost of a 'knuckle-shuffle' was only
one steiner of beer – about two bob! When some of
the squaddies realised what was on offer they literally
formed a queue, waiting their turn and watching
their mates having a 'knuckle-shuffle'. After their
turn, some would immediately go back to the end of
the queue and enjoy another pint of beer while
waiting their turn again.

We went from pub to pub, having a pint in each,

until we came to the place we had been told was the greatest – the Hole in the Wall. As we walked in, some girls came up to us and asked for a beer. Some of them were tasty, really good looking. They didn't seem like tarts at all. We sat and chatted and bought them drinks and then they asked us if we wanted to go downstairs.

With a drink in my hand I went off arm-in-arm with my girl, a dark-haired, well-built young woman who could speak English well. She seemed about 25. I knew what was going to happen but I wasn't prepared for the scene. Around the room were seven or eight couples, all standing against the walls, the girls in various stages of undress and the blokes enjoying knee-tremblers. I think I lasted less than 30 seconds.

That night, having watched innumerable nude shows and dirty films and enjoyed as many tarts as we could handle, we slept off the gallons of beer in the car. The next morning, tired, hungover but happy, we would go swimming at the local baths, clean up, have a shave and a shower and go for a good meal. By six o'clock we were ready for another night of sex, drinking and full-blooded, debauched German entertainment. It seemed like seventh heaven.

Somehow, though, there always seems to be some stupid bastard who wants to spoil life and I met such a person on camp at Bielefeld after I had been there a few months. He was a Regimental Police NCO who seemed to have a giant chip on his shoulder. He seemed determined to make everyone's life a misery. For some reason he took a dislike to the REME soldiers and would pick on us at every possible opportunity. He seemed to take a particular dislike to me. He would watch us day and night and discipline us for the most petty misdemeanours, such as having a button undone, smoking without permission or walking instead of marching around the camp.

The animosity between him and me built up over a couple of weeks. Every time I walked out of my billet or out of the workshop he was there, waiting to pick me up for whatever petty reason he could. He couldn't put me on a charge but he could send in a complaint to the officer in charge of the REME workshop and he did just that a number of times. The officer, however, suggested we just 'humour the little shit'.

We tried but it became most difficult. One particular morning I had been awake most of the night with toothache and was late for the workshop muster. As a result, I left the billet without all my buttons done up and the RP NCO bawled at me, 'Hey, you, come here!'

'I can't stop,' I explained. 'I'll be late,' and hurried off.

He ran after me, grabbed my arm and started to bawl me out. I turned round and landed him one, smack on the side of the face. He went down. I left him and ran to the workshop leaving him sitting on the ground. 'I'll fucking get you,' he screamed as he struggled to his feet but I took no notice.

Within minutes the Regimental Police arrived at the workshop and marched me to the guard room. Two hours later I was standing in front of the RCT commanding officer, charged with assaulting an NCO. He told me he had no option but to court martial me. I was flabbergasted.

Three weeks later I faced a court martial held inside the barracks. I pleaded guilty and claimed mitigating circumstances. My defending officer told the court that the NCO had been picking on REME soldiers over the previous weeks and pointed out my blameless record and good conduct since the day I had joined the army. Despite that, I was given six months' detention at Colchester, the Military Corrective Training Centre. When the CO read out the sentence I could have killed the little shit who had put me behind bars for six months.

During the next two weeks I was put through hell while waiting to be transported to Colchester. My provo sergeant weight-training mate was put in charge of me for that fortnight. Every day he had me up at six a.m. He would inspect my kit which had to be immaculate otherwise he would throw it back at me and tell me to start again. All my kit and bedding would have to be laid out perfectly and I would be dressed in full combat kit with a full pack on my back. For the next hour he would make me double all round the barracks, square-bashing on my own, never giving me a moment's respite.

After breakfast my hours would be spent in polishing the guard room floor on all fours, heavy duty gardening and cleaning the cookhouse pots and pans. Some evenings he would take me out again and give me more strenuous double-time work with a full pack. All my spare time was taken up in polishing my kit. I was shattered and angry. I felt that the army and my provo sergeant were being unfair to me.

The provo sergeant never told me why he was being so hard on me. I wondered why he acted so tough towards me when he had previously shown me nothing but friendship. Only after arriving at Colchester did I realise that he had been bloody kind in preparing me for the tough Colchester regime.

Colchester seemed like a mad house. On arrival, the NCOs, who would rule our lives with a rod of iron, were waiting to welcome us. And what a welcome. From the moment of being handed over by the two MPs who had escorted me from Germany to Colchester, the shouting and screaming began. Ordered into a small hall, we were told to lay out all our kit and then take off all our clothes and lay them on the floor.

As I stood to attention, stark bollock naked, one sergeant came up to me and said, 'So, you're the one who likes taking a swing at NCOs? Do you want to take a swing at me?'

'No, Sergeant,' I replied.

'You don't call me sergeant,' he screamed at me. 'From now on, throughout the entire time you are in this establishment you will call me and everyone else "staff". Do you understand?'

'Yes, staff,' I replied.

'And don't you ever forget it or you will be for the high jump.'

We were ordered to pack all our clothes into our kit bags and issued with the regulation Colchester uniform, a rough KF shirt, dark green denims and a dark green jacket. At the double we were ordered to run to our new billet, a Nissen hut, which was to be my home for the next six months.

After tea we were locked in our hut and told to make our kit ready for morning inspection. The next morning the Colchester regime hit us like a tidal wave. The relentless round of drilling, running, harsh discipline, hourly inspections and forbidding, scream- ing, shouting NCOs would not cease until we left the jail.

I knew that I had to survive the first few weeks, no matter what happened. I knew that I had to tough it out to show that I could take whatever the screws threw at me. My training had helped, in some funny way my father's treatment of me had helped and my provo sergeant in Germany had helped. In many ways I was already conditioned to take the toughest discipline the army could hand out. Somehow, after the first couple of weeks, I actually began rather to enjoy Colchester.

After the first month of hell, those deemed to have earned a good behaviour stripe were granted small favours. We were permitted an hour's TV a night and the door to the Nissen hut was not locked at lights out. We were also given more army training and permitted to use live ammunition on the rifle range. To me it seemed rather strange that soldiers incarcerated in a high security jail should be allowed to use live ammunition. When I raised this point with one of the screws, he explained that we were not, in fact, in jail but only attending a corrective training establishment. They could have fooled me.

After four months came a moment of absolute bliss. Marched before the adjutant one morning, I was told that I had earned two months' remission for good behaviour.

When I finally left Colchester, I realised I had never been so fit in my life. I could run five miles without even feeling puffed and I could strip a rifle, a sub-machine gun or an LMG blindfold. My shooting had improved out of all measure. I had also learned my lesson. Never again would I step out of line, nor would I let any other little runt so antagonise me that I would lose control.

I was posted to 10 Field Workshop at Tidworth on Salisbury Plain for a couple of months, working on major repairs before being sent back to Borden for a new six-week course on the repair and maintenance of Chieftain tanks and armoured personnel carriers. The work was interesting and enjoyable but at the back of my mind I knew that repairing vehicles would never satisfy my urge to become a real soldier. To me that meant joining the SAS. Not for one moment did I forget my principal objective.

A few months later I was asked whether I wanted to become part of a forward repair team whose job in wartime would be working close to the front line, repairing vehicles in double-quick time, sometimes under fire. The work was tough and challenging but we won respect from those we worked with. They knew the pressure we were put under, sometimes working all night making sure vehicles, tanks, APCs or whatever were roadworthy before first light. It came as quite a shock to find sergeant-majors coming to visit us in our makeshift workshops, bringing tea and bacon sandwiches. They would treat us with respect at all times, the first time that had happened since I had joined the army.

A year after my posting to Tidworth, I summoned up the courage to try, once again, for a posting to the SAS. I filled out another application form and again I waited, wondering why on earth no one contacted me. I heard nothing.

None the less I was enjoying myself. Tidworth was a town full of pretty girls and most of them seemed to want to be involved with the army. During the twelve months I spent there I think I dated eight different girls, all of them great fun and wanting to enjoy life to the full.

Perhaps the most beautiful girl was the daughter of a Maltese mother and English father, aged about eighteen, who I fell in love with instantly. We dated, we went out to the pictures, we drank, we went for walks in the woods, we partied. She allowed me to kiss her but would allow nothing more whatsoever. I tried everything I had learned, from gentle persuasion to non-stop passion, but not once would she permit anything more than kissing. I hated it but secretly admired her.

Fortunately for me there were others who needed no persuasion or passion but wanted sex as much, if not more, than I did. I had great fun.

Little did I realise it at the time but during my fifteen months at Tidworth I would meet a girl who would have a profound influence on my life and would, literally, save my sanity.

Maria would pop into the Victory cafe in Tidworth High Street for tea and a cake in the afternoons and, on occasion, I had seen this good-looking girl leaving the cafe and had noted her long, shining, dark hair, which reached down to the middle of her back, and her legs which were long and near perfect. She always seemed to have a spring to her step.

I had no idea, of course, who she was or what she did for a living. Neither did I believe that we would ever meet because whenever I saw her I was in an army Land-Rover in my REME uniform driving to or from camp. Whenever I drove past that cafe I would slow down and look to see whether she was there. What I would have done if she had been I don't know but I thought of her frequently.

Then, suddenly, one day she appeared, as if by magic, only a few feet away from me. We were both attending the weekly disco held above the NAAFI at the 14th Hussars camp at Tidworth. At first I wasn't sure it was the same girl. She was wearing a black leather mini-skirt with metal studs down the front and a white blouse and, to my delight, she was standing alone.

The more I studied her, the more convinced I became that she was the same girl who frequented the Victory cafe. I had a quick pint of Tartan bitter to give me courage and then asked her to dance. I had to know, of course, whether she was the same girl so I asked her about the Victory cafe. She told me she often popped in in the afternoon and I confessed to her that, for weeks, I had been her secret admirer. I felt a little miffed when she told me she had never noticed me.

I have never fogotten the music for that first dance with Maria. 'Yellow River' became our song and, when arguments later arose between us, we only had to hear that tune to forget the problem and realise that we loved one another.

For the rest of that night we danced all the slow, smoochy, romantic tunes together and had a couple of drinks whenever the music became wild. We both sensed that we wanted to be together, to learn more about each other rather than dancing to rock'n'roll.

Maria lived about three miles from Tidworth. She was the daughter of a steeplejack, an ex-soldier who had met her mother while he was stationed at Tidworth twenty years before. I hoped she would stay longer at the dance but at 10.30 she had to leave as she had booked a taxi to take her home from the barracks. We made a date for the next week.

We met the following week at the Victory cafe. I could tell from the first moment our eyes met that evening that we both felt the same about each other. She looked beautiful and seemed as happy as I felt.

We talked and talked. I discovered that she worked at Tidworth Post Office, a ten-minute walk from the cafe. I learned about her parents and that she was the eldest child. There were also twins, a brother and sister aged five, and her sister Janet, twelve. I was surprised when Maria confessed to me that she was only sixteen for she had led me to believe she was eighteen.

I somehow knew that Maria would be someone very special in my life because I felt differently towards her. Unlike some of my previous girlfriends, I didn't want simply to race her off to have sex. I wanted to get to know her, to talk to her, to kiss and hug her. It seemed strange to me for I had never felt like that before about any girl. It gave me a warm feeling.

Of course, sex did play a major role in our life together. After dating for a couple of weeks we were holding hands, kissing and smooching in the back row of the Tidworth cinema, hardly watching the films at all. Afterwards we went for a stroll in the woods at the top end of the village. It was August and the weather was lovely and warm. We made love under a tall umbrella pine tree.

Within a few weeks Maria's parents invited me for the proverbial Sunday lunch. From his own experience of army life, her father naturally knew the type of existence I enjoyed in camp and took pity on me. He also knew how soldiers love a home-cooked meal. From the beginning Maria's parents made me feel at home. They showed me nothing but kindness and generosity.

A few doors from Maria's home a young couple had set up home with their baby and we offered to baby sit. The couple spent at least two nights a week attending dinners and other functions and we gladly cared for their young child. Within minutes of them driving off we would be making love on the pile carpet in front of the gas fire. We would spend three or four hours lying there naked, talking, making love, having a drink and then making love again. It was wonderful. I had fallen in love.

However, the army conspired to make sure we were soon parted. I was detailed to visit Kenya with the Airportable Platoon, a quick-response light aid detachment, trained to fly anywhere within 24 hours. At the end of September we were despatched to service and maintain vehicles the Royal Engineers were using to construct a major new road from Nairobi to Lake Ngooro. We stayed for eight weeks, alternating between two weeks in the bush and two weeks back at base in Nairobi.

Some of the lads went wild in Nairobi. Every night they would go to the famous Starlight night club. They could not believe there were so many beautiful girls in one place and most of the girls were available, as well as being great fun. The lads would tease me no end because all I wanted to do was have a quiet drink and the occasional dance. They persuaded some of the girls to try to seduce me but I didn't want to know. They thought I was mad.

When I returned to Tidworth I knew immediately I set eyes on Maria that I was absolutely right to have shied away from the temptations of Nairobi. She looked happy and excited and sexy. We spent

Christmas together at her parents' house. It felt as if we were on honeymoon save for the fact that her parents were at home over most of Christmas.

Throughout the last months of 1969 and the first few of 1970 the television news would focus on the troubles in Northern Ireland which, at that time, seemed to be little more than a genuine civil rights movement, with the minority Catholics demanding more equality in jobs and housing. The British Army had been called in to separate the warring factions and were welcomed as heroes by the Catholics who treated them as saviours. That would not last.

The cheers, cups of hot tea and sticky buns which greeted the first British soldiers were soon forgotten as the Catholics became suspicious of the army. In a matter of only a few months they became openly hostile towards them; the problems of Northern Ireland were fast escalating from a minor civil rights political irritation to a major confrontation between the Catholics and the British Army.

At the beginning of February 1970, we were informed that two platoons of 10 Field Workshop would be despatched to Belfast for a four-month tour of duty. We were warned that we would have a dual role, working as REME technicians and also doubling as infantrymen, taking our turn patrolling the streets of Belfast with the infantry. We had no idea what to expect but we would soon learn.

A traditional Belfast welcome awaited us. Cold, driving rain swept in from the sea as we drove the vehicles off the ferry and made our way down grim, rain-drenched streets to a warehouse in Victoria Docks. The brick-built warehouse, with corrugated roofing, concrete floor and a damp, cold atmosphere, would be our home for the next four months. We looked around our desolate billet, wondering how on earth we would find anything to enjoy in what seemed a God-forsaken hole. Yet I sensed a tinge of excitement in the air. I would not be disappointed.

We would spend much of our time repairing vehicles and fitting the Land-Rovers with metal shields to protect the windscreens from the stone-throwing rioters. At other times we, too, were out on the streets, along with the infantry regiments, trying to contain the never-ending round of riots which took place virtually every night. At that time the gunmen had not begun targeting soldiers and the only trouble would come from rioters throwing petrol bombs and stones which were easily fended off with shields. Containing the rioters provided excitement and was far more interesting than repairing vehicles back at base.

On occasions we would be facing a hundred or more rioters chanting anti-British solgans and throwing petrol bombs at us for maybe three hours. Within minutes of them going home, however, we could walk down the same street to buy a packet of fish and chips with no one taking the slightest notice of us. We appreciated that. The rioters were bombing and stoning us because we were the only available target for their pent-up frustration and anger at the way they, the Catholic minority, had been treated in the north for so many years.

Before our tour of duty ended, however, the Catholics and Protestants had begun the occasional gun battle, although their weapons at that stage were only handguns. One day we were sent down to a flashpoint, where the Protestant and Catholic communities faced each other just outside Belfast city centre. We arrived to the sound of revolvers going off and clambered gingerly out of the vehicles to see if we could stop the shooting.

We watched the gun battle continue as we tried, with loud hailers, to persuade them to stop firing. We needn't have worried. There was not a cat in hell's chance of them ever actually hitting one another. It was no wonder at that stage that no one seemed to receive any gunshot wounds because the combatants on both sides would simply hide on one side of a corner, poke the gun round it and fire into the unknown without any idea whatsoever of what the target was. Indeed, there were no targets. It seemed that the sound of the revolver going off gave them sufficient satisfaction. However, that would not last.

Towards the end of our four-month stint, at the end of June 1970, a major riot took place in Belfast, which went on for nearly three days. We were on duty for 36 hours without a break because army intelligence had heard that the Protestants were planning to burn the homes of Catholics in the Ardoyne area. Our task was to protect the district. At the end of that shift, we were shattered. None the less, we were the lucky ones. We were on our way back to Tidworth and I was on my way back to Maria.

Six weeks after arriving back at Tidworth I had just finished work on adjusting the front brakes of a ten-tonner when two Land-Rovers came to a halt outside the workshop. I wandered out to have a fag and see what they wanted. Four soldiers clambered out of each Land-Rover and came over to me. To my amazement they were all SAS. Throughout all the time I had been at Tidworth I had never seen one SAS soldier, let alone eight of them altogether.

'Is the ASM about?'

They were referring to the senior warrant officer in charge of the workshop. I nodded towards his office and two of them went to talk to him. The others stood around. One of them came over to me and asked, 'Where do we find your commanding officer?' I pointed out his office in the headquarters building and they walked away, leaving their Land-Rovers parked outside the workshop.

Twenty minutes later the CO's clerk, a mate of

mine, came running over to me and said, 'Paul, the
CO wants you.'

'What the hell for?' I asked, wondering what I had
done wrong.

'Don't ask me. He just told me to come and get
you.'

With some trepidation I doubled over to the headquarters building, trying to clean my oily hands as I
went. I was, of course, in my dirty workshop overalls,
looking a right mess. I marched in, saluted and
wondered why the hell he wanted me. Two of the SAS
men were also in the room. My heart began to race.
Perhaps, after all, *they* wanted me.

'Bruce. It's about that application you put in some
months ago. Are you still interested in going on a
selection course for the SAS?'

'Yes, sir,' I replied, my heart thumping.

'Right. Go and get yourself cleaned up; hand in
your bedding and get packed. You're off in twenty
minutes.'

I saluted, turned and marched out. I could hardly
believe what had happened. Here, suddenly, out of
the blue, the ambition I had nursed for more than a
year was about to come true. I was so elated I could
hardly pack my gear.

I ran back to the Land-Rovers where the SAS were
waiting.

'Get in,' is all one said to me. I threw in my
clobber and clambered inside. If I had known the
adventures and experiences I would have to undergo
during the next two years I would never for one
minute have considered getting in that vehicle.

As we sped in convoy towards Hereford I suddenly
remembered Maria. We had a date that night and I
had not only forgotten to phone her but I hadn't even
given her a moment's thought. I felt a pang of guilt
but told myself that my life's ambition of being given
the opportunity of joining the SAS had so excited me

that she would understand when I phoned and explained everything.

We drove in silence. Already it was very different. Whenever I went on a trip with REME mates there was nonstop chattering during long road journeys. When we stopped for a bite to eat at a roadside cafe that afternoon all of them took off their SAS berets and slipped them inside their jackets, walking in bare-headed. I gave one a sidelong glance. 'It doesn't pay to advertise,' was the curt reply to my quizzical look.

As we sat down to eat, they introduced themselves. 'We don't talk too much to hopefuls because so many never make the grade. It's silly to get too friendly too quickly. When you get badged – if you get badged – then we can be mates. All right?'

I nodded and carried on eating. I wondered how anyone could tell who was in command because they wore no insignia. For all I knew they could all have been private soldiers, NCOs or commissioned officers. Only after some time with the SAS did one learn to understand and interpret the codes of behaviour which would indicate who was in command.

The SAS man in command that day was a five foot ten inch tall, wiry, even muscular, clean-shaven man with dirty blond hair. I noticed that he seemed like a coiled spring, ready for instant action but prepared to take things quietly and calmly until action was required. They all seemed to exude an air of confidence. I felt safe in their midst, as though nothing could touch them.

Three hours later we arrived at Hereford and I glanced at the large board outside the main gates – 'Headquarters. Regiment SAS' – my pulse raced. As we drove slowly through the gates the guard looked inside the Land-Rover and nodded. The driver nodded back. No one said a word.

CHAPTER THREE

THE ATMOSPHERE IN the SAS barracks at Hereford was very different from anything I had experienced in the army, anywhere. I was told to drop my case and kitbag in a wooden hut, a billet in the Sterling lines, named after the founder of the SAS. The hut, which housed just eight men, would be my home for the next twelve months.

On the surface there appeared little difference from any other army barracks: an iron bedstead, a metal locker, a wooden bedside cabinet, a mat, a light over the bed, the floor highly polished, the room neat and tidy but not excessively so. I smiled. Well, I thought, despite everything one had heard, it seemed the SAS had no special privileges, no luxury, when it came to army life.

Five minutes later I walked down to the cookhouse a hundred yards away. My new mentors were eating happily and they motioned to me to come and sit down with them after choosing my meal.

It was then that I noticed the difference. It all

seemed remarkably quiet. There was none of the hubble that one always associates with army cookhouses when squaddies sit and eat, natter, argue and laugh loudly. Everyone appeared so calm, so disciplined. It was quite unlike normal army life. These troops knew they were privileged – the élite – that none of them had anything to prove to anyone else. They all showed respect to one another, exuding confidence and self-discipline.

There were perhaps twelve or fourteen other hopefuls who had arrived for the same selection course. In total there would have been about 60 potential SAS recruits, all at various stages of training. Within 48 hours six of those who had arrived with me had left the camp, sent back to their units. Some had been declared unfit even to start the course. They were the ones who chatted too much, who swaggered too much, who were too extrovert in their behaviour, their walk, their talk. The SAS wanted quiet, serious, dedicated types. No wide boys, no show-offs.

No potential SAS soldier is ever told that he has failed the course. They are simply RTU'd (returned to unit). No one tells them the reason for their failure. They are simply called in to see an officer who informs them that they are being returned to unit. Many have no idea why they have failed. They are simply left to work that out for themselves.

The morning after their arrival, every new recruit reports to the commanding officer for an interview. He asks a few obvious questions. In my heart I hoped I would give the right answers.

'Why do you want to join the SAS?' he enquired gently.

I told him that my father had been in the Long Range Desert Group during the Second World War and he nodded. I added: 'I believe I have what my father had. And I believe the SAS should be my career.'

'Do you realise how hard the next few months will be?'

I told him about the provo sergeant, the former SAS man who had related some of his experiences to me while I was serving in Germany. He nodded again. 'So you haven't come here in a blindfold. You have some idea of what this place is about.'

'Yes, sir.'

'All right, thank you. You can go.'

The fact that I hadn't been RTU'd meant that I had passed the interview. Now it was time for the hard part.

During the next few days we would learn from the SAS instructors what to expect. We were lectured about the traditions of the SAS, its short history and about some of the gallant men who had served with the regiment. We were shown some old films showing the sort of training and exercises we would be put through during the next two years.

Basic training in any regiment lasts a maximum of twelve weeks. I had done my basic training at the REME depot in Arborfield. I wondered how they could make our training last for two whole years. I would soon learn.

Throughout those first few weeks we were left in no doubt that we could be RTU'd at any time for making mistakes which our instructors believed should not be made. For example, a unit of four men went out on exercise and, although equipped with maps and a compass, still managed to get lost. All four were immediately sent back to their units; not even permitted a second chance.

The first two weeks were a test to see whether we were fit enough to continue with the course that the instructors knew all too well would be excruciatingly rigorous. There were cross-country runs which began at six miles and, fourteen days later, were increased to twelve miles. No one wanted to be the last man home because we all feared that that might lead to failure. As a result, the runs were deadly serious affairs; no one talked, laughed or fooled about; everyone was determined to finish the run and to be one of the first home.

Because the SAS demands absolute fitness, all new recruits are given the option of returning to their units in order to get fit on the understanding that they will be permitted to return to Hereford when they feel capable of tackling the punishing regime. Some took that option but I carried on.

After a run in the morning, the afternoons would generally entail a route march, starting at ten miles and working up to twenty miles, all with a 40-lb pack. Once again, this was not like any other army route march. The pace never relaxed and the sweat poured off us as we seemed to find every known hill around Hereford. Somehow, the marches appeared to be uphill all the way out and uphill all the way back again!

Circuit training added to the demands being made on our bodies. That, too, was tough: press-ups, sit-ups, bar work, sprints, bunny hops; every exercise intended to increase muscle and stamina.

Map reading would become the most serious and vital lesson during this early part of training. During briefings from SAS instructors, we had learned that we would be operating in units of four if we ever made the grade. Armed with a map and a compass, a unit could expect to be dropped in the middle of nowhere – a desert, a jungle, the icy wastes of Norway or the Brecon Beacons – and still find its way back to base. The greatest importance would be put on map reading throughout my entire time with the SAS, for they knew that to become lost in the type of operation we would be carrying out would probably end in death or, worse, capture.

Every day one looked forward longingly to a

glorious hot shower at night and the bliss of one's bed. None the less, the harder the training, the better one felt and the more confident one became.

I managed to write only one letter to Maria, telling her what had happened, explaining my instant removal from Tidworth and hoping she would understand. I also told her that I missed her and would look forward to getting a weekend pass but a weekend pass would be three months away.

Unlike the army proper, no one in the SAS ever mentioned taking leave. Most regular soldiers complain like hell if they don't have plenty of long weekend passes but the SAS men consider their life such a privilege that leave is considered unnecessary. Relationships, and many, many marriages come to grief when a man joins the SAS.

Even during training we never knew when a weekend pass would be granted and no one wanted to ask. Total commitment to the regiment is considered far more important than commitment to a relationship. Everyone accepts that. If they don't, they drop out and return to their units.

During the training programme some men did fall by the wayside because of relationships back home. Letters would arrive from grieving girlfriends and lonely young wives, unhappy, upset and tearful that the man they loved had run off to join the SAS, leaving them alone and miserable. Understandably, some of the young wives, particularly those who were pregnant or had young babies, found life difficult. Some men did decide to return to their units rather than risk the breakdown of relationships or marriages. However, only a few took that way out. Most were determined to see the course through; to join the élite whom we all believed the SAS to be.

My confidence grew a little after those first two weeks of hellish training. I had managed not only to survive but felt incredibly fit, ready for the next stage.

One worry never left me during those weeks and that was the possibility of injury. A number of men did suffer injuries, usually ankle sprains or hairline fractures. Those men were permitted to return to their units until they had recovered and then rejoin the regiment. However, very few did return to the SAS, almost as though their injury had knocked the stuffing out of their desire to hack the hard SAS life.

Having knocked us into some sort of fitness, our instructors now felt we were ready for more rigorous endurance tests. The next phase would last three months. Three to four times a week we would be sent out to the Brecon Beacons, sometimes four or eight in a team and sometimes totally alone. Teams would be despatched every fifteen minutes or so to ensure that the pace would be kept up. If another team happened to catch up, it was greatly frowned upon. As a result, of course, one marched like hell, never slacking, determined not to be overtaken.

Endurance marches would range from eighteen to 30 miles a time in full battle order, with a 40-lb pack and a Belgian SLR (self-loading rifle). We would be given between six and ten map references – not easy ones, like a church or a building, but perhaps a rock or a couple of trees. We would either have to leave something at each one or collect what had been left by the instructors. At some map references the instructors would be waiting to greet us, not only to check on our progress but to see if all of those taking part were in good physical shape.

The instructors would always appear when the weather was bitterly cold or wet to check whether we were coping with the conditions and not suffering the effects of exposure. Only the year before, two SAS hopefuls had died on the Beacons from exposure, having wandered off course in a severe snow storm. The SAS might be tough but they didn't want people to die attempting to make the grade.

Back at Hereford an SAS 'Spearhead' rescue squad, a helicopter team, were always on stand-by in case any soldier got into difficulties and had to be 'cas-evaced' to hospital. During those three winter months of 1970, the chopper was called out on a few occasions but fortunately not for me, nor for mates in my team.

Some instructors were not averse to turning the screw when we were at our most vulnerable. On occasions we would arrive at a map reference absolutely shattered, feeling the effects of exhaustion, hunger and cold. They would be sitting in a Land-Rover with an urn of hot tea and sandwiches.

'Fancy a nice cup of hot tea and a cheese roll?' they would shout as we approached them. Anyone who stopped and took their offering was allowed to complete that day's endurance march but, on arrival back at Hereford would be called before the chief instructor and told he had failed the course. The following day he would be on his way back to his unit.

There was, however, another reason why they made their offer. Some recruits genuinely did feel like jacking in the training and returning to their regiments and this provided a way out for them. It also provided the instructors with the proof they demanded from their recruits – proof of superhuman tenacity, aggression, self-denial and discipline.

Another dastardly trick, designed to whittle out the faint-hearted, would come at the end of a gruelling endurance march. Shattered, hardly able to walk another step, we would arrive back at the billet ready for a hot shower, a meal and sleep. An instructor would appear at the door and pick out a couple of men, telling them to go and carry out some boring, totally unnecessary duty, like checking bulbs or the water levels in the twenty trucks we used.

It is difficult to imagine the reserves of mental

strength needed in those circumstances, when the body is crying out for a hot shower, rest and food, to have to drag oneself out into the bitter cold to carry out an inessential task. Those who couldn't hack it would be RTU'd the very next day.

On other occasions, exhausted and ready to drop, we would arrive at the final map reference where vehicles would be on hand to take us back to base. Sometimes, when we thought the march was at an end, we would be told that the trucks had rendez-voused at the wrong place and that we had another three miles to march. Summoning up enough strength in those conditions can be very hard but we had to do it.

On the marches, we were provided with hard-tack and a full water bottle. After we had done a few of these 'hell runs', however, we would learn a few tricks ourselves and would smuggle Mars Bars into our packs or fill the bottles with Ribena rather than plain water, all of which would give us more strength to endure the tests.

Sometimes we would be told in advance that, at certain map references, food and drink would be officially provided. When we arrived at the spot the food and drink would be missing, although the instructors would be there in a Land-Rover. 'Sorry lads,' one of the instructors would say, 'we were only winding you up. No food or tea during today's march.'

Those occasions often helped to inject a little humour into the march. 'Thanks for fuck all,' would be a typical comment or, later in the training, the instructors would receive the wry comment, 'Well we didn't believe you anyway.' Most of the recruits, how-ever, would take it in good heart, knowing full well that the antics were all part of SAS training. We all knew that nothing would ever come easy to us and it didn't.

The same might happen back at base. We might return to our billets and be told that the cookhouse was out of order and no food would be provided for two more hours. All of these tactics were designed to test our reactions, to see whether we could take the mental stress as well as the rigorous physical strain. We all knew that the instructors were pushing us to our limits, and beyond. Surprisingly, very few recruits did crack through anger, frustration or strain. During my three months of winter endurance marches, only a couple of blokes exploded when pushed too far and, of course, they were on their way back home within 24 hours.

It was on those occasions that I realised how fortunate I had been in having spent four months at Colchester nick. There I had learned to take all the shit that could be thrown at me. I had learned not to retaliate, not to give in, not to show that the system was getting to me. It undoubtedly helped me to survive Hereford.

Throughout those first few weeks I never permitted myself to relax for an instant. The regime was so similar to that which I had endured in Colchester that I half knew what to expect. I realised that it was their job to keep up the pressure, the momentum, to make sure we would be equipped to cope with any disappointment and trying situation without reacting unprofessionally. Instinctively, when anything untoward occurred, I prepared myself mentally to expect the worst, to expect a surprise. In that way I never was caught off-guard, and although I did sometimes get pissed off with some of their games, I never let it get to me. I would sometimes smile to myself at night when I finally collapsed into bed that I could thank my lucky stars I had spent four months inside. I could not have received a better preparation, neither mentally nor physically, but I doubt if they ever realised that.

From the moment I set foot in SAS headquarters, I was determined to make the grade, to win my SAS wings. To me nothing else mattered. Once a soldier is presented with his SAS wings he can wear them until the end of his army career, no matter what regiment he joins. With those wings on your arm you automatically win the respect of everyone associated with the army. I had set out to achieve that aim, to prove to my family, and especially my father, that I could achieve at the very highest level. Those ambitions would keep me going even when, on a couple of occasions, I really felt like chucking it in.

We all experienced 'lows' at one time or another. I had tried to keep in contact with Maria but found it difficult. I would go to bed after tea at about seven o'clock, intending to write her a long letter, but exhaustion would overcome me before I had written more than a couple of paragraphs and I would find myself falling asleep. As a result, her letters became fewer and fewer. After a while I realised that I was missing her company. We had had a good relationship. I had found Maria fun to be with; I could laugh with her and enjoyed her get up and go. She had a good sense of humour and we liked doing the same things. When I did have the strength to think about sex, I also realised how great our sex life had been.

As her letters became less frequent, I found myself becoming angry and upset that she seemed to have forgotten me. I wondered whether she had found someone else and that didn't help. My parents hardly ever wrote. My mother would drop me an occasional line, perhaps once a month, but my father never did. As a matter of fact, my father has never written a letter to me in his entire life. My mother would pass on the odd comment from him but he would never write himself. That pissed me off too.

On those occasions I had to dig deep into my reserves but it did seem very tempting to jack in the

SAS and return to a cushy life with the REME at Tidworth. It would also mean that I could get on with my own life and perhaps make a go of it with Maria. No matter how I felt deep down, however, I would never let such thoughts take over. Time and again I would say to myself, 'Remember those wings. You mustn't give up until you've got them.'

We all knew that at the end of the endurance training we would face the biggest test of all, what the SAS term 'the long drag'; a 40-mile endurance march across the mountains with 60 lb on our backs and carrying an SLR. To put added pressure on us, the march would have to be completed in eighteen hours.

We were woken by the duty guard at five a.m. and given a full breakfast. By six a.m. we were in the trucks, headed for Talybont reservoir, our starting point. On this march we were all alone, with no one for company. We began at ten-minute intervals and were given twelve map references to check into before completing the 40-mile test.

As we started out, the wind was blowing a gale and sleet and bitterly cold rain beat into our faces. It would have been difficult to have found a worse day to undertake such an exercise. We cursed the weather but knew we had to put it behind us and concentrate on the job in hand.

Each reference point was situated at the top of a hill or mountain so we were marching through horrendous terrain, the gradient making life very difficult and very testing. At each reference point an instructor waited to check us in, to see if we were fit to continue.

Despite the terrain, we had to average three miles an hour, which is only walking pace. However, when a 60-lb pack and mountainous terrain are added to the equation, three miles an hour is so tight that, at every possible opportunity, it becomes necessary to run just to keep up the average. On one occasion, as I clambered up a slope, I lost my footing and found myself rolling over and over down the hill. I managed to stop and looked up to see that I had fallen perhaps 60 feet. I was covered in dirt and mud, my clothes sodden to the skin and I still had twenty miles or more ahead of me. As I struggled to my feet, I really didn't think I would complete the march.

On a couple of occasions panic gripped me. I could hardly see in front of me because of the sleet slicing into my eyes, mingling with the sweat drippling down my forehead from beneath my woollen commando hat. I found it all but impossible to read the map and I was exhausted.

On the mountain peaks the sleet gave way to swirling mist which made it extremely difficult to check one's route with the compass. On those occasions I had to put all my faith in the compass because there were no visible signs to which I could refer, I managed a wry smile, believing that the instructors must have prayed for such appalling weather conditions to make sure we were given the toughest possible test. Being totally alone made one feel more exposed, more vulnerable, and that increased the psychological pressure.

To cap it all, I slipped on a stone as I was descending a hill at the double, and fell over, twisting my ankle. I swore like a trooper, angry that I had missed my footing and fearful that they would fail me. I got to my feet and tried to put my foot down but the ankle hurt. Gingerly I continued down the hill, hoping the pain would go away. Thankful that the ankle could take my weight, I determined to carry on. I had only a mile to go and knew that I had to make it.

Many didn't. Twenty per cent of those who began failed this test and every one was sent back to his unit the following day. It didn't matter that, until that moment, they had passed the course with flying colours. Failing that very stiff trial was sufficient for the instructors to fail the recruit. It seemed a tough decision but that is the SAS. Failure will never be tolerated. There are no excuses.

Even during that gruelling march our instructors hadn't played straight for, after we had completed the march within the eighteen hours demanded, they casually let us know that we had, in fact, been given twenty hours to do it in. They hadn't told us because they didn't want it to seem too easy!

That particular year the 'long drag' had been one of the toughest ever but that march has never, ever been postponed or cancelled because of bad weather. Indeed, it seems that the worse the weather, the happier the instructors become because it then becomes a true test of a recruit's physical and psychological stamina.

That night there were many long faces. The six who had failed were upset and annoyed as they faced being sent back to their regiments. Besides myself, there were others carrying minor injuries, and everyone had walked himself into the ground. As we changed and showered an instructor came in to congratulate everyone who had succeeded in conditions which he described as 'horrendous'. We had passed the toughest test the SAS ever throws at recruits.

He announced that everyone would be given seven days' home leave, starting the next morning. We looked at each other, suspecting from experience that this would be another SAS wind-up. We expected them to cancel the announcement later that night. Somehow they didn't. It was true.

With trepidation in my heart, I phoned Maria at the post office where she worked, hoping that I could see her during my leave. I didn't know what to expect and feared that she might have given me the old heave-ho and found a new boyfriend. I needn't have worried. I could tell from the sound of her voice that she wanted to see me. Indeed, she said, 'Fantastic, fantastic, I can't wait. This is wonderful news. How long have you got?' When I told her seven days she replied, 'And seven nights?'

The next day, dressed in civvies, I was on my way to Tidworth and Maria. Another recruit, who had a car and lived in Southampton, offered me a lift. As we drove along I couldn't help smirking to myself. The worst was over and I had survived. I now knew that I had a good chance of gaining those wings. That sense of achievement comforted me and gave me confidence. Slowly, I was beginning to realise what the SAS was all about. I was learning.

I had been wrong to doubt Maria. She had imagined that I had been off with other girls during my time at Hereford, little realising that I hadn't even set foot outside the camp except for forced marches and training runs. She could hardly believe the extensive training we had been through but, towards the end of the seven days, she began to understand.

One evening, while we were waiting in a queue to go swimming, a girlfriend of Maria's, who I also knew, came over to chat. I had fancied her at one time but we had never even kissed. She told Maria that she thought I had a lovely hairy chest and, jokingly, said she would like to rub her hands all over my body. Maria went berserk. She caught hold of the poor girl and shook her, shouting at her to keep her hands to herself. She also told her in precise terms to 'fuck off'. I had never seen Maria behave in that way and, anyway, as I thought the girl had only been joking. However, it showed the strength of Maria's feelings towards me. It had surprised me but it also made me feel good; she did care.

Until then, I had believed that the strength of her passion for me had been primarily sexual; now I realised that Maria was genuine in her feelings. I did not know what to do. The training at Hereford would take a total of two years and the instructors had not told us how much leave we would be given during that time. I presumed that leave would come more often now that basic training was completed but I wasn't sure; after all, this was the SAS.

Maria and I discussed this at length. She was still only seventeen and I tried to reason with her that we shouldn't rush things; that I didn't know where I would be serving after training was over. I knew it could be anywhere in the world. She became upset whenever we discussed the subject but I didn't want to make any commitments. I had no idea what the future would hold but I did realise that the SAS was now my life and that nothing, not even Maria, could stand in my way. I did not, however, tell Maria that fact during our wonderful week together.

Back at Hereford training continued as hard as ever. Officially, it is described as continuation training. It comprises some of the most important training an SAS man receives and lasts fourteen weeks.

Operating behind enemy lines is the essence of SAS work when on active service. One of the first lessons our instructors drilled into us was that being part of the SAS would never be the same as belonging to any other regiment in the British Army. We would never be considered as canon fodder, never be given suicide missions and we were under the strictest orders never to take chances that might end in death. The first duty of all SAS men is survival.

That lecture made us all feel special. It was a wonderful boost to morale after the hell of those marches. It was intended that it should be, of course, and that we should appreciate that becoming a member of the SAS – the Firm, as its members always call the regiment – was the highest accolade any British soldier could achieve.

'Bought the farm' is the SAS expression for getting killed. Throughout the army many and varied phrases are used to describe being killed in action but we were left in no doubt by our instructors that getting killed was not an option for SAS personnel. They explained how it would work. If any SAS personnel ever get killed while undertaking covert operations, their deaths are not officially recorded. At the precise second of death the dead man is officially returned to unit. As a result, the SAS never officially suffers any casualties. It made me realise that if I died during an undercover operation I would be killed as a member of the REME and as though I had never been part of the Firm. I didn't like that but there wasn't anything I could do about it. The only time that rule changes is during a recognised war, such as the Falklands or the Gulf War, when SAS deaths are officially recognised by the regiment.

However, the SAS isn't completely inhumane to the men who have given their lives for the regiment. On the edge of the parade square at SAS head-quarters in Hereford stands a 30-foot-high clock tower on which is inscribed the name of every SAS man who dies in action no matter where or in what circumstances. In SAS parlance it is a memorial to those who 'didn't beat the clock'.

We were told that the SAS always operated in four-man units. If necessary, that number could be doubled, trebled, etc., but each unit would always comprise four men. The NCO instructors emphasised – jokingly of course – that no one suggested a sixteen-man unit because whenever sixteen SAS men operate together an officer is put in command.

In reality, of course, some SAS commissioned officers are bloody good blokes and it is a nonsense to believe that SAS soldiers consider all officers to be wankers. They don't. The officers who make the grade in the SAS are as tough and motivated as any trooper. Occasionally the SAS does attract Hooray Henrys, but not for long. They are soon sussed and RTU'd like anyone else who doesn't absolutely make the grade.

Officers in training for the SAS do precisely the same course as all other ranks. They have no special privileges. Indeed, they invariably become one of the lads. Elsewhere in the British Army all officers are saluted all the time and are always addressed as 'sir'. In the SAS, troopers salute an officer first thing in the morning but, after that, we are all on first-name terms and the officer becomes as much a mate as anyone else during training. On active service operations officers and men muck in together for they all realise that their lives depend on each other, regardless of rank.

When a private or an NCO is finally 'badged' as a member of the SAS he might stay with the regiment for only a matter of months. If, however, he remains fit and motivated, then he might remain in the regiment for the rest of his army career. For officers, however, it is a different matter. Officers from other regiments who come to take an SAS course are permitted to stay for only three years before being sent back to their original unit. None the less, their SAS training is just as tough and strict as it is for everyone else, with just as much chance of being RTU'd if they don't make the grade.

Our first field lesson covered the arcs of fire when a four-man SAS unit is out on patrol. Those arcs of fire were drilled into us until they became automatic. As the instructors explained, keeping to the correct arcs of fire could be the difference between life and death for an SAS unit. One error wouldn't mean just your own death but the deaths of your three mates.

Whenever the unit moved through enemy territory, in line or diamond formation, the same rules would apply. The point man would always face the front, watching everything ahead; the second man would face to the right, the third to the left and tail-end Charlie would bring up the rear. He would forever be turning full circle, watching his back. There would be no excuses for breaking that formation and everyone would be left with no doubt as to where his responsibility lay in watching his arc of fire.

We would practise this on exercises *ad infinitum*. Other recruits, with an instructor in charge, would be sent out to ambush an SAS squad and we would be sent out as though we were in enemy territory. At this stage of training only blank cartridges were used but anyone who wasn't watching his arc of fire would receive an almighty bollocking from the instructor.

Failure in this exercise didn't mean an immediate RTU, thank God, because, naturally, the trained SAS instructors were capable of wiping out a recruit patrol on every single exercise. No matter how professional, how keen-eyed, how on the ball we tried to be on those patrols, we could guarantee that the SAS instructors would find a way of opening up on us when we were least expecting it. We could never win. We understood that. After 'annihilating' us, they would come down and explain where we had gone wrong but we never seemed to learn enough to beat them.

The secret lay in instinctive, greased-lightning reaction to the first burst of fire. The plan was to find positions where the patrol faced the 'enemy' and then reach a decision either to attack and destroy the enemy or to beat a hasty retreat. 'Never get killed' was always uppermost in your mind on those occasions. As the instructors repeated *ad nauseum*: 'There are no such things as dead heroes in the SAS'.

One of the most renowned specialities of the SAS is the craft of taking up positions in enemy territory, living rough in the open for days or weeks at a time and only leaving one's safe haven to ambush enemy patrols or carry out night raids on enemy positions.

The training took weeks. Despite the high level of commitment demanded, however, we also had some fun. At first, a four-man unit would be sent out for a day's exercise and told to lie low and wait for an 'enemy' patrol to pass by. Invariably, we would be stunned to find ourselves looking down the barrel of a rifle – the instructors would have crept up on us somehow, without us realising they were even in the area. How they did it we never knew because we had all been keeping watch as though our lives depended on it. Somehow, they had become invisible and that was the lesson they wanted to teach us. It took weeks but, eventually, at the end of the continuation training, we, too, had learned the basic secret of becoming invisible.

The fun began when we had been in training for four weeks. We were told that an infantry regiment would be out on exercise somewhere on Salisbury Plain and that we were to act as their enemy. We were sent off as four-man units to find a place in which to hide and wait. It was surprising to discover how much we had learned in so short a time because the other regiment didn't seem to have a clue about how to patrol in enemy territory. On virtually every occasion even an inexperienced four-man SAS unit like us could 'wipe out' a platoon of 24 men.

We had even more fun against the tank regiments. They would be warned that we would attempt to attack them at night, blow up their vehicles and kill as many men as possible. They waited for us, their area protected by flares which they had placed around the camp. We would approach before dawn when some were sleeping and others were tired at the end of the night watch; we would place dummy bombs on their vehicle tracks and retire, having put a few of our own trip flares around their camp. On the way out we would deliberately set off one of their flares and then sit back and watch. Chaos invariably followed. Attracted by the flare, they would rush for their weapons, often setting off the flares that we had left, thus causing more havoc. When the exercise umpires came to inspect their vehicles they would realise that we had infiltrated their camp with no one suspecting we had ever been near. Indeed, we usually managed to 'wipe out' their unit as a combat force.

On one occasion, when exercising against the 11th Hussars, a light armoured regiment, we managed to infiltrate the camp to find the commanding officer's personal tent unattended. We nipped in and stole all the regiment's maps, their military orders and even the CO's binoculars. We heard later that there had been hell to pay, with the CO going wild that his troops had been so pathetic as to permit us to infiltrate his own personal quarters without detection. We were learning.

Throughout these fourteen weeks of training we were not permitted to think that endurance tests had ended once and for all. Every couple of weeks we would be sent out on solo endurance marches which were designed not only to keep us superbly fit but also to make sure that our map reading was razor keen. The instructors never let us forget that map reading was one of the most vital lessons we had to master for they knew that when the training was over and our covert actions began in earnest, map reading could mean the difference between a mission's success or failure. As they explained, the SAS didn't take kindly to failure.

One morning in April 1971, I sensed a buzz of excitement in the cookhouse, something I had not experienced since our training had began five months before. We learned that three SAS units – twelve men – had returned from Northern Ireland where they had been carrying out undercover operations. We soon discovered that they had been in action both north and south of the border. Of course, we never knew exactly what type of action they had been involved in but we had some idea from what we had been reading in the newspapers. We knew that a number of soldiers out on street patrol in Armagh had bought it, blown up by mines. We had read of IRA gunmen targeting British soldiers and knew that a number had been killed or wounded during the past few months. We knew that any number of nail bombs and petrol bombs had been thrown at soldiers on street patrol.

Throughout the summer, rioting had been taking place at different times in both Belfast and London-derry. The more serious rioting, often accompanied by sniper fire, had occurred around the Falls area of Belfast where Catholic and Protestant families lived in close proximity.

We had watched on television the tens of thousands of Protestants who had marched on 12 July, celebrating the two hundred and eighty-first anniversary of the Battle of the Boyne in 1690. One hundred thousand people had turned out to cheer the 27,000 Orangemen as they marched with their pipes and bands from the centre of Belfast to a field five miles away at Finaghy.

Six huge bombs had gone off along the very route the marchers would take, yet, fortunately, no one was injured.

During that march 5,000 troops had sealed off the Catholic area of Belfast, another 4,000 police had stood guard along the route and 6,000 British troops had stood by at eighteen towns and villages across Northern Ireland where celebrations were held.

Despite the fact that everyone talked about SAS missions in foreign lands, I began to wonder if more SAS troops wouldn't be shipped over to carry out covert work in Ulster. What seemed surprising,

however, was that within SAS headquarters at
Hereford there was no secrecy about the operation
the SAS men had just carried out. Everyone talked
about it, excited that twelve men had gone out under
cover, living rough for weeks on end, and all had
returned safely.

Although we had, as yet, never been involved in
active service with the SAS, we were made to feel
part of the regiment, encouraged by the sense of
camaraderie that always existed in the regiment. No
one boasted of what they had done, no one asked any
questions and we would never know about other
men's missions. We had learned that SAS men never
boast about their actions for that would be considered grossly unprofessional.

The next phase of our training involved living
rough for up to seven days at a time. We were lucky
in that we were training in April and not the dead of
winter for, as the instructors told us, training in mid-
winter was painful and demoralising.

We would be sent out in a four-man unit equipped
with an SLR and ammunition, with one of us carrying
a light-machine gun, thunder flashes in lieu of
grenades, plenty of hard rations, Ribena and water.
We were dressed in full combat gear, tough, light
ankle boots, puttees, combat trousers, a KF shirt,
sweater, weatherproof combat jacket and a thin,
nylon disruptive-pattern smock. We were probably
carrying 60 lb each.

These exercises usually took place on the Brecon
Beacons. We would be given a map reference which,
in theory, would be in enemy territory perhaps 20 to
30 miles from Hereford. We would be expected to
practise moving through enemy territory, travelling at
night and holing up somewhere during daylight
hours. We were strictly forbidden to make fires,
hence the hard rations. We weren't even permitted
to boil a kettle. We were not even allowed to crash

out in a farmer's barn or make use of any other form of man-made protection. The orders stipulated that we had to keep away from all human habitation and, indeed, we had to make believe that everyone we came across was the enemy so that we moved through the country unknown and unsighted.

At the map reference we were ordered to lie low and keep out of sight and to take up an ambush position, waiting for enemy patrols to appear. The plan would always be to find a suitable bushy area under which we could hide, indeed, almost disappear. Having scraped away the undergrowth, the plan was to saw off some of the low branches with a 'flexible' saw and set them above you, thus giving further protection from wind, rain and any possible enemy. It could well be that we would have to stay there for a week or more, so the greater the protection, the better one's security was.

Quite often we would be on our own but within sight of each other. After setting up our hides we would hold a briefing to decide on our course of action when an enemy patrol did come into sight. From that moment on we would maintain absolute and complete silence, even if we were lying there for a week. It was very, very boring.

The great test was to try to keep awake, to maintain interest and not to sink into a semi-trance. After a while, the birds and any other wild animals in the immediate vicinity would settle down and accept our presence, even though we had invaded their habitat. Unwittingly they become our own personal guard dogs for if any intruder approached they would hear them and react earlier than we ever would. I would deliberately train myself to take little notice of any side noises that might have been possible enemy incursions but to wait until the birds, and any other animals we had come across, alerted me to intruders.

Sometimes, of course, those intruders were not

human beings but other animals but that helped to keep me on the ball. The main difficulty was remaining watchful. We all knew that if we didn't stay alert we probably wouldn't stay alive. If our instructors came upon us without any reaction from us or, heaven forbid, discovered us asleep, we ran the grave risk of being RTU'd.

We would have been briefed, for example, that our 'enemy' target was a platoon of soldiers wearing blue arm bands, which would mean not reacting at all to any other soldiers in the area. As a result, it meant keeping absolutely silent whenever others passed by, almost holding one's breath for fear they might hear.

When the target platoon did, in fact, come into our line of fire, we would wait until they reached a position where we could all open fire at the same instant. We had to ensure that the entire platoon, of perhaps twelve men, would be wiped out at once. If anyone survived, he would be given a *coup de grace* in the back of the head. There would be no question whatsoever of letting any member of the enemy squad survive for he might somehow report our whereabouts and that would be courting disaster and death.

Having taken documents from one of the 'dead' soldiers, to prove that we had succeeded in our mission, the next task would be to high tail it back to Hereford, once again moving at night and making sure no one saw us during daylight hours. To keep us alert on the way back to base, we would have to ensure that no one tailed us. If we suspected that someone was following, we were instructed to lay an ambush.

When on the move by night, it was vital to find the 'perfect' cover in which to sleep during daylight hours without the possibility of being seen, heard or discovered accidentally. It would also be necessary to ensure that we could not be spotted from the air. One of us always stood guard – two hours on, six hours off. A piece of cord would be attached by the man on duty to the wrist of the man next on duty. This method of communication may seem dreadfully old fashioned but it worked perfectly and, more important, it was silent.

There would need to be one entrance as well as a separate exit, in case of emergency. We would always sleep with our boots on, ready, if necessary, to move out at speed. Our rifles would always be within arm's reach and we would never unpack our gear.

Claymore anti-personnel mines would be laid at strategic positions about twenty yards from our base. As we had been told in training: 'If someone tries to creep up on you, being blown to bits tends to put them off.'

Moving across country was another art we had to learn. There were few hard and fast rules; it was principally a matter of common sense plus a natural affinity for the surroundings. Cover, shade, woods, trees – all provided some protection from enemy patrols. Woods, preferably forests, were useful because they afforded great protection from night vision equipment and portable radar apparatus.

Our instructors also emphasised the necessity of training in the evasion of sniffer dogs. They would impress on us the number of German Shepherds and other powerfully built dogs that Iron Curtain countries put great faith in. Throughout training, our instructors always put great emphasis on the security measures adopted by Eastern bloc countries, making us believe that the SAS could expect to be asked to undertake covert action behind the Iron Curtain.

When on a lead, the average dog is only as fast as its handler and dog handlers are not renowned as fast walkers or as men with great stamina. The odds were therefore stacked in favour of the SAS unit who were trained to move across country faster than anyone else. However, if a handler released his dog to follow us and attack, we were trained to kill.

We would sense from the barking that the animal had been set free and one of the squad would be detailed to confront the animal. He would take off his combat jacket and wrap it around his left arm. In the method it had learned in training, the dog would lunge at the man, burying its teeth in his forearm. We were trained never to run away but always to stand and face the animal. Having attacked and buried its teeth in the man's left arm, the dog would then be totally exposed to a knife. As the dog hung on the arm, we would split it open from stomach to sternum. Once it was on the ground, we would cut its throat to put it out of its misery. Thank God, however, I never actually had to do it.

For the remaining four weeks we were taught the art of survival in difficult, and even impossible, country. The instructors drilled it into us that a rifle, a gun, a knife – any weapon – is useless for survival when compared with plain, ordinary water. Without water you're dead. They rammed home to us the knowledge that it only takes three days without water to kill someone. We knew we could last three weeks without food but not without water. We had to practise collecting water using polythene sheeting. We also learned to catch grass snakes. On occasions we would catch a grass snake and barbecue it, having taken out the guts and opened out the flesh. It may sound disgusting but, in reality, it wasn't that bad and tasted rather like chicken.

We were taken for nature walks which always caused the odd joke and much laughter, but our instructors would tell us to cut the cackle by reminding us that paying attention to this lesson could mean the difference between life and death. We were taught what we could and could not eat; what was poisonous, nutritious, tasty and bloody awful. Even so, as the lectures continued, I could still never imagine myself scrabbling around on the ground searching for the correct insects to eat, no matter how hungry I became.

We were encouraged to search for fish and given instructions on how to catch them without sitting on a river bank for hours on end. We would set a line and hook and then leave the fish to bite while we went off setting up snares for rabbits, game birds or whatever. Despite this, throughout our training I never managed to hook a single fish or catch a rabbit. It made me wonder what might happen to me if I ever did find myself starving to death in some foreign country.

There seemed to be more important things to learn. One of the principal reasons for operating behind enemy lines is to acquire sensitive information or search out targets for bombing raids or artillery fire. It was therefore necessary to be highly skilled in transmitting information back to base, either by wireless or Morse code. That took some learning. Eight words a minute was the goal and for many that was almost impossible. Many of the lads spent hours each evening learning and practising Morse code among themselves. Once learned, however, one never forgot it, and after a while, it came as easily as the two-times table.

Throughout continuation training, SAS instructors would also lecture us, sometimes twice a week, on terrorism and the ways and means terrorists use to achieve their objectives. We learned about the forces guiding the terrorists' political thinking and their fanaticism. Much of the content of these lectures had been gleaned from British forces fighting the communists in Malaya and from the American Special Forces in their war against the Vietcong.

We began these lectures by focusing on jungle

warfare and then spent some time learning about Middle East terrorism, but later the instructors turned their attention to the IRA. We were led to understand that many of the Catholic population in Northern Ireland were terrorised as much by the IRA as by the Protestant paramilitary gangs. We learned that, just as terrorist organisations around the world coerced young men to fight for them by threatening their families, so the IRA used precisely the same tactics among the Catholic community. We came to believe that many young men were not diehard, indoctrinated terrorists but young people who could be persuaded to lead a peaceful life rather than risk death or serious injury fighting for a cause they were not totally committed to supporting.

We were also informed that some younger IRA fighters, some of whom were only teenagers, believed that they had 'God and right' on their side and were only too ready to die for their beliefs. We were led to understand that IRA gunmen would order whole estates to come out of their homes and riot against the British military; we heard tales of children being beaten up at school if their parents hadn't been out rioting on the streets often enough; and we knew, because we saw reports on television, of the tarring and feathering of teenage girls who dated British soldiers or even attended dances where soldiers congregated.

During the early part of 1971 we could see from television reports that the situation in Northern Ireland was deteriorating rapidly. IRA gunmen were taking over the policing of many Catholic areas and British soldiers patrolling the streets were becoming everyday targets. Deliberately, the IRA promoted a policy of dividing the Catholic people from the soldiers who had been sent to Ireland to protect them not only from loyalist paramilitary organisations but also from police harassment at the hands of the hated B-Specials.

By the summer of 1971 the camaraderie that had once existed between the average Catholic family and the British soldiers had totally broken down. The cups of tea, cigarettes and sticky buns which had been freely offered to the soldiers when they first took up their duties in Catholic areas, had gone. The IRA had to find a way of separating the Catholics from their protectors. They did so by targeting the soldiers, first during rioting and then by encouraging gunmen to hit the soldiers while on patrol.

The IRA knew the army would have to retaliate and, of course, they did, often causing mayhem as they tried to single out gunmen, chasing, following, arresting and sometimes shooting them. As the summer of 1971 went by, the antagonism between the Catholics and the army deteriorated to such a degree that open enmity developed. Now the IRA could boast that they were protecting the Catholic community not only from the Protestant majority but also from the British army. They had succeeded in creating a siege atmosphere, a situation which could only benefit the IRA in their real campaign of fighting for their dream of a united Ireland.

We understood all of this but had little idea how we would be involved in fighting such urban terrorist activity. Most of us had originally believed we would be heading for active service in the Middle East but, as the lectures went on, more and more we realised that we might, indeed, be heading for the cauldron of Northern Ireland.

CHAPTER FOUR

A T THE END of our fourteen-week continuation
training we were rewarded with another leave,
only this one would not be so generous – a
mere 72-hour pass, hardly enough time to get home,
have a bath, a meal and a drink with some mates
before catching the train back to Hereford.

I decided to go home to see my parents and
brothers and sisters in London as I hadn't seen them
for months. My father asked how things were going
but he didn't want to join me for a pint or talk about
my training. My mother wanted me to pack in the
SAS and return to the REME. At least my brothers
and sisters seemed proud of the fact that I had
become a member of Britain's crack forces.

However, one incident back home showed me why
SAS soldiers hide their identity and keep a low
profile. I had warned my brothers never to tell anyone I had joined the SAS, so they would tell people
instead that I had joined the Paras.

Unfortunately, one of my brothers had been

boasting in the pub about his elder brother being a Para and a couple of likely lads, who I had known as a teenager, decided to act tough. While I was buying drinks at the bar, one of them came up, stood beside me and deliberately trod on my foot. I just gave him a dirty look and carried on buying the beers.

'I thought you Paras were meant to be tough,' he said attempting to ridicule me.

My brother saw what was happening and came steaming in, punching the guy in the face. His mates jumped in and, of course, I then had to become involved. I couldn't see these blokes getting the better of my brother, so I pitched in. Within a minute most of the pub was in turmoil, bottles and glasses flying everywhere and punches and boots going in. No one seemed to know who they were fighting or why, with everyone throwing punches at whoever came into reach. I grabbed hold of my brother and dragged him out of the pub, leaving the rest fighting.

I had a few words with him but, thank goodness, he had learned his lesson; he would never brag about his elder brother again. It also made me realise how careful I had to be. I knew that I would not be the most popular SAS recruit back at Hereford if I got nicked for brawling.

Back at Hereford we packed our kit and drove to Abingdon, Oxfordshire for parachute training. For me, this would be the best part of the entire training schedule. One reason was that if I passed this successfully I would be badged, awarded my SAS wings.

For the first ten days we drove to Aldershot each day for confidence training, using the Parachute Regiment's assault course. Para NCOs were in charge of this part of our training and they drove us hard. However, because of our endurance training we were probably twice as tough as the great majority of Paratroopers.

Surprisingly, a couple of our lads were RTU'd from the assault course because they had never known that they suffered from vertigo. Their realisation came about when we had to make a six-foot jump from one piece of scaffolding to another with a 40-foot drop below. A safety net had been put in place, but these lads still could not make the jump. They could never become fully-fledged SAS men with such a mental block.

As well as jump-training from specially built scaffolding (a mock-up of a Hercules transport plane), we also had to learn how to fold and pack a parachute correctly. We all learned this exercise quickly because we knew our very lives depended on it.

Then I had to face my first ever jump from the sky – the celebrated balloon jump. For me, this would be horrible. Having strapped on our parachutes, four of us and a Para instructor climbed into the basket, and the balloon began silently and slowly to climb into the sky. Every time I looked down the ground seemed to be diminishing and I thought I would never make the jump.

The instructor hooked me up as I was the first in line. He opened the sliding gate on the front of the balloon's basket and tapped me on the shoulder. I thought at that instant, 'I've got to do it. I have to jump,' although it was the last thing I wanted to do. I shut my eyes and jumped. There was an instant of terror, a fear that the 'chute wouldn't open and then, before I realised what was happening, the parachute opened and I felt the jerk of the harness.

I shall never forget the joy of seeing the 'chute open and the feeling of weightlessness in the open air. I had somehow gone from near death to a new life – it was the next best thing in life after an orgasm. From that moment I knew I would always be apprehensive when parachuting, always wondering if the 'chute would open, and that every time that fear would be followed by a sense of ecstatic joy when it did open and I floated down to earth in peace, quiet and serenity.

I concentrated on my landing, bending my knees as instructed and rolling over on to my side. Everything went like clockwork but I was relieved when I realised I was on *terra firma* once again and in one piece. In fact, so elated did I feel, and the jump seemed to be over so quickly, that all I wanted to do was go up again to relive the experience.

As a result, I was looking forward to the eight static-line jumps we would be doing over Salisbury Plain during the next three weeks. Before each and every jump I would become nervous, knowing about everything that could go wrong, but all the jumps seemed to be over too quickly as we were only falling from 600 feet.

In between jumping we also attended lectures designed to teach us the intricacies of parachuting into enemy territory. We knew that if we were ever to operate behind enemy lines, the odds would favour parachuting into position rather than being choppered in. We were also taught how easy it had become for the enemy to trace, engage and shoot down aircraft over their territory and how vulnerable we would be in such circumstances. They tried to reassure us by pointing out various ways in which the enemy could be wrong-footed but, in our hearts, we realised how dicey it would be. Those lessons were not very comforting but we had to know the worst.

For our first free fall we travelled to Brize Norton and clambered into a Hercules. Our first three jumps were up to 10,000 feet because above that level oxygen must be used. Most parachutists are encouraged to open their 'chutes after a few hundred feet but we were trained to free fall until just above 2,000 feet to safeguard against being seen by enemy forces below.

By the time we completed the course we had become quite sophisticated parachutists. Using wing-style 'chutes, we could fly across the skies for up to 25 miles, which was great fun, and still ensure that we could land on the proverbial sixpence. A couple of times during the early part of training I did land in trees, which was bloody uncomfortable. Fortunately, I suffered no serious damage, just cuts and bruises as punishment for misjudging the landing.

Those accidents caused much laughter and piss-taking but everyone screwed up in one way or another. Our instructors told us it was all part of the training.

The highest jump was at 26,000 feet. We were above the clouds and freezing cold as we waited for the green light to flash on, our signal to leap out of the aircraft. Floating through the clouds was an eerie experience, not knowing what we would see when we left the cloud cover.

Parachuting at night caused even more concern. A luminous patch had been sewn on to the black night 'chutes so that we could all see each other after leaving the aircraft at the rate of one man every two or three seconds. Once the first man had jumped there would be no waiting for those following; we would simply walk along the aircraft and out into the sky. The plan was for all of us to land within a few feet of each other but, at first, that didn't always happen. On one occasion one bloke landed in a lake hundreds of yards from where the rest of us had come down successfully. It was an hour before we found him, soaked through and freezing cold.

From that incident, however, we all learned a valuable lesson. As the instructor pointed out: 'If that had happened on active service no one would have wasted time searching for the rogue parachutist. He would have been left to his own devices, for time wasted in searching for him could have put the rest of the unit at risk or screwed up the entire operation.'

Everyone was given the DZ (drop-zone) map reference so that if, by chance, a bloke got swept off course then he knew where to rendezvous. Everyone also knew that the unit could not, and would not, wait too long before moving off.

On landing, we had to be prepared to begin fighting immediately. Three men would be designated to defend the DZ while the rest gathered the kit together. The unit leader would have to decide whether it was possible to fight their way out of trouble or consider calling up a chopper to pull the unit out.

When parachuting, we were equipped with D-rings on each shoulder, attached by webbing to a harness around the upper body. In a real emergency, when a rescue chopper could not land, the crew would throw out lines which we would hook on to the D-rings. When all four men had hooked up, the chopper would whisk us away until it was safe to land and we could clamber aboard. We practised that frequently. Sometimes it got rather hairy but it provided a great feeling of exhilaration as we were carried along above tree level for perhaps a mile or more.

Following our final successful jump at high altitude, we were all invited into the sergeants' mess at Brize Norton for a great piss up. After the months of grit and determination, that night was a blissful relaxation; the pints of beer came thick and fast and everyone was singing and shouting, laughing and thankful that we had finally made the grade. Many of those who had started out had fallen by the wayside but we, the select few, had somehow managed to hack it.

I had dreamed of this moment and now I had done it. It felt bloody wonderful. Part of me wanted to cry with sheer relief that the initial training was over and I could hold my head up high. Before I became too maudlin, however, I had another pint and put those thoughts behind me.

Throughout our training we had all got on quite well together. We all realised that if we were going to pass the course we would need to remain friends, help each other when necessary and show a certain camaraderie towards each other. It seemed to me that most of us were of a certain type, quiet, even taciturn, determined and, perhaps more important, committed to the SAS.

We knew that on our return to Hereford we would receive our Para wings and would finally be officially welcomed into the SAS, the tortures of the past eight months over. We also knew, for we had been told a thousand times, that in the SAS the training never ends. Even those men who have been in the regiment for years still undergo training whenever they are not involved in active operations. In that way, SAS units are always in peak condition, their training always under review, so that they are capable of turning out on a mission within 24 hours, superbly fit, highly trained and ready for action. Unofficially, the SAS had adopted the famous Martini slogan of 'any place, any time, anywhere'. Some suggested it should become the SAS motto.

Back at Hereford, the eight of us who had survived the rigours of the course were ordered to report to the CO. We marched in, saluted and he handed us our wings and the sand-coloured SAS beret. He also formally congratulated us and welcomed each of us in turn to the regiment. He also issued a word of warning: 'You will find this beret harder to keep than it has been to win.'

I would never forget those words but at the time I could not comprehend that anything could be tougher than the blood and sweat I had shed gaining that SAS beret. I had not the slightest idea what the future would hold nor could I have understood at that time the enormous stress and strain the beret and wings would bring me.

We all realised, and most of us secretly hoped, that we would soon be putting everything we had learned into practice. We half-expected to find ourselves in some strange foreign country, probably somewhere in the Middle East, on active service, desperately trying to remember all we had been taught.

By July 1971, the newspapers were full of the Northern Ireland troubles. We knew that some SAS units were operating there for it had become the unofficial talk of the Hereford camp.

After a 72-hour pass we were told to report back to Hereford. We were not surprised to be ordered to undergo an eight-mile cross-country run. It seemed that we were back at the beginning of our training course. As we hadn't done any intensive training for several weeks, we did feel knackered. As I was about to strip off and take a shower, an SAS instructor walked in and told me to report immediately to an NCO in another hut. I walked in to find two blokes, total strangers, dressed in civvies standing at the end of the hut and a single chair in the middle of the room. 'Sit down.'

I obeyed, wondering what on earth this was all about.

They began questioning me, asking me what I had done over the weekend. In fact, I had decided to relax and go off on my own, armed with my binoculars, to do some serious birdwatching. I hitch-hiked to Llandovery in South Wales to study the red kites which were under threat of extinction in Britain. I had travelled down on the Saturday morning, returning on Monday afternoon, taking a sleeping bag, living rough and eating in cafes. I had really enjoyed myself, alone, away from the army and watching these wonderful birds.

Before I had time to explain, one said, 'We hear you have been down the pub bragging that you're in the SAS. Is that right?'

'No. That's untrue,' I said, 'I never went to any pub over the weekend.'

They refused to believe me. They told me they had someone who would recognise me, who could identify me, who would be prepared to put me in the frame. They told me I was lying through my teeth and that this man would tell the truth.

I denied it all. I told them the guy must be mistaken. I was beginning to become angry with their accusations, angry that they would not believe what I was telling them.

They then demanded that I relate to them, in every detail, precisely where I was, how I had spent the time, where I had been staying, giving them names and places and asking if there was anyone who could prove my word was true. I couldn't name anyone.

Understandably, they didn't believe me. They refused to believe that I had been totally on my own throughout the 72 hours with no one able to identify me or come forward to support my alibi. I was in a fix. I hoped these two geezers would go and find their witness so that he could disprove their allegations.

They carried on questioning me for more than an hour. I became confused because they were repeating, over and over again, the allegations which I knew to be false. Suddenly one told me, 'Fuck off out of here. We'll be seeing you later.'

I left the hut feeling totally bemused, hoping that I had heard the last of their accusations. I had a hot shower and tried to forget about the whole business. Then I went over to the cookhouse for lunch and ran into two mates.

They told me they had just had the strangest experience and related precisely what had occurred to me too. They had been ordered to another hut and made to answer the same allegations which they, too, had vehemently denied. I told them I had undergone the same treatment.

We tried to figure out who the SAS man could be who had been in Hereford pubs bragging and shouting his mouth off. We couldn't think that any one of us would have acted in such a way.

That evening as I sat down in the cookhouse with my tea, an SAS instructor who I knew quite well came over and whispered in my ear, 'Whatever you do, tell them fuck all. Just tell them a load of bollocks.'

'What do you mean?' I asked.

'Just remember what I said,' he replied and walked off.

Now I was totally confused, wondering what the hell was going on; wondering who I had to tell 'fuck all' to and, more important, why? Finally, I went to bed, began to read and fell asleep still confused as to what had gone on that day.

I woke with a start, with the hut in pitch darkness and someone shaking my arm, telling me to get up. Luckily, I had gone to bed in my underpants because I was given no time to put on anything, not even a T-shirt or trousers.

I was still half-asleep as two men pushed me towards the end of the hut and out of the door. I couldn't see their faces but something told me they were probably the two strangers who had interrogated me earlier that day. I was half-dragged, half pushed across the open ground and into another hut. I was roughly pushed into a chair. I began to come to and reckoned that I was probably in the same hut where I had been questioned the previous day.

They shoved a black bag made of cotton material over my head. My hands were tied with cord behind the chair and then there was silence. I tried to hear what was going on; I strained to listen in case they spoke, to give me some idea of what was happening. For all of five minutes I was left alone with not a word or a sound coming from inside that room. My heart began to thump.

'What was this parachute course like that you've just been on?' One man asked.

Remembering what my SAS instructor had advised me, I denied I had been on a parachute course.

He said, 'You've been in the SAS for eight fucking months and you haven't been on a parachute course. That's bollocks.'

'I ain't been here for eight months, I've only just arrived,' I lied.

'Bullshit,' one replied, 'Don't you lie to us.'

'I'm not lying,' I protested.

For the next two hours the two men kept up a relentless barrage of questions, sometimes asking me things about my life in the army which I knew to be true but which I denied vehemently to them. They even questioned me about my time in the REME, about things I had done, all of which were true. I kept wondering what the hell all this questioning was for; convinced that they still believed that I had been in a Hereford pub boasting about being a member of the SAS.

Then the insults really began. They were fucking and blinding, calling me all the names under the sun, insulting my parents and all the time calling me a lying bastard. Then, suddenly, I heard a woman's voice in the room. She was saying, 'Who's this old slag Maria from Tidworth?'

'I don't know who you're talking about,' I lied. 'I don't know anybody called Maria.'

The foul-mouthed bitch continued: 'Don't you fucking lie to me. Not only do you know this Maria but we know that while you have been here she has been fucking every Tom, Dick and Harry around

Tidworth. She's nothing but an old slag, nothing better than a fucking whore.'

Like a bolt from the blue I understood. I knew Maria wasn't like that. I knew this bitch was telling lies. The penny dropped; this was the feared interrogation training we had heard rumours about but never been told about officially. Our instructors had never mentioned interrogation training but we knew, from what we had heard, that one day we would be put through this training. I did not know what to expect but I convinced myself in that instant that this was it.

They kept asking me questions. I would answer whatever came into my mind but I did not tell the truth. I found my mouth had become dry and was feeling terribly thirsty. I asked if I could have some water.

'You're getting fuck all, you lying shit, until you start telling us the truth,' they replied.

They continued asking questions, about the training, the SAS, my past, everything and anything. I started to get angry. Suddenly, I felt a shot of pain across my legs as though I had been struck with a cane. Then another swish and the cane hit my other leg. 'What the fuck's that for?' I asked.

'Every time you lie to us you'll get another one. And they'll get harder and harder until you tell us what we want to know.'

'I've told you everything,' I lied again. The cane swished again, cutting across my naked thigh.

I had a sudden fear that they would hit my bollocks. I thought of crossing my legs to protect myself but realised that if I did that then they were certain to go for my balls and I knew that would really hurt.

They began to slap me across the face whenever I answered them. It didn't matter what I said but, every so often, with no warning, one of them would

Catholic mourners carry crosses through 'Derry after thirteen people were killed on Bloody Sunday, January, 1972.

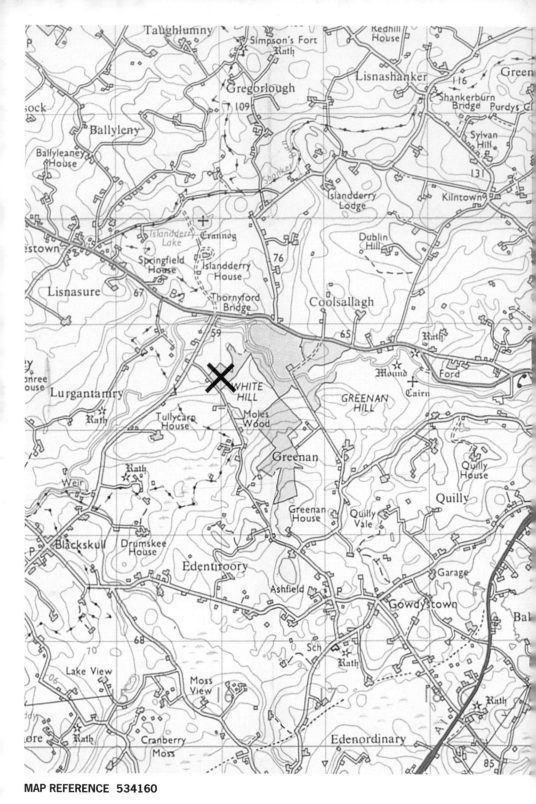

MAP REFERENCE 534160

The first burial ground off Blackskull Road, between Dromore and Lurgan. The SAS unit dumped most of the bodies in deep trenches on the edge of the wood during their first seven months of action. The burial site is marked by a cross.

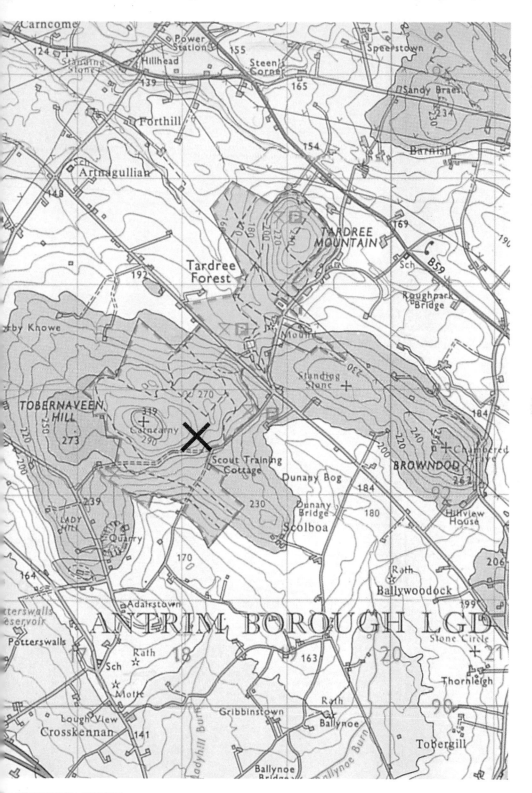

P REFERENCE 925182

e second burial ground deep in Tardree Forest where the remaining victims were
ried in a specially dug trench. The cross marks the grave.

The place on White Hill where the SAS unit parked their car before making their
victims walk the few hundred yards to their place of execution on the edge of the wood

Top: Villawood Road, Greenan, the road along which Paul Bruce and his three SAS colleagues drove, taking their prisoners to the place of execution.

Middle: The author Paul Bruce points into the conifer wood off Villawood Road, where the bodies were buried.

Below: The author Paul Bruce in front of the fresh line of conifers planted since his SAS unit dumped the bodies of IRA suspects.

Top: The turning off the main Lurgan-Dromore Road pointing towards Blackskull and the wood where IRA suspects were dumped.

Below: The author Paul Bruce points to a spot on the border with the Republic, one of the meeting points where IRA suspects were handed over for execution.

well-fortified British Army border post manned by uniformed British Army troops.

Top: A British Army patrol, Belfast, 1971. The gas masks were protection against CS g
used by the troops to disperse demonstrators.

Below: Troops try to halt a Civil Rights demonstration in Belfast, 1971.

smack me across the face or use the cane on my legs. Neither was really painful but what shook me was the fact that there was no warning; every hit or slap came as a shock and that disoriented me.

I don't know how long the interrogation and physical abuse went on because, after an hour or so, I lost track of time. I judged it must have continued for about two more hours but I may have been wrong. It could have been longer. I began to lose touch with reality. I kept telling myself that this was only interrogation training, that it would soon be over, that they would take off the hood and tell me everything was fine and I could go back to my billet and get some sleep. And yet part of my brain began to doubt that because the blows and the questions were very real indeed.

I wanted to go for a piss. Suddenly, all I could think about was wanting to go for a slash but I kept my mouth shut because I knew that they wouldn't let me go; indeed, they would probably have loved to see me pissing in my pants while they laughed at me and took the mickey. I was determined not to give them that pleasure.

It seemed odd because I was both desperately thirsty and desperate for a piss. I kept asking for a drink but they never once gave me even a sip of water.

I began to have doubts about what was going on. I couldn't believe that this was only training. I knew the SAS system was tough and the training rigorous but this seemed beyond credibility. But if it wasn't training, what the hell were these people after; what did they want with me; why were they determined to slag off poor Maria and insult me and my parents.

At times I became angry. I swore at them, told them I was telling the truth and told them, including the woman, that they were all a bunch of cunts. I told the bitch: 'How dare you slag off Maria. You have no right to do that. You're calling her names because you're probably the biggest whore around Hereford.'

For that I earned three hard swishes with the cane across my thighs. They hurt. Not once did they laugh; not once did they change their approach to me; not once did they give me an inkling that this was all a game and that it would soon be over. Occasionally, throughout the interrogation, I told myself that, once I was free, I would kick the shit out of these three bastards, particularly the bitch who had been slagging off Maria.

Then one said casually, his voice filled with menace, 'We're going to leave you here to think about things. When we return we want you to tell us the truth, or else. Do you hear? We haven't touched you yet. Tell us more lies and you'll really pay for it. We're fed up with all your fucking lies.'

They must have been gone for the best part of an hour. During that time I tried to rationalise what was happening. Deep down, I suspected that if they were determined to hurt me they would attack my bollocks. That worried me.

They returned and immediately resumed the same relentless questions that they had asked a thousand times before. The blows came raining down on my face and my legs and thighs were hit repeatedly with the cane. I came to fear the swish, knowing that a split second later I would feel the cane cutting across my legs and thighs. It was not knowing where or when I would be hit next that upset me, not the actual pain. I could take that. But I didn't know whether I would be able to stand it when they began grabbing, kicking or hitting my balls. I just hoped to hell they would leave them alone.

I lost track of time; I lost track of what to say to try to put an end to this bloody agony. I thought of telling them the truth; sometimes I was within an ace of jacking in the whole bloody interrogation and telling them truthfully the answers to all the questions they had asked about the SAS, the training, the parachuting, everything. And yet something made me keep up my tissue of lies. I kept thinking of the advice my SAS instructor had given me, 'Tell them nothing'.

And it worked.

Suddenly, I felt the hood being taken off my head and I blinked at the light. I looked around and saw the two men and the woman who had been tormenting me. I was trying to pull myself together, to gather my strength, when one of the men said, 'It's all over. You did well.'

The sense of relief was unbelievable. All thoughts that I had nurtured of kicking the shit out of them vanished in a second. All I wanted to do was have a slash. I was near to bursting point. I also desperately needed a drink.

One told me it was ten o'clock at night; that I had been under interrogation for twenty hours; that now I was free to go and do whatever I wanted, have a meal, have a drink, have a shower or just go to sleep. All I wanted was a slash, a shower and bed.

As I drifted off to sleep, my thoughts returned to the interrogation. On the one hand, I was happy that I had survived without breaking down but on the other I thought that if ever I found myself in a situation where I needed to break someone to find out information, I wouldn't be as gentle as my interrogators. I would go straight to the balls and inflict as much pain as possible as quickly as possible to get the result I needed. Then I fell asleep wondering what the hell I was doing in the fucking SAS.

The next morning I discovered that three of my mates had been given the same treatment. We were all knackered.

Later, we were debriefed by our instructors. They told us the reasons for giving us what they said was a little taste of the type of interrogation we could

expect if we ever fell into enemy hands. They emphasised that they had only given us 'a taste' of the
treatment we could expect. We all realised what they
meant; that if anyone was trying to gain information
from us in earnest, they would ignore all the niceties
and brute force would be used from the very beginning. It didn't warrant thinking about. What we had
experienced was bad enough and we had been
questioned and abused by our own instructors.

They told us that everyone has a breaking point;
that the bravest man in the world will always be
broken at some point; that the reason for holding out
if we ever found ourself under interrogation was for
two specific purposes – to give our SAS comrades
time to escape or to give as much time as possible for
any counter-attack to be launched which might result
in our own release.

Our instructors told us that the time had come for
revision, coupled with two weeks of intense physical
training, runs, route marches and gym work. We
returned to basics: weapon training and map-reading
and more firing of live rounds on the ranges, using
SLRs, SMGs and the Browning pistol. They seemed to
be preparing us for the real thing.

Usually at this stage, most SAS recruits then enter
another phase of training, a further three months of
continuation training. This might entail intensive
medical training, at the end of which an SAS recruit
would be capable of treating broken bones, snake
bites and other ailments and diagnosing various
fevers, as well as tending to the wounded with some
degree of professionalism. We missed out that three
months of extra training but we didn't guess why.
Our SAS officers knew that where we were destined
to operate there would be no need for medical
training or desert survival techniques. However, we
would need to be very experienced in all forms of
weapons training.

Throughout the summer months Maria and I had drifted apart but the hell I had been through defending her during the interrogation nagged at me. I found it difficult to forget her; to forget how good our relationship had been. I kept thinking of her lovely face, her laughter and the great times we had had together. I wanted to rekindle what we had enjoyed before and I wrote from Hereford but she didn't reply. I wondered if the bitch in interrogation had actually known about Maria, whether she had known that she really had been putting it about in Tidworth. Part of me wanted to know the truth; part of me didn't.

When I heard nothing, I knew I had to put Maria behind me; to forget her. Secretly I hoped we would meet again one day and who knows what might happen. Deep down, however, I was jealous, jealous of who she was seeing, who she was kissing, who she was fucking. I hated it.

Hearing nothing from Maria, I spent my seven days' leave at the end of August at home in London, enjoying home cooking, a few pints with the lads and the sheer bliss of not having to think for a second about the army, the SAS or bloody training. I met Betty, a good-looking, fair-haired, twenty-year-old florist who worked in Walthamstow. One of my younger bothers introduced us and we hit it off straightaway.

She knew I was in the army and that I had only seven days' leave and realised that I wanted to have a damn good time and forget all about the army. She seemed only too happy to enjoy those days with me. I didn't tell her that one of the reasons why I needed her company was to try to forget about my affair with Maria. We went out drinking and went around London together, to museums and art galleries, sightseeing like any tourists. She helped me to forget Maria and we would spend every night making love at her home till we fell asleep exhausted. It was exactly what I needed after nine months of hard, bloody training.

After a few days back at Hereford, getting fit with cross country runs and circuit training, I would meet the three other men who would become closer than my brothers during the next twelve months.

I was told to report to the company sergeant-major's office in the headquarters squadron. Sitting on the sergeant-major's desk, smoking a cigarette and chatting away, I saw a hard-nosed, suntanned, young SAS sergeant with collar-length dark hair and a Zapata-style moustache. He had long sideburns which came to below his ear lobes. He looked very fit, strong and healthy, about five foot nine inches tall, with an athletic, boxer's physique. His suntan was deep and I realised he must recently have returned from some Middle East operation. Later, he would tell me of his experiences in Oman.

'This is Don,' said the CSM. 'Don, this is Paul.'

An Eastender, Don said casually, 'How's it going?'

'Fine,' I replied.

'Good,' he said as he looked me up and down. He knew I was an Essex boy although everyone else in the SAS took me to be a Londoner.

The CSM said, 'We're just waiting for a couple of others. Take a seat, we'll be with you in a minute.'

I sat and waited for a few minutes, letting them chat together. They were talking about the CSM's children who were in married quarters at Hereford.

Then, into the office came the two men we had been waiting for. I was rather surprised because I knew them both. We had bumped into each other on occasions at the camp. They had not been part of my outfit but in another unit going through the same training regime at the same time.

The first, Benny, was about five feet seven inches tall, with dark hair, a dark, swarthy complexion and a small, military-type moustache. He was in his early twenties, stockily built, strong and fit, and the one thing I immediately noticed about him was the size of his hands and feet. They were really big, out of all proportion to the rest of his body. Wherever we would go later, to pubs or clubs, the women would flock around him. They believed the old adage that you can tell the size of a man's cock by looking at the size of his hands. In Benny's case it was all too true, for the size of his todger was remarkable. He loved the attention.

With him was JR, another typical SAS type, about five feet eight inches tall, strong-looking, athletic and light on his feet. He would bounce about rather than walk. Dark haired, with a fair complexion and grey-blue eyes, he would become the comedian of the group. In his early twenties like me and Benny, JR seemed to be bursting with energy, unable to keep still. His reactions were like greased lightning. We would always be telling JR to calm down, relax and take things easy but he couldn't.

We would say of JR that he was such a tight bastard that he would peel an orange in his trouser pocket and cut it up and eat it on the quiet so that none of us even realised he was doing it. A Northerner with a good sense of humour, he would be fun to have around. But he had a failing that we would discover later.

The CSM introduced us and we all shook hands, nodding to each other but saying nothing. He told us, 'You will soon be going to Ulster because there is a nice little job someone wants you to do out there.'

Our faces dropped. We had all hoped to travel to the Middle East; we didn't fancy Northern Ireland with its hard, cold weather. We had seen enough of the place on the television lately.

Not waiting for any response from us, the CSM continued, 'You will be going out on a week's exercise in which you will have to take evasive action, keep a low profile and not be discovered. We will be sending out some men to search for you and capture you. You must all make bloody sure you are not captured because they will be told that if they do capture you they will be permitted to interrogate you a fucking sight harder than the other week. So make sure you don't get caught.'

He went on, 'Don here will be in command. From now on you will look on him not only as your commander but also as your mother. Do everything he tells you and learn as much as you can from him. He's done it all and he knows how to operate. This is a chance for you three to learn what the SAS is all about. He knows the score.'

The CSM continued: 'From now on you will have to get used to having live ammunition and your firearms with you at all times; not just during the day, but twenty-four hours round the clock. After leaving here you will go to the armoury and take out an SMG each and two magazines of 7.62 mm. You will have to sign for them and woe betide anyone if you as much as lose one round, let alone your weapon.'

It was the usual old army bullshit but, somehow, coming from this CSM it sounded more intense, more urgent. This would, after all, be the real thing.

'After that you will go to your billet and pack as though for an exercise. Pack as little as possible because for the next seven days you will be on the run, moving fast across country. You will not want to take the kitchen sink with you. In fact, the only thing of importance you will be taking with you is your weapon and ammunition; nothing else really matters except, of course, your compass.

'This is a test. If you can get through this week on the run you will be told to stay out for a further two weeks, living off the land. By the end of that time you will have got to know each other well, better than your own brothers. Where you lot are going you will need to read each other's minds and know precisely how you are all going to respond under really stressful conditions. This is the best way of getting to learn about yourselves and each other.'

He concluded, 'That's about it. I don't want to see you for three weeks.'

He did not say 'good luck'. We had already learned that no member of the SAS ever uses the phrase 'good luck'. The reason they don't is because they never believe in luck; their training, professionalism, stamina and natural ability are considered far more important than any luck could ever be.

We trooped out, a little bewildered by what had happened. None of us were specialists, except Don, and we had thought that our training would last for at least another six months before we were sent on an operation. We could have understood it if we had been specialists in medical, signals, explosives or whatever, but we had no specialist training.

Outside the CSM's office Don gave us a quick, short briefing, adding to the official one from the CSM: 'Just take your sleeping bag, a ground sheet, a mess tin, irons, one set of spare clothing and a commando knife. One other thing, make sure you bring your Post Office savings book.'

We looked at him bemused. With a grin, he added, 'Don't worry. Once we get through this first week we are going to have the time of our lives.'

That brought smiles to our faces even though we did not completely understand what he had in mind. It sounded good, however, and he was our new 'guv'nor'. Anything he said would be all right by us.

An hour later we were walking out of the Hereford headquarters, heading west towards the Black Mountains and the Brecon Beacons beyond, with our weapons, ammunition and kit. We headed off along the main roads on to country lanes before heading out across open country.

I felt a twinge of excitement. Although we weren't yet operating in hostile country, this seemed far more real than anything we had undergone during training. We knew we had to escape capture, that there was an object to the exercise. We knew that passing this test successfully would mean going to Ulster on a real mission.

That first day we must have travelled twenty miles for Don set a hard, fast pace. We had one stop, at a bakery on the edge of Hereford, where we stocked up on steak and kidney pies, pork pies, sausage rolls and a couple of pints of milk each. We had never before been permitted to do anything like that when out training and we realised instinctively that, in Don, we had someone who did indeed know the ropes. Stocking up on pies may have been a minor point but it instilled in us the feeling that we could have confidence in him.

'It's far better eating this stuff', he quipped, 'rather than spending hours trying to catch some poxy fish which we couldn't even cook.' Already, he seemed like a man after my own heart.

That first night we were halfway up a hill at the edge of the Black Mountains where we found a drystone-walled shelter used in winter to keep the sheep together in snowy weather. We took the usual precautions, taking turns on guard, although we had kept our eyes peeled during the march out and had seen no sign of troops anywhere. None the less, we were taking no chances.

The weather wasn't particularly bad, alternating between showers, wind and sun. As it was early September, the nights turned cold in the mountains but our sleeping bags were warm and the food we had brought along kept us reasonably happy. I would have preferred a lovely steaming-hot beef stew at night but the cold pies were certainly better than poxy cold fish.

For the next three days we headed in a zig-zag line upwards into the Brecon Beacons, always keeping a sharp look out for the troops trying to find us. We didn't know whether they would be following us or were perhaps ahead of us, so we could never afford to relax.

Every couple of hours we would find some high ground and Don would go alone to a commanding position and scan the entire countryside with his binoculars. We also took the precaution of making use of the mountain streams, walking along them for a few hundred yards, just in case the troops following had been provided with dogs to track us.

To make the task more difficult for the following soldiers, we would never simply cross a lane when we came to one but would walk down it for perhaps a couple of hundred yards before going off to the other side.

When we met flocks of sheep we would walk along with them for a hundred yards or so. At first they would automatically assume that we had hay with us but when they realised we had nothing for them they would leave us to walk on alone. That helped in two ways. It made it more difficult for the trackers to follow us and it also made it more difficult for sniffer dogs for the smell of the sheep would put them off our scent.

We began to think that the CSM had conned us. We had seen no one following us and believed the CSM had just said what he did to keep us keen and make us march harder and longer than we would otherwise have done. Then, on the fourth day, Don went to make another recce and came back much faster than he had done before. 'There are four men about a mile and half behind us. I'm virtually certain they're the ones sent to find us. Let's go.'

He decided that our best chance of evading them would be to turn 180 degrees in a wide arc and come up behind them. That march took us a good hour and we must have covered a few miles, despite having to keep behind cover at all times. When we found their trail the four men had disappeared from view but Don suggested that we use their footprints so that, if they did succeed in following our 180 degree arc, they wouldn't be sure they were still on our trail.

After following them for half a mile or so, we came across a metalled country lane and so we legged it, as fast as possible, for five miles or more, running for perhaps a mile and then walking for a mile, and so on. We hoped that we had succeeded in throwing them off the scent.

We had seen no helicopters and were virtually certain that no following units had any idea of where we were. If they did come across us it would be totally by chance. Don suggested that we try to reach the other side of the Brecon Beacons before the seven days were over because he had an idea as to where we might spend the next fourteen days. He was fairly certain that we were now safe from our trackers and that the unit following was probably still searching for us in the opposite direction. To celebrate, he told us that, the next day, we would have our first hot meal since we had left camp seven days before. 'We'll have a barbecue,' he said. We looked a little surprised, wondering where he would find the steaks and sausages.

JR commented, 'I can't see any fucking sausages out here.'

Don replied, 'There are plenty of frigging sheep around, aren't there?'

None of us had ever killed a sheep and we had no idea how on earth you skinned it afterwards. It didn't seem a very bright idea but we just hoped that Don was not only a good hunter but also a skilled chef.

The following evening we made camp in the corner of a field, miles from any buildings or country lanes. Don disappeared to find a likely lamb, taking me and JR with him. Benny was left behind to start a fire.

At first Don tried to sneak up on a lamb with the intention of slitting its throat. However, it seemed to us that the sheep knew what he was after. They would let him approach to within six feet and then run away, leading him a merry dance around the field. For twenty minutes he failed to catch one and was becoming more and more pissed off. He was also feeling a prat in front of us – a respected, well-trained, professional, experienced SAS sergeant unable to catch one defenceless sheep.

Fed up with chasing about, Don decided to put an end to the charade. He put a magazine on his SMG, saying out loud; 'Right, you little bastards. I'll teach you to take the fucking piss out of this desert hero' and he opened up at point-blank range, killing six of them, while the others scattered.

JR and I looked at each other, speechless. We had never seen anything like it. I thought to myself, 'I wouldn't want to upset him in a pub.'

After the shock of the killings, we all burst out laughing, including Don. He realised he had gone over the top and I thought he must be a bit loopy to react to sheep in that way. I wondered how he would react if the enemy ever tried to take the piss out of him.

We had a look round to check that no one had heard the sound of the SMG and then looked at the sheep, trying to find one which hadn't been riddled with bullets. We were fortunate; one of them had been shot just once, through the head. We dragged the other five sheep to the edge of the field and threw them in a ditch before covering them with branches.

We took the other sheep back to our camp, hung

it up by its hind leg from the branch of a tree and cut its head off to allow all the blood to drain out. When it had stopped bleeding, Don took his knife and skinned it. He had obviously done this before because the whole operation took him only fifteen minutes and seemed absolutely professional.

We wasted most of it, simply cooking the legs on spits over the fire. They took more than two hours to cook thoroughly, with each one of us taking a leg and holding it over the flames like a spit roast. Most of the time we spent laughing about the whole episode. We hadn't had much to laugh about during the previous four days and the affair helped to ease the atmosphere. The sheep tasted fantastic; our first hot meal for days. We hadn't realised how hungry we had become.

I asked Don how he would account for the rounds he had used.

'Haven't you heard of the six Ps?' he asked.

'No, never,' I said. 'What are they?'

'Proper planning prevents piss poor performance,' he said, speaking slowly and emphasising all the Ps.

'I understand,' I said.

'And another point,' he added. 'I always carry spare ammunition. Don't forget that. You never know when it might come in useful.'

After we had devoured the food we felt better, more comfortable and at ease with life. The fire still burned and we began chatting together for the first time since we had set out. We told each other about our lives and backgrounds and Don took this opportunity to describe how he had been killing gooks out in Oman. 'Not much different from killing those sheep,' he said, and laughed.

I couldn't imagine what it would be like actually to kill someone or, for that matter, even an animal, especially like that. I had all but pissed myself laughing when Don took his machine gun and had opened up on a flock of sheep but I stopped laughing when I realised that one day I would have to do things like that myself. I didn't give it much more thought, however, for we were going to Ulster not the Middle East; there would be no gooks in Ireland.

While we were heating the water for our coffee at dawn the following day, Don announced that we were off to Milford Haven, the oil refinery port on the Welsh coast. 'Shit,' I thought. 'That's more than a hundred miles away; that will take us four or five days.'

He told us that he knew of a place where we could hole up in peace for a couple of weeks, relax and enjoy ourselves. We had wondered how we were meant to survive for three weeks with no rations. We knew we should be living rough and we wondered whether we were expected to survive the entire time on insects, birds and any vegetables we came across. It had made sense to us when Don told us to bring along our Post Office savings books despite the fact that it would mean spending our own money. We had seen hardly anything, except sheep, during our seven-day trek, that could have kept four hungry men happy.

However, we hadn't counted on Don's initiative. 'Fuck marching,' he said after an hour on the road, 'It's time we took things a bit easier. We'll hitch-hike.'

We looked at each other. We thought that was against the rules but who were we to argue. Don was in command.

As we waited for a lift, Don said, 'Let me give you some advice. You don't live rough if you don't have to; and you don't march for miles when you can ride. You only march when it is imperative to do so.'

Because we were in army uniform, people happily stopped to offer us lifts but we would only accept a lift if there was room for the four of us. In all, the journey took about twelve hours and we rode in eight separate vehicles. It was wonderful driving along at 60 miles an hour, watching the country fly past rather than humping our packs, hour after hour, along lanes and across country.

We finally drove into Milford Haven in a transit van at about nine p.m. We thanked the driver and began moving out of the town to a house where Don said we would be able to stay in some comfort. An hour later we arrived at an old, detached cottage, a few hundred yards off the beaten track up a tiny little lane.

JR commented, 'This looks like fucking luxury to me.'

The cottage consisted of one large room with the kitchen off and a small hall where the stairs led up to two bedrooms and a bathroom. In one bedroom was a double bed, which JR and Benny shared, and I slept in one bunk bed with Don in the other. After seven days of sleeping rough, this place seemed like the Ritz.

It was obvious that Don had stayed there before. We all had a steaming hot bath, the first for a week, a shave and general clean up. Then we slept for eight hours solid with no one standing guard. We knew we were safe and the front door was locked and bolted.

We packed our weapons and ammo in polythene and buried them in the back garden in what must have been the original cold store. On top of that we piled compost. We felt they were safe enough from any casual passerby.

I began to suspect that someone knew we were going to stay at the cottage because the refrigerator and the larder were packed with enough food for a large family on a two-week holiday. That couldn't have been an accident. Later, we asked Don whether the cottage had been specially laid on because we were going to be roughing it in Ulster for a long time; this being a sort of holiday during which we would get to know each other by living, eating, sleeping and relaxing together.

He replied, 'Surely you don't think even the SAS would make us live rough for three weeks and then ship us straight out to Ulster, not knowing what conditions we might have to put up with there.' It made sense.

The first stop the next day would be the nearest launderette to clean all our gear. During the following two weeks we travelled most days to Haverfordwest, about five miles away. We would search out the best pubs, go to a few discos, have some good meals and hope to meet the odd, good-looking girl. In fact, we all scored.

One night we decided to throw a party back at the cottage. We invited some girls we had met, plus their brothers and their girlfriends. That night about sixteen of us had a great night with lots to eat and drink and everyone bonking all over the house. That seemed to go on most of the night. They thought we were four young lads on holiday. The girls gave us their addresses and we all said we would be in touch. That, of course, was out of the question, but we hoped they had enjoyed themselves.

By the time we arrived back at Hereford, having hitch-hiked most of the way, the four of us were bosom pals. We had all come to know each other really well and happily accepted Don's authority. He was a natural leader but never authoritarian. We respected him for that and it made the relationship between us all that much easier and more comfortable.

When we walked in to see the CSM, he said with a wink, 'I see you've been really roughing it.' He knew all right. He probably had a good idea what the next twelve months would be like as well, but he said nothing about that either.

CHAPTER FIVE

TWO DAYS LATER, and dressed in civvies, we were driven to Liverpool in a Land-Rover and caught the ferry to Belfast. The overnight crossing could not have been worse; a gale-force wind sent waves crashing against the ship and half the passengers spent most of the crossing being sick. We couldn't have had a more unpleasant welcome to Northern Ireland.

Belfast looked dull, drab and very wet. The innocent thoughts I had cherished of serving with the SAS in the sun and sand of a Middle East country evaporated in the damp mist of Belfast as we walked off the ferry into heavy rain.

Before leaving Hereford we had been briefed by a major who first gave us a potted history of the political troubles during the past few years and then explained, in greater detail, what had been happening in Northern Ireland during the past few months. A large map of Ireland covered the wall. It was coloured in different shades, showing the Catholic,

Protestant and mixed areas of Belfast and Londonderry, as well as dividing the six counties into their
relevant religious and political zones.

He told of the British Government's decision,
under Prime Minister Edward Heath at the end of
July 1971, to change dramatically the army's role in
the Province from a non-active, defensive one to an
active one.

During the previous few months the IRA had
become far more active, gaining much greater
credence and control in Catholic areas and proving
themselves the protectors of the beleaguered Catholic
minority. The major said that Friday 23 July 1971
had marked a watershed in government policy
towards the handling of the IRA, with British forces
in the Province being ordered on to the offensive
instead of maintaining the passive tactics they had
adopted since the troubles began in 1969. On that
day, 1,800 British troops, backed by hundreds of
police, had swamped Belfast, Londonderry and eight
other towns in the Province, searching the homes of
known IRA members and sympathisers, looking for
activists responsible for outrages.

Home Secretary Reginald Maudling, revealing that
10,000 British troops were now stationed in Northern
Ireland, told the Commons that day: 'The army's
operation in Northern Ireland this morning marks the
beginning of a new phase in the battle against the
IRA. 'It is our duty not only to contain disorder and
violence but to search out the men and organisations
responsible. In this new phase the security forces will
act with vigour.'

However, the army's new tactics brought a swift
and devastating reply from the IRA, illustrating the
power they possessed to galvanize the Catholic
minority into action. Within days, tens of thousands
of IRA supporters and sympathisers took to the
streets, demonstrating against the British troops in

some of the most violent riots encountered by the army.

During the following weeks, attacks on army patrols escalated alarmingly, with petrol and nail bombs being hurled. Bomb explosions also blasted targets in Belfast and Londonderry.

The officer explained that the two wings of the IRA, the more politically inclined Official wing and the hard-line Provisionals, appeared to have buried their differences and to be working together. The two wings had issued a joint statement at the end of July, stating that the IRA would be stepping up its campaign of murder, sabotage and terror in its efforts to attain its military aims as well as in its determination to push for the abolition of Stormont, the Northern Ireland government.

The impact of the highly controversial policy of internment in the Province was also explained to us.

The major told how internment had been introduced on Monday 9 August, after a weekend of mayhem when IRA gunmen with loudhailers had toured Protestant areas in the Ardoyne, telling families: 'Get out of your homes and leave, otherwise we will burn you out.'

This shock tactic had resulted in hundreds of families quitting their homes in fear, seeking shelter at police stations; others had taken refuge in school buildings which were guarded by police and army patrols. A real sense of fear had gripped some Protestants who felt vulnerable to IRA threats and intimidation.

Before dawn on Monday 9 August, police, backed by troops, had raided hundreds of homes in Belfast and Londonderry, arresting 300 IRA suspects and sympathisers under sweeping new powers taken by the Stormont Government with the full knowledge and approval of the British Cabinet.

Announcing the new policy of internment, the

Northern Ireland Prime Minister Brian Faulkner said, 'We are quite simply at war with the terrorists. We are now acting to remove the shadow of fear which hangs over too many people.'

As he spoke more than 200 Protestant families in the Ardoyne removed all their belongings from their homes and then set fire to their houses, thus making them uninhabitable by Catholic families.

That day the first major sectarian shoot-out between Catholics and Protestants took place in Coalisland, when 100 Catholic gunmen staged a gun battle against 60 Protestants.

Since internment, the officer told us, the level of violence, especially against British troops, had escalated alarmingly and different tactics were now necessary to destabalise the IRA and wreck its morale. 'That is why you lot are being sent to Northern Ireland.'

Forty-eight hours after the wholesale arrest of IRA suspects, the Stormont Government announced the result of its internment policy, claiming that 70 per cent of suspects sought had been arrested and interned, including a high proportion of the IRA leadership.

There would, however, be a high price to pay for introducing internment, a policy which the IRA had predicted but which took out of action the great majority of their leadership. Within the first 48 hours of suspects and sympathisers being detained, bombings and shootings across the Province cost 22 people their lives.

Then we were given certain information which began to make sense to us. The major told us of a recent briefing by Brigadier Marston Tickell, Chief of Staff Northern Ireland Command HQ, when he had stated that, following internment, the intelligence services expected flying columns of IRA gunmen and activists from the south to infiltrate the north, to keep up the political pressure and further increase the degree of violence and terror.

Brigadier Tickell said, 'To put a stop to these flying columns we intend to switch much of the British Army's activities to the border area where troops will be moved into the unmarked border zone to keep watch.' He also issued a warning, which he had received from Special Branch, that the IRA intended to make a dramatic political gesture by capturing a small border town and declaring a great victory.

Our briefing officer added, 'You and all British troops will find yourselves in a war of attrition against these terrorists who are now armed with automatic weapons as well as revolvers. They also have the capacity to make and distribute gelignite bombs across the entire Province. I can tell you that your mission will be no picnic.'

To bring us up to date, the major explained what had occurred in the four weeks since internment. Two thousand families, about 10,000 men, women and children, had been forced to leave their homes; most parts of Belfast had become religious ghettos; many more sectarian gun battles had taken place; and widespread bombings were causing daily harass-ment of the general public. As a result, he said, a mounting tempo of fear and insecurity had gripped the entire Province.

Our briefing officer also told us of the political problems that had arisen over the border issue in the area where we would be operating.

He told us of meetings which had taken place between Prime Minister Edward Heath and the Irish Premier Jack Lynch, in which Heath had demanded that the Southern Ireland police and army should do much more to stop the smuggling of arms and men across the border into the north. Lynch had sug-gested that United Nations troops should be invited to patrol the border but this idea had not found favour with Heath.

The major gave us no clue of what our duties might be in Ulster. It is probable that he himself had not the slightest idea of the secret undercover operations we would become involved in. That information, he explained, would be given to us after we arrived in Ireland and had reported to 39th Brigade Headquarters at Thiepval Barracks in Lisburn.

He had given us much to think about. Now we were ready for some action.

In the pubs and bars of Belfast in October 1971 the talk was still of the bombing of the Four Steps Inn on the Shankill Road, when two people were killed and 25 seriously injured after a bomb ripped the pub apart. Targeting pubs was a new phase of the IRA's terror tactics. On that night, hundreds of Linfield Football Club supporters had stopped at the pub for a drink after their team's European cup tie against Standard Liege at Windsor Park. As a police spokesman said at the time: 'There were hundreds of people milling around the pub at the time; it was a miracle that more people weren't killed.'

At Belfast Dock, a Royal Transport Corps driver in a Land-Rover met us and drove us and our baggage to Sydenham Docks where the prison ship HMS *Maidstone* was anchored. The sentries waved us through the gates and the Land-Rover pulled up outside a sandy-coloured Portakabin which would be our home for the next few weeks.

Inside, we were pleased to see that a television set took pride of place in one corner of the room. There were two sets of bunk beds on either side, a desk, four chairs, a gas-bottle cooker, a large wooden wardrobe and, at one end, a tiny room with just a wash basin, shower and loo. In the middle of the desk a modern, grey telephone had been placed, through which we would receive instructions from the Lisburn headquarters. Over the windows were thin, green, cotton curtains, which looked more like sacking.

We hadn't been in the Portakabin more than a few minutes when Don told us, 'Don't make yourselves too comfortable, we won't be staying in this place long.'

'What do you mean?' someone asked.

'Look,' he said. 'That's the main gate over there, about fifty yards away. Any bastard could drive up to those gates and hit us with an RPG or something.' We were learning.

We decided to eat at the REME cookhouse, situated at the end of a large hangar about 60 yards away. The grub was good and far better than we would have put together in our Portakabin.

The wry comment from the REME lads was that the food was so good because the cooks tried to spend hours producing really tasty meals so that they wouldn't have time to go out on street patrols with everyone else. It worked; the food was good and they didn't go on street patrols.

A couple of hours after we had unpacked a Q-car – an ordinary-looking blue Morris Marina with Northern Irish plates, driven by an Ulster Defence Regiment soldier in civvies – arrived to take the four of us to the Lisburn headquarters.

We went in civvies, wearing jackets over our jeans to conceal the 9 mm Brownings we had tucked into the waistbands. These were the only weapons we had brought over from the mainland. We would never be without them throughout the following twelve months.

'I feel just like James Bond,' quipped JR as we drove into the 39th Brigade HQ. No one else said a word.

We were whisked through the main gates and stopped outside the headquarters building which was guarded by armed UDR soldiers. 'You will be meeting

Brigadier Kitson, Commander of the 39th Infantry Brigade,' we were told. 'He may want to have a few words with you.'

We had heard much of the legendary Brigadier Frank Kitson, an army officer who had served in Kenya, Malaya and Cyprus. During two years in Kenya in the 1950s, Brigadier Kitson's fame spread through the army because of his radical policy of 'turning' around captured terrorists and leading them out as 'counter gangs' against the feared Mau Mau.

It had been assumed that Brigadier Kitson, who had won the MC (Military Cross) twice over, had been brought in to command the 39th Infantry Regiment because of his acknowledged expertise in counter-insurgency. Kitson's professional hallmark was the practice of treating field operations and intelligence gathering as inseparable functions. He found himself trying to apply some of his Kenya expertise to Northern Ireland.

Someone once said that, under a peaked cap, Kitson looked like a gauleiter with his cold, staring eyes, pale, wintry expression and strangled voice. In the two years he served in Ulster, Kitson, an ambitious, efficient, searching, spiky man with a chilling stare, became the IRA's most hated and feared military target.

Before being sent to Ulster Kitson had published a controversial book, *Low Intensity Operations*, which had made him a figure of cult-hatred on the far Left. Kitson's theories addressed the proposition, once endorsed by Prime Minister Edward Heath, that internal subversion and civil anarchy represented the dangers of the future, rather than conventional war. As a result, considerable effort, particularly in Irish Republican political circles, centred on caricaturing Kitson as a systematic and callous anti-democrat. That argument could not be sustained, however, for Kitson, an honourable and sensitive officer, was a man whose respect for democracy probably ran deeper than it did in most of his critics.

Kitson, who always believed passionately in the British Army, quickly won a reputation among his senior officers in Ulster for ruthless, even brutal, action, if he believed it could be morally justified. The IRA would come to fear and hate Brigadier Kitson for his successful methods in combating them, often taking them out before they could strike.

As a field officer in Malaya, Cyprus, Kenya and Germany, Kitson had won the respect and affection of his men; some officers found him forbidding but others well-nigh worshipped him and his military virtues.

The son of an admiral, Kitson would serve for two years in Ulster before being appointed to the élite position of Commandant of the School of Infantry at Warminster in Wiltshire in June 1972. He would go on to become GOC 2nd Armoured Division in 1976, and Commander in Chief of United Kingdom Land Forces in 1982. He would be promoted to general and be rewarded with a knighthood. Because of his ruthless approach towards the IRA gunmen, he would remain at the top of the IRA's hit list even when he left Ulster.

The most senior army commander in Ulster when we arrived was General Sir Harry Tuzo who had been appointed GOC and Director of Operations Northern Ireland in 1971. He would still command that position when we left Ulster in October 1972. However, we were not destined to meet him.

Having been escorted to the headquarters building, we were personally greeted by Brigadier Kitson who shook us all by the hand and then invited us upstairs to a large briefing room with maps covering the walls.

'Your lads have arrived,' Kitson said as he handed us over to a Royal Signals officer who came into the room to greet us. 'He'll look after you,' Kitson said and left the room. We would not see the controversial brigadier again during our tour of duty but we believed that he was the man responsible for the war of attrition that had recently started against the IRA. Kitson knew that the men best able to carry on that war were members of the SAS.

Also in the room that morning were a couple of men in civilian clothes, both around 40 years of age. They listened with interest to everything the signals officer said. We believed they were senior intelligence officers.

We were given a cup of tea and a cigarette while the officer addressed us, although most of the time he seemed to be directing his briefing towards Don.

'At this point in time,' he told us, 'there are three SAS units in the field on active service; one in Southern Ireland and two patrolling the border. They are engaged in passing information back to Lisburn, informing intelligence of IRA movements of arms, ammunition and men from the south, across the border and into the north.'

After ten minutes the signals officer handed over to a warrant officer who had come into the room while the officer was speaking. I never knew what mob he was in because he wore no beret, but he wore a leather strap with a warrant officer's crown on his right wrist.

The signals officer left the room and the two men in civvies appeared to relax more, moving to join us around the table. The WO also sat down and more tea was brought in.

During the following hour the three of them took turns to brief us on the way we would fit into the SAS operation on the border. They informed us that, according to the latest intelligence reports, most of the IRA's senior ranks had been rounded up and were interned in Long Kesh, leaving perhaps as few as 60 senior IRA professionals in Belfast and London-derry. They believed the rest of the IRA's forces consisted of unprofessional sympathisers and kids who hardly knew how to handle a gun.

We had been brought in to try to contain the situation and make sure the IRA could not organise or train more professional gunmen and bomb makers. The information being gathered by the SAS units and other agencies was now being used to create a state of uncertainty and unease among the two wings of the IRA, the Officials and the Provisionals.

Intelligence believed that if the pressure was kept up in the field, there would be every chance that the IRA would not have sufficient trained men to sustain a bombing or shooting campaign in the north. With violence and bombings contained, an opportunity would then arise for the politicians to thrash out a solution.

He told us that the SAS had been brought into Ulster at the start of the troubles in 1969 but had, unbelievably, been permitted to operate in uniform which was now perceived as a serious mistake. It also meant that none of those SAS units who had served in Northern Ireland could return to work in covert operations. As he put it, 'That was a major cock-up.'

He went on, 'That is why you will be operating throughout your time in Northern Ireland in civilian clothes. You must let your hair grow down to the collar and spend most of your days in jeans and sweaters. At no time during your tour of duty in Northern Ireland will you ever wear uniform. And on no condition must you wear anything at all that could suggest you are members of the armed forces. Not even underwear.'

He went on to detail our unit's particular job. He said, 'You will be part of an abduction and assassination operation.'

I didn't even blink. It came as no surprise to me. My heart flipped but somehow I had thought this was coming, although I still wondered exactly what we would be required to do.

He went on: 'Hopefully, you will only be involved in border work. You will receive instructions to go to a map reference to collect IRA gunmen trying to infiltrate from the south. We know the IRA are at this moment training as many young gunmen and bombers as possible and it will be part of your duty to prevent these killers from entering Ulster.'

Don asked, 'And when we have them in our possession, what do we do with them?'

The warrant officer replied, 'Later on I will give you another map reference. This will be the place where you will dispose of them. The area will be prepared before you get there. Everything will have been taken care of. You will just have to deliver them.'

'What exactly do you mean?' asked Don, wanting to make sure that he understood precisely what the officer was saying.

Without trying to hide our role, the warrant officer said starkly, 'It will be your duty to kill them. You will hand them over dead.'

My mouth went dry and the palms of my hands began to sweat. I hadn't imagined that we would actually have to kill someone in cold blood and deliver them to someone else to be got rid of. I had no idea that this would be part of an SAS mission. It seemed unreal, like a bad dream. I couldn't imagine that the SAS would be called on to kill people like that. To shoot them in war I could understand, but this . . .

I knew these IRA bastards had to be dealt with; that the bloody IRA campaigns of bombing and shooting had to be stopped, and at all costs. But this? 'Shit,' I thought.

The warrant officer must have understood what we were thinking because he added forcefully, 'If you have any qualms about this mission, forget them. If those bastards ever got hold of any of you they wouldn't just kill you; your deaths would be far fucking worse than anything you could imagine.'

He went on: 'Unfortunately we are not operating on our own. We come under the joint services intelligence wing and therefore we will also have to become involved with the grasses, the MRFs – Military Reconnaissance Force – the IRA members who have agreed to work for us rather than spend the next twenty years in jail. On occasions you will have to act on their information and you must never forget that some of these bastards will, in fact, be double agents. And that can spell danger for you all.'

The warrant officer also gave us our password, 'Nemesis'. He told us: 'If ever you get arrested, stopped at a police road block or picked up by any army patrol, you must go along with whatever the officers say and then demand to speak to their commanding officer. When you get to him you must give him the one word 'Nemesis' and ask him to contact 39th Brigade headquarters and ask for the intelligence duty officer. We'll sort out the rest. Don't forget it, the word is Nemesis,' and he spelt it out: N–E–M–E–S–I–S.

At the time we had no idea what the word 'nemesis' meant. Later, when I looked in the dictionary, I smiled. Nemesis was the mythological Greek goddess of retribution and vengeance, often interpreted as any agent of retribution or vengeance. I thought to myself how clever those bastards were to think up such names. It was perfect.

He told us the Marina we had arrived in would be our vehicle but that we would need to change it from time to time.

'Any questions,' asked the warrant officer.

'Yes,' Don said,

'What?'

'We are not staying at that Portakabin at Sydenham. It's just not safe.'

Don didn't ask the question; he just told them straight. The warrant officer and the two civvies looked at each other.

'Something will be sorted out,' replied the warrant officer.

At the end of the briefing, however, the warrant officer did have some good news for us. We were told we would all be promoted to sergeant for the duration of the mission so that we would have a decent wage. That brought a smile to our lips.

JR asked with a grin, 'Could I have three stripes to sew on my leather jacket?'

The warrant officer replied, 'I'll pretend I never heard that request.' But he was only joking.

The briefing was at an end. 'Fancy a bite to eat?' Don said as we walked to our car. We all nodded.

During lunch at a cafe in Lisburn, we picked up a newspaper which reported on the front page that the Official IRA's publicity bureau had issued a statement concerning alleged SAS operations in Belfast and other parts of Northern Ireland. The statement alleged that members of the SAS were planting ammunition and weapons on innocent civilians to whitewash the brutality of the British Army.

We looked at each other and shrugged. We didn't know whether it was true or false but it certainly meant that we could expect no mercy if we ever fell into IRA hands.

We did not mention the briefing or the newspaper report during our fry-up meal at the cafe but we could hardly wait to reach the safety of our base to discuss everything that had happened that morning. We didn't really know how the operation would work but hoped that Don did. Benny asked the one question we all wanted answered, 'How many blokes are we going to have to knock off?'

'Impossible to tell,' Don replied. 'It could be just one or two or it may be one every week. Maybe more than that. We just can't tell. And they've no idea either,' jerking a thumb in the directon of Lisburn.

He went on: 'Now listen. We are not going to let this get personal. We have a job to do. We can't let our feelings get involved. These blokes are killers, intent on killing you and me and as many soldiers and police as they can. It's going to be our job to get rid of them and nothing else.'

Before we left Lisburn, Don had been informed in a private briefing that a meeting would be arranged between the four of us and three IRA informers, the 'Smerfs' as we decided to call them, as soon as possible. Don didn't like the idea of working with them but we had no option.

He said, 'We are going to have to meet these bastards but I don't like the idea. We can't trust them and we mustn't trust them. There must never be any hint that we are SAS because we are the number one targets of the IRA. We know the IRA are shit-scared of us but we cannot take any risks.' We all nodded. I felt relief that we had Don to lead the unit – someone who had been around, who knew the score.

That night we went out together for a drink. We had been shown the Protestant areas where it would be safe for us to have a drink without any risk. However, we knew that, on occasions, even the Protestants could turn against us for a variety of reasons. We knew we could trust no one totally because we had seen on television some Protestant yobs, draped in Union Jacks, hurling bricks and stones at British soldiers patrolling the streets. It didn't make sense to us but it did make us realise that while we were in Northern Ireland the only people we could trust would be ourselves.

Benny asked Don how many other SAS units were involved in the operation. Don explained, 'There are always two units out there on the border at any one time.'

'Does that mean they stay there living rough the entire time?' asked Benny.

'No,' Don replied. 'There is a rota system; at any one time two units are always out living rough. Each particular unit stays out for a month at a time then takes two weeks' rest back at Palace Barracks in Hollywood, Belfast.'

Before going out we had had to find the best possible way of concealing our 9 mm Brownings. Sticking them in the waistbands of our jeans was useless because they could have fallen out while getting in or out of the car and could be easily seen.

We decided on a shoulder harness. We cut a slit in our T-shirts and jumpers, leaving a convenient hole under the left armpit. In that way we could wear the harness underneath the T-shirt but would be able to draw the 'millie' – as we called the 9 mm Browning – quickly in any emergency. It worked really well, no one could tell we were carrying weapons under our leather jackets.

After all we had heard that day, we needed a drink. We were anxious to get on with the job and yet apprehensive about what we would have to do. It seemed better to relax, have a good drink and talk about other things.

While Don went back to the 39th Brigade headquarters, we stayed in the Portakabin and read the papers. The IRA were boasting that during the first seven days of October they had killed two British soldiers and wounded at least sixteen. We were certain it was bollocks.

Benny quipped, 'They can say what they like but wait till we get started.'

Don returned with a briefcase full of surprises.

When he opened it we could see sixteen pistol barrels, extractors and firing pins for our 9 mm Brownings, all laid out in blue velvet, designed specifically for all the parts to fit perfectly. We had never seen anything like it before in our lives. It looked more like a professional hit-man's gear.

He explained that all the pieces in the briefcase had long since been declared unfit for use and officially destroyed. However, in reality, they had been taken out of service and put aside deliberately for just such an eventuality. He explained that we would need weapons that could never be traced; and all the Browning parts were such that they could never be identified as being part of our individual weapons.

'Make sure', he said, looking at each one of us, 'that you never get them mixed up with parts of your own weapons.' (After about four months, in fact, we did get rid of four of the sixteen spare parts, throwing them into the sea somewhere south of Larne. We had used them too often.)

After a day lazing around watching television in our billet, we drove to north-west Belfast, to a pub in a mixed area, to meet the three 'Smerfs'. Before we went into the pub, Don pulled a photograph out of his pocket and took a good look at it. The photograph looked like a kiosk picture and was of a woman seemingly in her late twenties, with shoulder-length, fair hair.

As soon as we entered the pub we saw her seated on the left in a booth towards the back, the quietest part of the pub. We ordered a pint of beer each and Don went over to her, to check that we did have the correct person. Then he signalled for us to join them.

Although the area was mixed Catholic and Protestant, I felt uneasy. This was the first time in my life that I had been confronted by the enemy and I felt vulnerable just sitting there, a perfect, motionless target for any gunman. The Browning under my arm gave me some confidence as I wondered whether we had been led into a trap. I looked around the pub, checking if there were any likely gunmen, but I couldn't tell. Benny, JR and I all seemed on edge and we kept our eyes on the doors as Don continued chatting with the woman. Thinking on it, I reckoned the four of us all knew how to handle our weapons and figured that if someone did try to shoot us we stood a better than even chance of fighting our way out. I tried to relax, to appear nonchalant but it proved very difficult.

The woman, who actually looked in her thirties, had bleached blonde hair and a sallow complexion. She introduced herself as Yvonne and spoke with a strong, hard Ulster accent. She told us the other two blokes would arrive shortly so we decided to split up, just in case we had walked into a trap.

Don and JR stayed with Yvonne and Benny and I went and stood near the bar, drinking. Ten minutes later the two men walked in and went straight over to Yvonne, Don and JR. Benny and I stayed where we were, so we didn't find out what they were all talking about until we returned to the Portakabin about ten o'clock.

Throughout the hour they were chatting, I felt uneasy. Many people coming in and out of the pub seemed to spend some time watching and trying to listen to what was going on in that corner. I mentioned this to Don later and we agreed that if we had to see these informers again we would make a rendezvous in a pub well outside Belfast.

It appeared that the three had been discussing our first job. They produced photographs of two men who they alleged were senior IRA officers, known killers, still at large in Belfast. They said the two men were living near the mainly Catholic Ardoyne area.

Don said we would have to try to check them out,

watch their movements and see if there was an opportunity to intercept them without arousing too much attention.

We first checked out the pub where the informants told us they drank and, sure enough, we found them sitting having a quiet Sunday lunchtime pint of Guinness. We left them to their pints but continued surveillance on them for the next couple of days. It soon became apparent that all they did was eat and drink in the pub most days and nights. One night after the pub closed we followed them home but when they walked into the Ardoyne we knew it would be stupid to follow so we went back to Sydenham Docks.

Each morning they would surface about eleven a.m., buy a packet of cigarettes in the newsagent's shop near the pub and then walk on to the pub for their first drink of the day. At that time of day it seemed there was hardly anyone about.

On the following Wednesday night Don said, 'I think it's about time we stopped poncing about and got this over and done with. He added, 'All we've got to sort out between us is who's going to actually pull the trigger.'

I didn't want to be the second one to volunteer so, without really thinking, I said, 'I'll do it.'

'Good,' he said. 'This is what we will do. I think the best time to hit them is in the morning either before or after they buy their fags. They'll probably be a bit hungover and their reactions will be slow.'

That night I kept practising drawing my pistol. I kept loading and unloading it, practising the draw, wondering if I would fuck up. The palms of my hands kept sweating until I told myself to get a grip and then I would practise some more. That night I lay awake, tossing and turning, thinking what could go wrong. I don't think I slept a wink, I was so worried about fucking up.

The next morning I was still nervous. I could hardly dress myself. I didn't want any breakfast so had just a cup of coffee and a cigarette. I practised some more and found I was shaking so much that I couldn't hold the pistol steady. I began to get worried that I would be unable to pull the trigger when it came to it.

Don nipped out to make a couple of phone calls. When he returned we all bundled into the Marina and drove off with JR at the wheel. We parked about half a mile from the pub. Don said, 'Don't worry, it'll go like clockwork; I promise you.'

I gave him a quick look, got out of the car and set off towards the newsagent on my own, my mouth dry, my hands sweating. Don followed about 30 yards behind and another 30 yards behind came Benny. JR stayed with the vehicle.

As I walked towards the newsagent I kept checking my watch to make sure I arrived right on time, praying the two men would keep to their normal routine. As I approached the corner opposite the shop my heart missed a beat. I could see them chatting away to each other and walking casually, as they had done every day, towards the shop. They didn't even notice me.

They went into the shop when I was about 80 yards away. I increased my pace, not knowing how long they would stay in there. I didn't want to miss them. I had planned to hit them as they came out. I looked through the glass door of the shop but could see that they were still being served so I pretended to be looking at something in the window. I glanced around but there was no one to be seen.

As I stood still, waiting impatiently, I felt my legs turn to jelly and thought I was about to collapse. My heart was thumping and my hands felt hot and sweaty. I couldn't keep them still. I felt beads of sweat on my forehead and was sure I looked just like a gunman waiting to shoot someone. For a split second panic overtook me and I wondered if I should just forget it and go back to the car.

As those thoughts raced through my head I saw the shop door open and the two men emerge. I noticed that one was opening his packet of cigarettes. As soon as I saw them my panic vanished. I just thought of what I had to do and my nerves held steady. Now I was acting without thinking.

My pistol was already cocked. I put my hand under my leather jacket, pulled out the Browning and shot the man on my left full in the face from about five or six feet. I then immediately shot the other bloke twice, once through the heart and once in the face.

I turned the gun on the first one again and shot him in the chest as he crumpled slowly to the ground. The glass in the door shattered and a spray of blood spurted out from the chest of the man I had shot first, covering half his body in blood.

I just stood there, trying to take in what I had done, wondering whether I should check if they were dead. But I knew they were. Suddenly I felt a pull on my arm. It was Don. 'What are you fucking doing... waiting to sign autographs? . . . Come on.'

We walked away fast, with Don looking around as though expecting something to happen. I looked around too, fearing that hundreds of people would have heard the shots and come running. But, thank God, there was no one around, the streets seemed virtually deserted. No one even came out of the shop.

Then I saw a dark blue Commer van driving towards us. 'Good,' said Don.

The van pulled up, two men got out and walked over to the men I had shot. We took no further notice and continued walking up the road towards the waiting Marina. JR pulled away quite slowly, not wanting to draw attention.

I sat in the back of the car shaking like a leaf. Yet, somehow, at the same time that I was shaking, I also felt relieved. I was just so glad, so grateful, that the operation had gone off so well, so easily, and somehow I hadn't fucked up as I had feared I would.

As we drove back to Sydenham Docks two thoughts kept going through my mind. The first was that it had been so easy to kill someone in cold blood; the second was how easy it would be for someone to knock me off in the same way.

Don brought me back to the moment. He turned round and said with a smile, 'You see; I told you it would be a piece of piss.' He paused and added, speaking to everyone in the car, 'As long as you don't think of them as human beings you're all right. Got it.' We nodded.

I asked him who the blokes in the blue van were. 'Don't worry about them. They're the laundry men; they do the cleaning up.'

CHAPTER SIX

N O ONE SAID another word as we drove back to the billet. I looked around at my colleagues to see how they were reacting to what had just happened. I had pulled the trigger but we were all in this together. It had been a team effort. I kept thinking about what I had done and, more important, how I had managed to carry it out. I didn't feel any guilt; I had been doing what I had been trained to do and these men would have done the same to me if given half a chance. They had probably already been responsible for the deaths of other soldiers, maybe innocent civilians as well. I told myself they deserved no mercy.

My thoughts rationalised what had happened and I began to relax as we drove back to camp, a fifteen-minute ride. I pushed the sight of the two men, lying in their own blood outside the shop, to the back of my mind, not wanting to dwell on it, not wanting to know whether they were married or had any kids. I hoped they were single men with no attachments.

That way it made my actions less brutal and helped to remove the pangs of guilt.

'Don't think of them as human beings,' Don had said. I knew his advice would be sound and I tried to do just that but it became difficult to divorce those two dead men from the fact that, until a few moments before, they *had* been human beings. I felt relief that the killings were over; I felt confident that I would never have to do anything like that again; it would be the turn of the others to face their moment of truth. I had carried out my task as I had been trained to do and it had gone well. In two months, I told myself, we would be back home in England, away from this shithole of a place that I had begun to hate.

Back at our base at Sydenham Docks, Benny put on the electric kettle and a cup of hot, strong, sweet coffee did wonders for me. Since waking that morning I had felt a strange taste in my mouth and the coffee helped. 'Anyone for gin rummy,' Don asked and we took up his suggestion eagerly, knowing that he was trying to take our minds off the events of that morning.

As we played, flashes of what had happened that morning kept invading my mind and I found it difficult to concentrate on the game. I kept thinking of the walk towards the shop with my nerves on edge and sweat on my forehead and the palm of my hands; worried, so worried that I would be unable to pull the trigger. Then the shootings. I tried to think of them but it had all been a blur as though I had switched into automatic mode, doing what had to be done but not really being in control.

I played a lousy game that day. I lost nearly every hand because my mind kept wandering back to what had happened, back to what I had done. I kept telling myself that I had only done my duty. Yet that thought would not stop the doubts racing through my mind.

Lunch came and went. The others all went over to

the REME canteen but I didn't want to know. I simply couldn't face the thought of food; it turned my stomach just to think of eating. I knew the reason of course but didn't want to face it. I knew I would get over my bad feelings soon enough. I kept telling myself that I was a soldier, a member of the élite SAS and here I was acting like a pathetic prat.

Wednesday night was disco night at Sydenham, when girls from Protestant areas would be bussed in to the REME recreation block which doubled as a disco. I looked forward to that evening, to having a few pints of beer. I knew that would help me to forget.

But the pints didn't taste good that night, although they did make me hungry and I must have eaten eight or nine packets of crisps as I forced myself to drink the beer. I looked round the dance floor but no one held any interest for me and I turned in early. I felt that maybe sleep would save me. I was wrong. Sleep seemed impossible. I heard the others come in and clamber noisily into their bunks, a little the worse for wear. Eventually I dozed off sometime after two in the morning but not for long.

An hour later I woke with a start, my body shaking with cold and sweat. I had been dreaming of the four of us running through the streets of Belfast, buildings on fire all around us and the streets full of men and women running in every direction. Every so often a sniper would shoot at us but we didn't know his whereabouts and we would fire at random, hoping to flush out the men with guns. All of a sudden I find myself running down a long alleyway with really high brick walls on either side. I am alone, with no one around. At the end of the alley I can see the shop where I shot the men. Then I relive what had happened but this time there are differences. My gun will not fire. I desperately try to release the safety catch but it is already off and still the gun won't fire.

The two men look at me and realise I am pointing my gun at them, intent on shooting them. They see my predicament, that my gun won't fire, and they go for their own guns. Sweat is pouring off me, my hands shaking as I realise that they are about to kill me. I see their guns come out of the waistbands of their trousers and yet I am rooted to the spot, unable to turn and run. Something is making me stand rock steady, unable to move, and yet I know that I am about to die. They have their guns in their hands and they are laughing at me as they release their safety catches and squeeze the triggers. I know I am about to die. At that precise moment I awoke.

That was the first time I experienced that nightmare but it would not be the last. Each and every time I have that nightmare I awake cold, sweating and shaking.

The next morning I awoke determined to put behind me all that had happened; not just the killings but the nightmare as well. I thought I had been plain stupid in letting the whole affair get to me to such an extent. I had blown up the incident out of all proportion and knew I must return to reality. I told myself I was behaving like a wimp.

I also realised I was bloody hungry and polished off a plate of bacon, eggs, sausage, tomatoes and fried bread. After that I ate two bowls of corn flakes and drank two mugs of tea. I felt better, more like my old self, and the terrors of the previous day began to fade.

JR wanted to chat to me about the shooting. He explained that sitting in the car waiting for Don and me to come back had been terrifying. He told me he had been fearful that we would get shot; that the mission would go wrong; that he would be left in the car waiting while IRA gunmen found him and moved in for the kill. I told him he had been silly to allow his imagination to run so wild but he wanted to know each and every detail of what had happened outside the newsagents.

I tried to tell him everything that had happened and how I had felt as I stood outside the shop waiting for the two men to emerge. He asked loads of questions but kept returning to one in particular. Over and over again JR asked, 'What's it like actually to kill someone?'

I didn't want to tell him for a thousand reasons. I knew that he would one day go through what I had been through when it was his turn to kill someone. If he was lucky it would happen in a gun battle somewhere, perhaps on the border. If he was less fortunate he, too, would have to kill someone in cold blood, just as I had. So I simply left out the details of the actual killing and talked of my feelings, of my emotions before, during and immediately afterwards. In that way I thought it would help him to come to terms with what we knew we would all have to do at some future date.

Don returned from a briefing at 39th Brigade headquarters and told us we were going on an expedition the following day. First, however, he had news for us. He explained that the killings we had carried out that week were not, in fact, a one-off mission. From time to time, we would be assigned to carry out other killings. Our targets would be IRA gunmen who had been identified by Special Branch and other intelligence branches, like MI5. He also informed us that MI6 had been operating in Southern Ireland for some time and they, too, would be responsible for identifying IRA replacements making their way from the Republic into Ulster. Our orders would all come through him from 39th Brigade headquarters where we had received our original briefing after arriving in Belfast.

Don told us that he had no idea how many gunmen we would be expected to target; nor could he tell us how long we would be staying in Belfast. 'It's a job that's got to be done and we've been assigned to do it,' he said. 'The sooner we get rid of these arseholes, the sooner we can go home.'

At that time we felt the troubles would be over in a matter of months. We had been told that, since internment, only about 60 or 70 IRA gunmen were in the north and that we would be one of the units used to deal with them.

Don went on: 'Today I have been given the map reference of one of our disposal points. In future, it will be handled differently to what we just did in Belfast. There will be no laundry men to clean up afterwards; we will have to take away the bastards we kill and we will have to dispose of them. The brass at 39th Brigade gave me the map reference of one place where we will dispose of the bodies. Tomorrow we will go and check it out.'

With rain beating down, the four of us set off in our blue Marina, the pathetic windscreen wipers making driving difficult, to find the map reference given to Don. We knew the spot was not far from the main Lurgan to Dromore Road.

As we left Belfast, the rain cleared and the sun shone sporadically through the clouds. I hadn't seen the beauty of Northern Ireland before, hadn't appreciated the countryside, which at times seemed as desolate as the Brecon Beacons, and at other times more like the farmland of Hampshire. 'Good bird-watching country,' I thought.

As we turned slowly off the main road we crossed a stone bridge spanning the fast-flowing stream below. I looked up and down the torrent of water, wondering if there were any sandpipers. Peaceful, quiet and in the heart of the country, it was an ideal habitat for sandpipers.

We drove slowly up the metalled lane to the precise map reference and noticed on our left the wood marked on the map. The trees, mainly deciduous, were a mix of oaks, beeches, elms and a few silver birches. On the edges of the wood were conifers, but most of these appeared to be immature, the majority of them only a few feet tall. Between the lane and the wood, 50 yards of scrubland was being cleared by a worker with a JCB digger.

Checking the map once more, Don said to JR: 'Pull in here. This is it. Map reference five-three-four-one-six-zero.' JR drove the Marina slowly off the narrow lane on to the piece of scrubland. The ground was wet and heavy but the sun shone brightly and the clouds had cleared, leaving a brilliant blue sky.

As we walked over to the farm worker I could hear birds twittering away and heard some crows cawing high up in the trees. I looked up and noticed that they were hooded crows, a large black and grey species, making quite a din.

The farm worker switched off the JCB and walked over to us as we approached. It seemed obvious that he knew we would be paying him a visit. We did not shake hands. Introducing the man, Don said, 'This bloke is one of us. He wants to see the back of the IRA bastards as much as we do. And he is going to supply us with holes to get rid of these scumbags.'

The farm worker appeared to be a typical Irish farmhand who had spent most of his life working outdoors. He looked about 30 and was nearly six feet tall, with dark, wavy hair, well down below his collar. He had ruddy cheeks and spoke with a strong Northern Irish accent.

I looked over to where the man had been working with the digger and saw a twelve-foot-long trench, about four feet wide and seven feet deep. We walked over to the trench which was approximately 60 yards from the lane and ran parallel to it.

'Come and take a look,' the man said. 'I think it'll suit your needs.'

'Should do,' said Don. The rest of us said nothing.

I realised that we were being shown a grave big enough to hold a number of bodies. My stomach turned over as the full realisation hit me that, more than likely, I would be expected to carry out more executions; that the two men I had shot in Belfast were only the first; I feared it would not be long before my turn came round again. I wondered if I would be capable of carrying out another execution; if my bottle would hold out.

As we walked back towards the car JR began throwing stones.

'What are you doing?' Don asked him, irritated.

'I've just seen a rat over there and I'm trying to get it,' he explained.

'Well don't,' snapped Don. 'You're behaving like a bloody kid. Get in the car.'

As we sat in the car Don explained, 'If you haven't already sussed it out, this is where we will be disposing of the customers that we will soon be picking up.'

We looked at each other and wondered exactly what our involvement would be. We didn't know whether we would be expected to kill these people or whether they would be delivered to us in American-style plastic body bags. I hoped that all we would be asked to do would be to bury whatever we were told to, with no questions asked. 'No questions, no pack drill – the old army adage,' I thought as JR backed the car out into the lane.

Benny asked of all in general, 'Who's organising this then, the fucking Mafia?'

Don commented, 'That's the first time I've ever heard the British Government described as the Mafia.'

We laughed, but not very loudly.

Benny went on: 'Seriously, all this must be taking some real organisation. I never realised that we would be expected to kill people and then dispose of their bodies in forests miles away from civilisation. This isn't real.'

'It is,' replied Don.

A few moments later Don turned to Benny and said, 'Were you wearing a fucking blindfold when you joined the Firm? We're not knights in shining armour, you know. We kill or we get rid of the bad guys. That's our job.'

After a moment's silence Don corrected himself with a chuckle, 'When you come to think of it, that's right, we are knights in shining armour.' He went on to remind us that the SAS emblem of a winged dagger represented Excalibur, King Arthur's sword, in effect making every SAS man one of King Arthur's knights. We liked that idea. It made us feel good, even privileged.

Don suggested we drive around the area to get a feel of the place, to check various landmarks, to make ourselves aware of each and every recognisable piece of the countryside and to see how deserted the area really was.

Having driven around for 30 minutes or more, we drove south towards the border. It was our intention to recce the area and Don wanted to show us the problems facing the British Army in trying to keep out the IRA gunmen who wanted to enter the north by crossing the border, rather than attempting to use small boats as others had done.

As we drove down we came across a typical Northern Irish country pub and stopped for lunch. We enjoyed a pint and a ploughman's lunch – a hunk of strong, mature cheddar, bread and pickle. We could have been on holiday anywhere in the United Kingdom countryside. It seemed a far cry from the reality of our life and we had only been in Northern Ireland for a little more than a week!

Using the narrow, hedgerowed back lanes, we

drove down to the border, checking our map every mile or so. We didn't want to cross the border accidentally, but we did repeatedly and deliberately cross into Southern Ireland. Don wanted to show us that the border was almost impossible to patrol effectively for there were no border signs, no landmarks delineating it, nothing whatsoever to tell the unwary traveller whether he was in Northern or Southern Ireland.

What seemed more extraordinary was the complete absence of any army or police presence on either side of the border. Indeed, it was impossible at any time to tell which country we were in without checking the map in very close detail. Even on the Ordnance Survey map the black line detailing the border was about a quarter of an inch thick, which, in real terms, meant it would have been about 100 yards wide. It seemed obvious that the mapmakers had not been able to trace the border accurately either!

We knew from our training in Wales that the border country could have hidden an SAS squadron of 60 men and it would still be impossible to see them with the naked eye. That showed us how easy it would be for IRA gunmen, with help from locals who knew the area far, far better than we ever would, to cross undetected into the north.

We drove in a circle from near Armagh to Dundalk in the south. We were, however, careful not to stop anywhere that we thought could be Southern Ireland territory. We just needed to check the lie of the land, to make ourselves aware of the problems that lay ahead as well as giving ourselves some idea of landmarks that we could check on our maps.

One sign that did help us during that car drive was the Irish tricolour, for the Republic's flag could be seen on farmhouses and cottages on both sides of the border. Those were houses, farms and cottages that we knew we should steer well clear of.

As we drove through what we would call 'bandit country', Don said, 'If anyone tries to stop us while we are in this part of the world and they ain't wearing British Army uniform, shoot the bastards.' He wasn't kidding. We were all carrying handguns in shoulder holsters, with a full magazine of ten rounds and a further three magazines each in our pockets.

His remark gave us a feeling of excitement, for that was what we had been trained to do ever since joining the Firm. Part of me really wanted someone to stop us and ask questions.

Back at Sydenham Docks that night, we sat around drinking tea and discussing the problems of patrolling bandit country. Don explained our role, 'We are now on stand-by, waiting for orders from Lisburn telling us where they want us to go and what they want us to do. It might seem boring hanging around doing nothing but I can assure you that we will be needed, and soon. I can't tell you when. What I do suggest, however, is that we concentrate on keeping fit.'

Next day we all went for an eight-mile run, dressed in track suit trousers, a T-shirt and baseball boots. We didn't kill ourselves, stopping every few miles, but when we did run we went at quite a pace. On the way back we ran through a Belfast City park and saw some youths kicking a football about. For a laugh, we joined in with them.

JR and I had both been more than competent footballers and the young blokes asked us if we would turn out for them. Later, we would find out that young men from both Catholic and Protestant backgrounds played for the local pub. They hadn't been doing too well of late and thought we might be able to help them win a few games. They played every Sunday and asked whether we would be available. 'If we're not working on that Sunday, sure, love to turn out,' we said.

A few days after our trip to bandit country we read in the papers that British Army Royal Engineers had begun blowing up cross-border roads in a bid to stop infiltration into the north. The engineers used plastic explosives, leaving large craters, twelve feet wide and six feet deep. They began the operation around Newry in County Armagh and at Monaghan in County Tyrone.

The operation would continue for ten days but not without stirring up much local anger. Within hours of the Royal Engineers moving away from a blown road the local people, aided by the farmers, immediately repaired the roads so that they were once more open to vehicles. Within days of the troops blasting a crater the locals had repaired it well enough to allow vehicles to move slowly along the road. We wondered what Lisburn's next tactic would be.

Worse would follow. After the first couple of days the IRA decided to intervene and the engineers would come under small arms attack as they began to prepare the roads for blasting. On one occasion in early October an army helicopter hovering overhead was hit by small arms fire but managed to return to base. No one was injured.

The war on the streets intensified around the middle of October 1971. Three British soldiers were hit when patrolling in the Short Strand, a Protestant area and two IRA gunmen wounded.

In other incidents seven Belfast City buses were hijacked one night and set on fire; British army troops found large quantities of arms and ammunition in the Catholic market area of the city, instigating severe street riots. In Londonderry troops fired on four IRA gunmen, wounding them.

The newspapers on Saturday 16 October 1971 revealed the extent to which the crisis had developed in a matter of weeks.

The previous day, two RUC officers had been shot

dead as they sat in a private, unmarked car in the Catholic Ardoyne area of Belfast; a soldier attached to the Green Howards was shot and seriously wounded in Belfast after being hit by 30 bullets; three armed hold-ups were carried out in Belfast; there were explosions in both Londonderry and Belfast; a bank was bombed in Greenhills Road, Londonderry; and masked men held up a bus at Drumaney in County Londonderry, firing shots at random to scare the passengers.

During that week the British Army had undertaken a large sweep in the Catholic areas of Belfast, arresting eighteen people and discovering arms and ammunition caches. As a result, hundreds of Catholic women took to the streets, protesting at Britain's internment policy as well as at the arms searches being carried out. At one point they laid siege to Mount Pottinger RUC police station. The officers had to be rescued by army reinforcements.

By that Saturday night the death toll in Northern Ireland had reached 112 since disturbances had begun in 1969. In the first year only thirteen people had died; in 1970 only nineteen had died; since the introduction of internment on 9 August – only three months before – a further 57 people had died.

With the IRA's extraordinary burst of violent activity, which had caused so many deaths and appalling injuries, we were anticipating being called on to take our share of the fight against the gunmen but during the next few days we lived the life of Riley, keeping fit during the day with runs and gym work, lazing around the billet watching TV and playing cards and spending the evenings visiting pubs in the Protestant areas of Belfast.

A REME staff-sergeant arranged for us to be invited to a Unionist Club between Belfast and Carrickfergus. The clubhouse, a wooden building built on a jetty at Belfast Lough, provided wonderful panoramic views across the sea. The walls inside boasted yachting trophies, shields and regimental plaques. In pride of place above the wooden bar was the Red Hand of Ulster.

The members, mostly middle-aged, respectable businessmen, big and small, showed us nothing but friendship and generosity. They knew, of course, that we formed part of the British security forces but they never asked us the name of our regiment nor about the precise nature of the work we were carrying out in Ulster. Indeed, they often seemed protective towards us, saying on occasion, 'Just make sure you keep clear of the evil bastards.'

One or two of the members must have been very wealthy for the yachts moored nearby were magnificent, expensive motor-yachts, worth a small fortune. On occasions, one or two would invite us back to their homes to enjoy a traditional Sunday dinner.

At the club I often chatted with a friendly, decent kind of bloke who spoke with a Northern Irish accent but who was, in fact, a recently retired English businessman. He had bought a bungalow in Carrick-fergus and was renovating it as a hobby. He moored his blue, 30-foot, ocean-going, four-berth yacht on the lock. He was a man who always stood his round and I would get to know him very much better during the next twelve months.

Throughout those first two weeks in Belfast we would often be wakened by the sound of rifle fire at odd times during the night. Sometimes the gunfire sounded really close but, to our knowledge, the Sydenham Docks complex was never the target of any direct fire. On occasions, of course, we also heard the unmistakable sound of a bomb going off, and we would try to judge how much gelignite had been used in each explosion.

It seemed that the call for us to continue our part of the plan to wipe out the gunmen would never come. Each morning we expected Don to be called into the Lisburn headquarters for our orders. We waited in vain.

On Monday 18 October we were surprised to hear that we had been ordered to hold another meeting with Yvonne, the woman informant we had met a couple of days after our arrival. This time, chatting in a pub in Lisburn, the woman told us of an IRA gunman who was staying in a safe house near Malone Road, South Belfast. Yvonne said bluntly, 'He needs to be killed. He has committed terrible atrocities.'

We wondered what made Yvonne tick. We had been told that she had once been an ardent IRA supporter but now worked for British intelligence. We wondered why she had agreed to turn traitor and now talked about her own side with such venom. She told us she had been informed that the gunman was staying in the house of known IRA sympathisers. She encouraged us to take the house by storm, at night or at dawn but Don didn't like the idea and told her so, saying, 'If we hit that house we would have to take out everyone in the place. We couldn't risk trying to find the one suspect we would be looking for. And that's stupid.'

Yvonne appeared to know the gunman really well because she admitted that he fancied her and wanted to go to bed with her. She suggested that she would take him to a pub on the Wednesday – two days away – get him pissed and then we could grab him when they were on their way home.

We agreed in principle to go along with her plan but, without informing her, we changed the operation. We knew that shortly after eleven p.m. in Belfast, with the pubs emptying, the streets would be full of people as well as troops and police watching out for trouble. The last thing we wanted was to be caught in the middle of a gun battle with police and troops having no idea of our true identity.

We arrived in our blue Marina shortly after seven p.m and parked in Malone Road, about 100 yards from the terraced house. We saw Yvonne and the man walk into Malone Road and move towards the pub about 200 yards further down the road. I was driving, with Don next to me in the passenger seat and Benny and JR in the back.

I drove past and stopped about twenty yards or so in front of them. As they drew level with the car, JR and Benny leapt out and Benny took out his pistol, thrust it into the gunman's face and told Yvonne, 'Fuck off. Get the hell out of it.'

JR quickly searched the bloke who made no attempt to fight or make a run for it. JR found a .38 Smith and Wesson, the old British Army style revolver, in the man's waistband. They forced him into the back of the car and off we drove.

We knew where we were going – to the spot where we had met our grave digger a fortnight earlier. We had only driven a few hundered yards when our man, recovering from the shock of being kidnapped, said, 'What are you Protestant bastards doing with me?'

Don, who was in the passenger seat, turned round and, looking him straight in the face, said, 'Look here you little republican shit. We're not Protestant bastards; we're just taking you for a little ride.'

The man tried to start a conversation several times during the 30-minute drive but every time he opened his mouth we would tell him to shut up and keep quiet. In an effort not to frighten him, however, Don told him nonchalantly that he was being taken to someone who wanted to ask him a few questions. That helped to settle him and he remained quiet for most of the journey.

It was dusk when we finally arrived at our map reference off the Lurgan–Dromore Road. We drove down the lane and parked on the scrubland off the road. He looked at us and we could see the fear in his eyes.

We told him to get out of the car but he refused. 'I'm not getting out anywhere,' he said, 'and certainly not here miles from civilisation.'

JR and Benny looked at each other. Benny knew what he had to do and told the man, 'Get out here and now otherwise I will fucking shoot you while you're sitting in the car.'

The man wasn't sure what to do. He began to get out and then sat back in the car again. In the end Benny half-pulled, half-dragged him from the car. He clung on grimly to the car door, refusing to let go.

Benny kicked him hard in the leg and ripped him away from the car door, sending him sprawling. As JR dragged the man to his feet, he turned to see that Benny had a pistol in one hand. He turned to JR who was now standing by him holding two guns, a pistol in one hand and a .38 revolver in the other.

The man must have known that he was about to be killed and refused point blank to walk. Benny kicked him repeatedly in the legs, shouting at him, 'Walk, you fucking bastard, walk, or I'll fucking kill you here and now.'

But the man refused, falling to the ground and screaming for help as Benny repeatedly kicked him in his efforts to make him get to his feet and walk where he was told. 'I'm not going,' he shouted, 'I'm not fucking moving. I'm staying here.'

Benny became agitated and began shouting, fucking and blinding at the man, not sure what to do. He had completely lost his cool and was in no mood to allow the man to argue with him. It seemed that the man would not agree to walk anywhere, despite the kickings. Benny knew what he had to do.

In the same split second, both Benny and JR aimed their weapons at the man on the ground and opened fire, hitting him in the back. Benny fired three shots, hitting him in the back and the head. His body jerked forward as the rounds hit home and he slumped to the ground.

I looked around, positive that someone must have heard all the noise and commotion. At that time our weapons had no silencers and Benny and JR had fired four shots between them, sending the birds in the trees chirping and squawking. I knew we were on the edge of a wood and a long way from any houses but it seemed that the whole neighbourhood for miles around must have heard what was going on.

After all the noise, the shouting and the screaming, the wood seemed to go instantly silent. We looked at each other, not sure how to respond. Someone said, 'Quick, let's get this fucking over as fast as possible.'

We all grabbed hold of an arm or a leg and carried the body towards the trench in a hurry. Without ceremony, we threw him in, turned and walked back to the car.

As we drove back to Belfast, Don turned to JR. 'Where's the gun?'

'What gun?' he said.

'His gun, the one you took off him.'

'I've got it here. I thought I'd keep it as a souvenir.'

'No you fucking won't,' replied Don. 'Clean it, get rid of all the fingerprints and throw it.'

Five minutes later we stopped by the side of the road and JR threw the gun as hard as he could into a hedgerow. The operation was over.

The following morning we had a chat about the previous night's work. We all realised it had been a fuck up; it hadn't gone well and we had made far too much noise removing the man from the car and dragging him along before killing him. If we were going to continue taking out people and disposing of them we had to think of a better way of keeping them quiet before killing them.

We hoped we would not be asked to continue picking IRA gunmen off the streets. We had been led to understand that our task would be more clandestine; this work was more like cops picking up some poor sod off the streets rather than SAS work.

Benny could not be consoled. All day he went around like a bear with a sore head, blaming himself for the mess up and refusing to listen to our advice. We knew that it wasn't Benny's fault; it was the actions of the man that had determined how the operation went. It was simply Benny's bad luck that his man had played up in such a manner, making his task that much more difficult.

Later that day Don went off to the Lisburn headquarters. He was determined to get us out of Sydenham Docks and into more secure billeting and, more important, he knew that we needed another Q-car. We had now used the Marina on two operations as well as being seen around the town in it – the same four men in the same blue Marina. It had to go.

He returned a few hours later with a dark blue Ford Cortina Mark II and told us we would be moving on Saturday. He said, 'You may not believe this but we are moving to Silver City.'

'Silver City?' we replied in unison, unable to believe that we would be billeted in Northern Ireland's biggest top security jail. Silver City was the name given to the infamous Long Kesh Prison, where all the senior IRA officers were kept, as well as the great majority of men picked up and interned under the Special Powers Act. Long Kesh earned its name of Silver City because, in the early 1970s, the corrugated iron walls shone like silver in the sunlight.

We wondered what life would be like there and felt sure we would miss the good food we had enjoyed at the REME canteen.

After a farewell drink with a couple of REME blokes on the Friday, we moved the following morning, managing to squash all our gear in the boot of the Cortina. We carried no ID cards, of course, but the officer in charge of the Long Kesh guard house knew to expect us.

We drove through the gates and about 120 yards along the road, turning right into a road lined with Portakabins. It looked more like a holiday caravan park than Ireland's biggest jail.

This Portakabin was more spacious and more luxurious than the one at Sydenham Docks. Although we now had much more room and four single beds, we still had to walk from the Portakabin to the showers and loos, about six yards away. In the bitter cold of winter those eighteen feet seemed more like half a mile.

At that time, Long Kesh seemed to house soldiers from every other regiment in the British Army. There were one or two infantry regiments and detachments from REME, the Royal Engineers, MPs, cooks and medical staff as well as scores of prison officers.

It seemed ironic that we had been moved to Long Kesh which now housed hundreds of IRA suspects. Earlier that week Prime Minister Edward Heath, after holding talks with Opposition Leader Harold Wilson, had agreed to set up an inquiry, under Sir Edmund Compton, to examine allegations of brutality and the torture of internees as well as others arrested under the Special Powers Act. Following the announcement of this inquiry, fierce debates raged in the House of Commons, Stormont and the Irish Dáil as critics blamed Britain for the situation in Northern Ireland – for neglecting the situation in the north for 50 years; for introducing internment; for blowing up border roads; and for permitting the torture of internees.

At the same time Cardinal Conway, Archbishop of Armagh and Primate of All Ireland, denounced the British and Stormont governments for using torture

to obtain information. We read about all these allegations in the newspapers and wondered what the hell
would happen if the part we were playing in the
troubles ever became known — that we were secretly
killing known IRA gunmen on orders handed down
by the British Army's senior officers in Northern
Ireland's headquarters. We believed those officers
would have received their orders from the Ministry of
Defence in London.

We also recognised that the actions we were
ordered to undertake would have had to be
authorised at the highest level. It seemed unlikely that
senior civil servants and ministers at the Ministry of
Defence would not have known about the missions
we had been ordered to undertake. We believed the
policy of picking up IRA gunmen and shooting them
in cold blood could only have been approved in
London.

We wondered how many more people we would
be ordered to get rid of.

CHAPTER SEVEN

T HAT WEEKEND THE fury of the Catholic backlash erupted in Newry. Not since the policy of
internment had been introduced in August,
three months earlier, had the mass of the Catholic
population made their feelings known in such a
violent way.

The spark that ignited the whole town occurred
when a local businessman strolled towards a bank in
Newry town centre to deposit his day's takings in the
night safe. As he approached the bank three men
rushed him and tried to snatch the bag holding the
takings.

The man screamed for help, refusing to hand over
the money. With great determination and courage, he
held on to the bag as the three hit and kicked him in
an effort to force the bag out of his hand.

Overlooking the bank, however, a British army
marksman had been placed on duty to watch for just
such an attack. Alerted by the man shouting for help,
he saw what was happening and, as the three men

ran from the scene, he shouted at them to stop. They continued running and the soldier opened fire, killing all three.

Within an hour the centre of Newry became filled with angry Catholics demanding that the soldier be strung up for killing innocent men. Two hours later more than 10,000 chanting, angry, rioting Catholics would not be calmed by the army's loudspeaker appeals for order.

Determined to avenge their dead friends and get even with their Protestant foes, other Catholics torched shops, homes and government buildings in and around the town. Fire brigades from towns twenty miles away were called in to deal with the flames that threatened, at one point, to race through the entire centre of Newry. Army reinforcements were called in from Belfast as the rioters stormed around the town far into the night.

Not since the troubles began had the Catholic minority in one town reacted with such venom and such determination to burn down every building they targeted as belonging to the enemy. The strength of feeling manifested itself three days later when more than 15,000 people attended the funerals of the three men.

It seemed to us in our Portakabin at Long Kesh that the IRA was far from being on the edge of defeat. From that one incident it seemed likely that they would win over a few thousand more recruits to their cause. What we had hoped would be a quick tour of duty in Northern Ireland now threatened to stretch into months, if not longer. I wondered how many more people we would be ordered to kill.

During that same weekend of 23–24 October we were also surprised to read that the security forces had shot dead four men and two women who had been planting bombs in Belfast. The six had been an IRA squad intent on bombing the city centre's premier hotel, The Europa, and the famous Celebrity Club in Donegall Place. Those killings would also be roundly condemned because not one of the six people shot dead had been carrying a weapon.

It was the first time that we had read of women taking such an active role in terrorist activities. Until that moment we had believed the women actively supporting the IRA had taken a back seat, leaving the men to carry out the shootings, beatings and bombings. I wondered if I would ever be able to kill a woman if ordered to do so. I doubted it.

On the morning of Monday 25 October 1971, Don told us that we would be starting the next phase of our task and he would have to visit Lisburn head-quarters to pick up a new shooter. This one, however, would be fitted with a sophisticated silencer.

While he was away all hell broke loose in the Long Kesh jail, hidden from our view by a ten-foot-high corrugated iron wall but only a few hundred yards from our billet. We had been alerted by a helicopter hovering above the jail and we could see flames shooting up above the jail and plumes of smoke drifting into the sky. On the ground there was non-stop activity, with people shouting orders.

On the television news later that day we heard the reason for the commotion. Two hours before the trouble the British Government had announced their decision not to set up a semi-permanent commission of inquiry into allegations of torture of Long Kesh internees by the security forces. It had also been intended that the commission would investigate allegations of the shootings of civilians by British troops. As we sat in our billet watching the BBC news we looked at each other. No one said a word.

We heard later that four prison warders had been taken hostage and held for two hours; the recreation hall had been set on fire and the inmates had wrecked their accommodation and barricaded themselves inside with their hostages.

Troops were called in to restore order, armed with pick axe handles and CS gas.

Two days later the Irish newspapers reported that the IRA had smuggled out a note from Long Kesh, detailing what had happened during the riot. The note claimed that, after the internees had set fire to the prison canteen and barricaded themslves inside one part of the jail, British soldiers had fought their way in after firing CS gas canisters into the block for fifteen minutes.

The note claimed that only when all was quiet, with some internees barely conscious, did the 300 troops storm the building with their pick axe handles. The IRA note claimed that the prisoners were beaten on their heads, faces, shoulders and arms, some suffering serious injuries. A number were admitted to the military wing of Musgrove Hospital with broken arms, jaws and noses and seventeen were detained. Allegedly, after the riot had been put down, a number of inmates were taken away for intensive questioning. Before the questions began, however, they alleged that soldiers had beaten them. For two days, the note claimed, soldiers looted and wrecked the H-block huts, taking whatever they wanted.

The Northern Ireland office issued a statement to the effect that troops had fought their way into the prison and some slight injuries had been sustained by the rioters. But the Northern Ireland Catholics' allegations against the British Army and the RUC had been gaining credence. For the first time a group of Catholic priests in the diocese of Armagh issued a statement 'condemning the cynicism of the Northern Ireland Irish Home Affairs Office in stating that only a small number of inmates had been slightly injured in the riot'.

When he returned with the new 9 mm Browning

pistol and the silencer, we asked Don why he always went alone to the Lisburn headquarters, suggesting that it would be safer for him to be accompanied by one of us, just in case.

'Two reasons,' Don told us, happy to explain. 'All you need to know is what I tell you. The less you know the better and maybe, one day, it could be safer for you not to know the people who are in command of our little operation.

'The second reason is that guarding Lisburn right now are members of the Ulster Defence Regiment and, quite frankly, I don't trust some of those bastards. It's bad enough that they have got to know me; it's better that they don't get to know the rest of our team.'

Don's scepticism would prove disturbingly accurate. Only months later we heard of two IRA members who had had the audacity and courage to join the UDR and who had robbed the UDR's armoury one night and escaped with a number of Sterling machine guns and self-loading rifles. It hadn't taken the police long to discover who had been responsible but it was too late; the two IRA men had vanished.

That night we decided to have a drink in the little pub near the rear of Long Kesh jail, which was situated between the jail, the old aerodrome and the race course, about 200 yards from the security gates at the back of the jail. So that we would not be seen travelling in and out of the main gates, we had been given our own key to those gates which we used at all times. The pub would become our local. We liked it because not only did it have a dart board but it seemed to us a very English type of pub and served what we wanted, typical English pub grub.

The following day we needed to dispose of the various parts of our 'millies' – 9 mm Browning pistols that we had used on our three victims. The barrels, extractors and firing pins had to go. We knew all too well that any good forensic investigation would identify our part in those killings if they ever got their hands on those bits and pieces.

So we drove out to Lough Neagh and threw some of the bits as far as we could out into the water. They must have hit the water about 50 yards from the shore. We then drove further out, to the coast, and slung the remainder in the sea, as well as breaking up the wooden case, with its dark burgundy-coloured velvet lining, and throwing that into the sea as well. We watched as the wooden pistol case bobbed away out to sea.

When we arrived back in the late afternoon Don insisted that we all went and ate a good meal in the cookhouse. Back in our Portakabin, he announced quietly, 'Right, now we've had something to eat, start to compose yourselves because we will be leaving here in one hour. We've got a little job to do.'

During the following hour we prepared for the job, stripping our 'millies' – oiling, unloading and loading them again. We would be careful to buff each and every round of ammunition before loading it into the magazine. Everything had to be sparkling clean so that nothing could possibly go wrong. Don never examined our weapons; that would have been an insult. We had been trained by the SAS and took pride in being totally professional.

We took our own Brownings, as we had done before, but the new 9 mm pistol, equipped with the silencer, would be kept in the glove box of the Cortina. The person responsible for carrying out the killing that night would be responsible for cleaning and loading the 'killer gun'. On this occasion Don had decided that he would pull the trigger. He felt he should be responsible for trying out the new weapon.

Don told us that this job should be a piece of cake for this would be a far easier task than the others had been. It would be the first time we were carrying out the task for which we had been designated.

He explained that we would drive to the map reference Lisburn had given him that morning and wait in the car to be contacted by another SAS unit. They would bring with them an IRA gunman who had been targeted and would hand him over to us. We would never know his name nor would we know what crimes he had committed. We had to take it on faith that the man was guilty. We presumed that he had been responsible for carrying out shootings or bombings.

Don explained that the men we would be dealing with had records of IRA involvement going back months and years. Some had fled south when the troubles began and were now returning to the north to organise IRA units and carry out killings. They had been targeted by MI6 operatives in the south, who informed Lisburn headquarters that these men were on their way back across the border.

Patrolling the border were at least two, four-man SAS units, living in the field in their combat kit as we had all been trained to do. They would stay out for four weeks at a stretch, in wireless communication, picking up IRA suspects who they ambushed as they made their way north. The SAS unit would then pass them on down the line. Those to be despatched would be taken by the unit to rendezvous with us at our map reference; some would be passed on for interrogation at Long Kesh; others sent for Special Branch questioning.

As dusk fell, we clambered into the Cortina and headed south. I drove, with Don in the passenger seat, while Benny and JR sat in the back map-reading and navigating. This time everyone seemed more relaxed, one reason being that Don would be carrying out the mission, which meant we could all breathe more freely.

There would be another significant difference. Our

other two hits had been in daylight with the victims unaware of what was happening. This time the victim would have been picked up some hours earlier, informed that he was being taken for questioning and, therefore, we believed, he would be more relaxed. He would have no idea that he was about to be executed. We realised all too well that this subterfuge would make our task that much easier.

Five miles from the border we passed a British Army foot patrol of twelve men, a platoon of infantry, armed with SLRs and dressed in combat gear and hessian-covered helmets. They glanced at us but took no notice and made no attempt to stop us. I looked at their faces and most seemed pretty pissed off with their job of patrolling the border. They probably felt as though they were targets, waiting for the IRA to take a pot-shot at them.

We pulled up on the side of the lane near the map reference Don had been given. I switched off the lights. Don told JR to get out and walk about ten yards behind our car to watch our backs, just in case of an ambush. Shortly afterwards I saw the flash of a red torch light about 30 yards ahead of us, in the hedgerow; the signal we had been waiting for.

'That's them,' said Don and got out of the car to walk towards them. I stayed in the car with Benny.

I saw two men walking down the road towards Don, one in full combat gear and camouflage helmet, the other dressed in jeans, a donkey jacket and boots. The SAS man had his hand on the man's soldier, guiding him towards Don.

Don approached the two men and took control of the man. The SAS man turned and walked back up the lane until he disappeared from view. The IRA man, about five feet ten inches tall and well built, seemed apprehensive, a little frightened but not agitated.

Don called JR over and told him to sit the man

between him and Benny in the back seat. Without a murmur the man climbed in.

'Let's go,' Don said and I drove off.

Don turned round to the man and said, 'Just relax; we're going to take you for a ride. We'll be handing you over to the RUC.'

I had to drive about 150 yards further down the road before I found a place to turn round because the lane was so narrow. Then we headed back to the wood where we would dump the body. We drove for about half an hour before we arrived at the spot.

As we drove, the IRA man began talking, telling us that he belonged to no terrorist organisation, didn't know anything about the IRA and couldn't understand why the hell he had been picked up. Don told him, 'It's nothing to do with us . . . we're not interested . . . you'll have to explain all that to the RUC.'

On arrival, I pulled off the road, parked and switched off the car lights. Don turned to Benny, 'Nip out and check that the RUC are waiting for us down the road.'

Benny hesitated, not immediately realising that Don was bluffing. He suddenly twigged, got out of the car and walked off down the lane. He came back five minutes later and said the RUC were waiting down the road.

Don ordered the bloke out of the car and Don got out too. The man had taken only a couple of steps when I heard the 'thump, thump' of the Browning, barely audible even in the stillness of the night. I saw the man slump to the ground, shot twice, once in the back of the head and once in the back.

JR said, 'I thought you would wait until we were nearer the spot. Now we've got to carry the fucker.'

I thought how callous JR had become and it surprised me.

Before we left the scene, Don bent down and

picked up the two empty shell cases. We wanted to leave nothing that could ever raise suspicion or, worse still, launch an investigation that could lead directly to us. Whenever we left the scene of a killing, we would always pick up every shell case.

Once again, we all grabbed the arms and legs and, between us, carried him to the trench. I noticed that only about half of the original trench had been left open; the rest was filled in. I also noticed that on the exact spot where we had dumped the other body, some young conifers had been planted. Once again, we threw the body into the deep trench and walked back to the car, making no attempt to throw any dirt on the body or cover it in anyway.

I wondered when the farmer responsible for burying the body would be around to carry out his duty. I realised that a dead body would attract predators very quickly, particularly foxes and crows, rats and other vermin. The job would have to be done speedily, perhaps before daylight. I looked around but saw nothing. I would imagine that he had been warned to stay clear of the area and begin his gruesome task at daybreak.

I shivered in the night air and felt the hairs on the back of my neck stand up, as though someone had walked over my grave. I wondered whether the cold night air was the cause or the killing we had just carried out. In my heart I knew the blame lay with the execution.

As we drove back to Long Kesh, however, I sensed a feeling of relief among the four us. This time the operation had gone as planned; there had been no last-minute hitches; no need to face the man before shooting him; the operation had been cold, clean, clinical.

We arrived back at camp before midnight and sat around drinking coffee and discussing in some detail how the operation had gone. Don would raise any points he thought needed airing, to ensure that things went even better on any subsequent mission. He suggested, although it was really an order, that in future operations the man sitting behind the driver would always get out of the car and act as guard as JR had done that night.

As we chatted, JR stripped the Browning and silencer and cleaned and oiled every piece before reassembling it. Two hours later we turned in for the night. I dozed off immediately and slept through the night without a dream or even the hint of a nightmare.

On waking the next morning the realisation of the killing the previous night hit home but I knew that I would have to forget it, push it to the back of my mind and get on with life. I had already discovered that this was the only way I could deal with the thoughts that, on occasion, would fill my mind and haunt me. Mostly, I managed to bury the memories by concentrating on whatever I was doing, whether it was cleaning my teeth, having a shower or enjoying a meal. I knew I had to forget everything we were doing or I wouldn't be able to cope. I told myself, time and again, that an SAS man doesn't question his orders. He does what he is told to do with complete professionalism. And I was determined to be a bloody good SAS man.

Thank God, however, Northern Ireland wasn't all about killing.

We lazed around the next day, found a launderette in Lisburn to wash our clothes, watched TV and read the papers. That night we went for a drink at the Union Club in Carrickfergus.

We hardly ever talked about each other's backgrounds, our families or our lives before joining the SAS. Of course, being young squaddies we talked about women but would never mention their names. For an entire year we would live in each other's pockets, living closer together than any family. For the greater part of our life in Ulster we would mostly go out together as a group and we would always work together, never alone.

I learned that JR, a Yorkshire lad, had lived most of his life in an orphanage and had become a boy soldier before joining the Royal Engineers. Benny came from Enfield, Middlesex and his background seemed quite normal, like mine. I learned that he had an elder brother and sister. Don came from Devon but was born overseas where his father, a career soldier, had been stationed at the time.

Because we were spending so much time together we all realised that whenever we went to a pub, club or disco we should split up and go our separate ways, although still keeping a watchful eye on each other just in case. We were all friends, of course, but realised that keeping apart as much as possible would make life easier when we had to be together, whether driving around in our Q-car or chatting together in our billet, where, of course, we would spend most of our time.

When we were confident of going to a safe area, perhaps to play football or to the Union Club, we would always hand in our pistols at the Long Kesh guard room until we returned. We would always pick them up immediately on our return, however, because we never knew how quickly we might be sent into action.

When we arrived at the Union Club, I went to have a drink with John, the Englishman who I had met on a couple of visits. We began chatting over a couple of beers and he invited me to Sunday lunch that week-end to meet his wife and family. He knew I was young, just 23; and away from home and he wanted to be kind and generous. I really looked forward to that Sunday roast; it seemed ages since I had enjoyed a home-cooked meal.

The following night we decided to go to the army disco at Sydenham Docks. The place was steaming when we arrived shortly after nine o'clock. It seemed half-full of squaddies but, more important, there seemed to be three women for every two blokes. We looked at each other and knew we were going to have a ball.

It seemed to be my lucky night. I had been standing by the bar having a quiet pint of bitter and looking around when I noticed an attractive, young, well-built, rather tarty blonde girl dancing with one of her girlfriends. She came over, ordered a drink and began chatting to me. I felt hooked.

She told me her name was Alison but I didn't believe her. She just didn't seem like an Alison, a name which, to me, conjured up Alice bands and pretty young girls. Instinctively, I realised this Alison knew all about life as she appeared openly raunchy. She was precisely the sort of girl I needed to meet that night to make me forget everything.

I asked Alison if she wanted to dance but she preferred to stand and drink. Only when the music slowed down did she want to dance. As soon as we started dancing I knew she wanted me, her hands went everywhere and she pressed her body to mine as though she had known me for ages.

She suggested we go outside for fresh air and I was only too happy to get out of the smoky atmosphere and find a chance to smooch. She didn't want to know. She led me to a line of half a dozen three-ton army trucks which, conveniently, had their tailgates down. 'Come on,' she said. 'Give me a lift up.'

I grabbed her arse and pushed her into the back of the truck before climbing in. She had picked up her coat on the way out and she threw it down on the cold floor of the truck and lay down. 'What are you waiting for?' she asked. 'I'm not wearing any knickers.'

I needed no second invitation and I had been right. Alison was dynamite. She demanded I screw her twice before she would allow me to leave. As we walked back into the disco she said, 'I'll see you again. I love a good screw.'

During that night of debauchery Benny's claim to fame would receive the attention of at least two girls and would earn him a reputation which lasted throughout our twelve-month stint in Northern Ireland. To say the least, Benny had been well endowed.

After going outside for a long session with the girl he had met that night, she returned to the disco singing Benny's praises. She proclaimed happily to her girlfriends: 'You've got to try him; he's amazing; it's the biggest I've ever seen; I can hardly walk straight and I definitely can't sit down.'

Sometime after midnight all four of us returned to Long Kesh with smiles on our faces. We had needed a good drink and a good fuck to unwind and forget, for a night, everything that had gone on since we had arrived in Northern Ireland. We felt better.

Spruced up and smartly dressed, I met John at the club for a pint before the long-awaited Sunday dinner. He drove us back to his bungalow about three miles away. The moment I saw his daughter Lizzie I knew we would hit it off. She confessed later that she, too, had felt the same way.

During lunch Lizzie and I would occasionally catch each other's eye and smile, and afterwards she asked me if I would like to go with her to take their dog for a walk in the fields behind their house. I readily agreed.

We spent more than an hour walking the dog, chatting, laughing and teasing one another. Lizzie was fun to be with. Her parents were from England and had lived in Northern Ireland for only a few years. Only five feet five inches tall, with brown hair, brown eyes and a lovely well-rounded figure, Lizzie, a shop assistant, had just turned twenty.

As we walked and talked I realised that Lizzie would be a wonderful companion for me during my tour of duty in the Province and, hopefully, would give me an interest away from army life. I also realised that the more time I spent with Lizzie the more respite I would enjoy away from my three mates.

Considering how closely we had to live together, the four of us got on bloody well, yet part of that relationship was built on the realisation that we were part of an SAS unit who knew they had to get on together, come what may. That helped. At times, however, I yearned to be on my own in the country, birdwatching or simply walking alone, without the necessity to carry a gun or the constant need to look over my shoulder.

I felt guilty liking Lizzie. I was certain I felt something for her, not only lust, and yet I wondered if my attraction was based on the fact that she had parents who lived in a nice house, who were showing me generosity, feeding me and making me feel at home in a way that I had never experienced in my life before. They made me feel more than welcome.

After insisting that I stayed for tea, Lizzie offered to drive me back to Long Kesh. As we sat in the car saying goodbye she lent over and kissed me on the mouth. I began to kiss her but she pulled away. I liked that.

As I walked into camp with a smile on my face I believed we would see more of each other. Inside, I knew I needed her.

CHAPTER EIGHT

AFTER MAKING HIS morning telephone call to Lisburn headquarters Don told us he would be away for a couple of hours and would see us all at lunch. He never made any phone calls from inside Long Kesh for fear that the call could be intercepted or bugged. Despite the fact that we were all allegedly fighting on the same side Don did not want there to be any possibility of people listening to his conversations with the intelligence services working at Lisburn.

He would make the calls from different telephone boxes and at different times so that there was no pattern to them. He would always walk to make his calls, not only taking different routes but in a way that made him seem unobtrusive, going about his daily duty almost unobserved.

If he was called into Lisburn he would take the car, leaving the camp by the back gate.

On his return on this particular Wednesday,

3 November, he told us: 'Look lively, we've got another job tonight,' and he added, 'We had better make sure we are all on the ball again'.

We were ready. That weekend two British soldiers had been killed in Belfast, one shot at point blank range as he sat in a car; the other killed when a bomb exploded in his billet in Cupar Street off the Springfield Road.

As well as those assassinations, something else had made us angry. We had seen on the TV news that weekend that 15,000 people had marched through the West End of London to Whitehall, protesting against internment without trial in Northern Ireland. We had heard the never-ending chant of the marchers, 'Victory to the IRA', repeated over and over again by the protestors, many of whom carried nationalist flags.

Only days before the march the government had announced that during the month of October the IRA had detonated 225 bombs, using a total of 2,381 lb of explosives. Many of those bombs had been intended to kill and maim British troops. The IRA didn't seem to care that some of the bombs also killed innocent women and children.

We also realised that not only were the IRA winning the propaganda war in mainland Britain but they had succeeded in gaining an increasing amount of support for their cause throughout the entire Catholic population of Northern Ireland. One woman in the Ardoyne, who had never supported the IRA, commented at that time: 'We never wanted the IRA but they seem now to be our only protection.'

It looked as if the briefing we had been given on arrival, only five weeks before, by the combined intelligence-gathering sources of the British Army, British intelligence, Special Branch and the RUC, had been either completely wide of the mark or perhaps deliberately slanted to give us the impression that the war against the IRA was all but over.

In those five weeks the number of bombings and shootings across the Province, but principally in Belfast and Londonderry, had escalated alarmingly. Every single night, without exception, the BBC Northern Ireland news was filled with reports of deaths, injuries, bombs, shootings and burnings. By the targets selected, we knew the IRA had been responsible for all but a few of them. Far from being nearly extinct in the north, the IRA seemed to be gathering strength daily.

We felt we could have been far more usefully employed on the border with the other SAS units, catching the IRA men infiltrating into the north, rather than just being used as an execution squad. All four of us would have much preferred to be dressed in combat gear and going out to capture these bastards in the way we had been trained, rather than donning jeans, sweaters and leather jackets as though we were going for a drink down the local. We did realise, however, that every man we took out meant that there would be one less killer on the streets of Northern Ireland. That gave us some justification.

As usual when we were waiting to go out on a job, we were all pacing up and down in the billet waiting to get on with it. I walked up to Don who was cleaning the silencer and the 9 mm Browning, 'I'll take the border special tonight,' I said, taking the shooter from him.

'What did you call it?' he asked.

'The border special,' I said. 'We've got to call it something. And that's all it's good for.'

'Yeah,' said JR, 'I like that; the border special,' and he laughed. His laugh, however, sounded more like relief because, in reality, it should have been JR's turn to pull the trigger that night.

After taking the gun, I stripped it down once more and made sure I had cleaned and buffed the rounds, placing them carefully back in the magazine before sliding it gently into the butt. I waited to hear the click, showing it was properly in place. I wanted no foul up.

We drove down to the border once again, with JR at the wheel and Don and Benny in the back navigating us to the map reference Don had been given earlier that day. We drove neither too fast nor too slowly, always keeping to the speed limits, trying not to draw attention to ourselves.

Shortly after eight o'clock we pulled up on a narrow, lonely road near the border and waited in the darkness for the rendezvous, wondering what our man would be like this time. Don climbed out and walked back, as arranged, about ten yards. We knew the area would have been secured because at least one other SAS unit would have made sure of that before we arrived. We posted a guard simply as an extra precaution.

I waited until I saw the red light from the torch. JR flashed our headlamps once and I got out and walked up the lane. I saw an SAS trooper, in full camouflage, carrying a pistol in his right hand with his SLR slung over his shoulder. He held his victim far more securely than the last time, gripping the man's neck as he pushed him towards me. 'Watch this one,' he warned. 'He's a lively little runt.'

The man, about five feet six inches tall, slim and with what I can only describe as a ferret-like face, looked confident, even cocky. Looking at me, he said in a Southern Irish accent, with a sneer, 'Who's this then, the Special Branch?'

I said, 'I'll take care of the little rat,' grabbed hold of him by the back of the neck, frogmarched him the ten yards to the car and put him in the back seat. Don climbed in after him and we drove off.

After driving in silence for a while our man asked sarcastically, 'And where do you boyos think you're taking me?'

'We're taking you to someone who wants to talk to you,' Don said.

He replied, 'I suppose you're the fucking SAS like those other fuckers who picked me up.'

'If we were the SAS,' Don said, 'you would already be fucking dead, sunshine.' He added, 'Now shut up, sit back and relax.'

When we arrived at the forest Don grabbed him by the jacket and half-dragged him out of the car. 'Out,' is all he said, 'Out.'

JR parked off the road and we walked across the grass towards the trees, the moon shining brightly in a near cloudless sky. We shivered in the cold; winter wasn't far away.

We walked a hundred yards or more towards the old trench but noticed it had all been filled in. Beyond it we saw that a new trench had been dug. Our man also saw it.

He said, 'What the fuck's this?' and turned towards me. I was about to pull the trigger as he turned and I just continued to squeeze it, hitting the man full in the face. I immediately re-aimed at his chest and pulled the trigger twice to make sure he would be well and truly dead.

As he fell to the ground I could see the small red mark on his face where the round had entered. I could see nothing on his chest but I knew I had hit the mark. Don bent down and checked his pulse. 'He's a goner,' he said.

Don grabbed hold of his shoulders and I took his legs and we picked him up and threw him into the trench. I picked up the three empty shell cases and the Browning and we walked back to the car without saying another word.

I felt good as we drove back. I hadn't liked the little runt from the moment I saw him. I hadn't liked his sarcasm or his attempt to put down the SAS. I wondered how many soldiers he had tried to kill and how many he had killed. I felt I had done my bit to rid the country of one more troublemaker who was prepared to go the whole hog to achieve his political aims.

Back at Long Kesh Benny made the coffee and I sat on my bed cleaning and oiling the pistol. Two hours later we were all sound asleep and looking forward to the following night – Thursday, disco night at Sydenham. Lizzie would be there.

As we walked into the disco a number of girls began whistling and cheering at Benny for word had spread fast.

'Who's a big boy then?' a number of them shouted at him as we walked to the bar for a pint.

Benny turned scarlet, put his head down, his hands in his pockets and walked with us trying to hide his embarrassment.

'You're supposed to keep a low profile in our mob,' JR joked, 'and here you are after one bloody night you've become a celebrity.'

'Not my fucking fault,' said Benny. 'I didn't think she would go shouting her mouth off.'

'If you're going to cause all this fuss,' I said, 'you'll either have to go to the doctor and have a few inches taken off or make sure you keep it inside your trousers for the rest of the time we're here.'

'Leave me alone,' Benny mumbled as he downed his first pint in one.

It would be only a matter of minutes, however, before a girl came up to Benny and, despite his embarrassment, succeeded in dragging him on to the floor for a slow dance. Don and JR teamed up with the girls they had met the week before and Lizzie came in looking good, smiling and happy. 'Nice to see you again,' she said as she walked up to me and gave me a peck on the cheek. It was as if we had been married for a couple of years, but she did seem happy to see me again. I tried to play it cool, of course, but I was genuinely really happy to see her.

Lizzie looked great and I felt proud to be with her as well as lucky. It felt good to have someone with whom, I hoped, I would have a proper relationship. I knew in my heart that I much preferred to have a steady girl than a one-night stand.

The evening went well and we danced, had a few drinks and chatted most of the time. We kissed and snogged through all the slow dances and it seemed good. Lizzie invited me to dinner again on the Sunday and said she would collect me from Long Kesh and take me to the club for a drink before going back to her home.

The lads enjoyed their night out and we all went back together in the car shortly after midnight. We made sure the route we took from Long Kesh to Sydenham passed through only safe areas for that same day the army had carried out the biggest house-to-house search ever mounted, starting at seven a.m. in the Catholic Andersonstown area, covering most of the Lower Falls and ending at lunch time. They were looking for known IRA suspects, weapons and bomb-making material.

As we drove back, we noticed the numbers of RUC police on the streets and felt sorry for them. We felt safe because we carried our pistols whenever we went out, except on disco nights. The police, however, were becoming increasingly targeted by the IRA and were getting very angry. In October 1971 alone there had been 155 separate attacks on police stations and police personnel and yet they only carried the old-fashioned, First World War .38 mm revolvers.

That week two police divisions had written *en bloc* to the Chief Constable, Graham Skillington, threatening mass resignations if they were not re-armed. Some demanded automatic weapons, like Sterling machine guns, others demanded armoured cars.

Two days before, Belfast had been rocked by a

massive bomb that had ripped through the Red Lion, a Protestant pub in Ormeau Road at Ballnafeigh, two miles from the city centre. Two civilians had been killed and 36 people seriously injured in the blast which had been timed to go off in the middle of the day when the area was crowded. Minutes later, another bomb exploded in a fashion shop, destroying it. The shops had been on either side of the RUC station but that wasn't touched by either blast. No prior warning had been given. It proved to us that the IRA couldn't care a damn for the people they purported to be supporting and protecting.

To make sure we kept fit we would, from time to time, go for hard runs around the disused aerodrome as well as lifting weights which one of the army cooks kept in a makeshift gym not far from our Portakabin. His weights proved really useful, providing us with something to do rather than hang around all day waiting for the next mission.

Meanwhile, Sunday came and went and I spent most of the time with Lizzie, taking her dog for a walk, having drinks in the club and then enjoying a good Sunday roast as well as tea. At ten that night Lizzie dropped me back at Long Kesh with a kiss and a promise of a date at the disco that Thursday.

We knew another job was imminent after Don had been told to report to Lisburn for another briefing. 'We've got another bloody Belfast job,' he said on his return. He explained what had gone wrong and why we had been ordered to sort things out.

Two of the former IRA supporters who had agreed to work for the Special Branch had apparently managed to kidnap a known IRA gunman, a former colleague and they had him chained to a bed in a house in Ballysillan Road, north-west Belfast. The two former IRA men, Mick and John, had begun to panic that their victim would be discovered and their cover blown. They had contacted Special Branch who

decided we would be the ones to dispose of him. They
wanted the job done immediately; they didn't want to
risk losing their informers.

Despite the urgency, we preferred to carry out the
operation under cover of darkness and arrived at the
scene shortly after dusk. Two minutes after we pulled
up outside the house, Mick and John came out with
their man, his hands tied behind his back. They had
obviously given him a real hiding for his face was a
bloody mess, with cut lips, black eyes and a badly
bruised face.

Don got out of the car and the two Irish informers
pushed their prisoner in beside me. 'Listen, you two,'
Don said to Mick and John. 'We don't want any more
fucking jobs like this, do you understand?'

'Well it had to be done,' one of them said. 'We saw
him, so we grabbed him; we had no option.'

'Bloody morons,' Don mumbled as he got back
into the car next to the prisoner.

As we drove away Don untied the man's hands
and, to reassure him, said, 'If you're co-operative and
answer the questions, you'll probably be handed over
to the medics to take care of you.'

His soothing words had the desired effect. The
man kept quiet and sat back rubbing his wrists.
Throughout the journey I would occasionally look at
his face and could see the mass of congealed blood
around his eyes and nose and the heavy bruising. He
looked a right mess, yet he hardly seemed to notice
the beating he had taken.

No one spoke during the journey as Benny drove
back to the forest where the execution would take
place. On this occasion I felt annoyed that we were
having to carry out someone else's dirty work. I
didn't mind so much when we were taking out known
IRA gunmen who the SAS had picked up on the
border, but I felt that this had nothing to do with us.

This would be JR's first execution and I wondered

how he would deal with it. I knew, from bitter experience, that when I actually pulled the trigger the effect
on me was far greater than when someone else
carried out the execution.

I should have guessed, however, that JR would
screw up and he did. As before, we thought he
wouldn't shoot the bastard until we had all walked to
the trench. Suddenly, I heard the 'thump' of the
silencer after we had taken only a few paces from the
car. Shot in the back of the head, the man fell to the
ground.

We just looked at each other, annoyed with JR for
making us carry the body nearly a hundred yards to
the grave. The man, in his thirties, must have been
more than six feet tall and weighed over fifteen stone.
The four of us struggled to carry him.

Benny commented, 'Thanks, JR. For fuck's sake
why didn't you let him walk?'

'I thought you'd like the exercise,' replied JR, 'It's
good for you.'

'Shut up,' said Don.

As Benny began to drive away, JR suddenly said,
'Christ. I've forgotten to pick up the bloody case.'

'Come on, JR,' said Don, 'you're acting like a
fucking amateur. Get out there and find it. And make
it quick.'

I got out and helped JR as we scrabbled around
on the ground in the darkness, trying to find the
single case. It seemed like an age but after about five
minutes JR found it. 'Thank God,' he said. 'I've found
it. Let's go.'

'About bloody time,' Don remarked as we got back
in the car, deliberately embarrassing JR further,
hoping his criticism would make him pull himself
together.

I could see that Don had been annoyed by the
whole affair, not only that we had been ordered to
carry out a job which had nothing to do with us, but

also by the lack of professionalism shown by JR. Don knew JR had fired the Browning earlier than he should have done because his nerve was near breaking point. Don knew he had forgotten to pick up the single case because he had not been thinking straight. To Don, these matters, small in themselves, showed that JR was not sufficiently self-disciplined, could not cope with stress and hadn't yet proved he was a good enough soldier to be part of an SAS unit. Don was proud of being a ruthless professional and he believed that everyone who wore the winged dagger should be of the same calibre.

A couple of minutes after leaving the forest the headlights of the car picked up an old, small, wooden sign, with black lettering that was only just visible to the naked eye. It read 'Blackskull Lane'. I looked at Don, unable to believe that this had been a mere coincidence. Then we checked our reference map and, a few miles away, we saw the village of Blackskull marked on the Ordnance Survey map.

'Someone's got a sick sense of humour,' said Benny quietly.

That week Amnesty International published a report alleging serious and apparently substantiated allegations of ill-treatment of internees held at Long Kesh. Amnesty urged that an independent international commission should be set up to investigate the allegations which detailed a number of cases which, they claimed, amounted to a *prima facie* case of the brutality and torture of internees.

The report said internees suffered severe beatings, were often stripped naked, were made to run barefoot over broken glass and were subjected to one particularly gruesome torture which had become commonplace in Long Kesh.

Prisoners' heads were covered with an opaque cloth bag with no ventilation and they were dressed in a one-piece boiler suit and forced into a search position with their legs apart. They were then left in a room filled with constant, high-pitched whining for up to six hours at a time. Some prisoners, they claimed, were driven to the point of insanity, others openly prayed for death to release them from their agony.

The report had been accompanied by a statement signed by 387 Catholic priests in Northern Ireland – 80 per cent of the Catholic clergy – alleging the torture and brutality of men arrested under the Special Powers Act.

We believed the British Government could never agree to such an inquiry for fear that the commission members might stumble across our activities. We knew what uproar would follow round the world if news ever leaked out that the British Government had employed their own crack SAS forces to act as execution squads in Northern Ireland.

Then the IRA revealed the depths to which they were prepared to stoop, even towards their own, by singling out totally innocent teenage Catholic girls for harassment and punishment.

On Tuesday 9 November 1971, Martha Docherty, a nineteen-year-old Catholic girl from the Creggan in Londonderry, was picked up by women from the area. In three days' time she was due to marry a young British soldier, Private John Larter, aged eighteen, from Suffolk in England, a soldier in the Royal Anglian Regiment who had planned to become a Catholic the day before his wedding. A month earlier he had been kidnapped by youths in the Creggan, shot through the hand and told to keep away from Martha.

The women tied Martha Docherty to a lamppost with lengths of wire, cropped off all her hair and then tarred and feathered her. Around her neck they placed a placard with the words 'Soldier's Doll' on it. For fifteen minutes 50 or more women stood around swearing and jeering at the petrified girl.

Despite the punishment, however, Private Larter

did become a Catholic two days later and the couple were married the following day in Elbrington Barracks, Londonderry.

Martha would not be the only girl to suffer. The following night Deirdre Duffy, only seventeen, was stopped by seven women while walking in Londonderry. Pushed into the back of a car and driven to the Bogside she was hauled out, tied with wire to a lamppost and tarred and feathered. Her offence was dating a British soldier.

At that time a total of 27 British soldiers serving in Londonderry were engaged to be married to local girls. The IRA did not approve and issued strict orders forbidding any girls to attend discos or dances at which British soldiers would be present. Any girl who did attend would be punished.

I felt deeply sorry for the girls and the IRA's treatment of them only enhanced my feeling of disgust for them. It appeared that they would happily bomb innocent people, hide behind the Catholic minority, and use terrorist methods against the troops, including sniper fire and remote-control booby-traps. They were only brazen when dealing with their own teenage girls or youths who had allegedly broken some IRA rule. Those poor little bastards would be taken away and beaten by three or four IRA thugs using sticks and batons. The more serious lawbreakers would have their knees shot away in what the IRA liked to call 'knee-capping'.

With those thoughts in my mind, I had few qualms at that time about the job I was being ordered to carry out. The more Northern Ireland seemed to be sinking into a morass of violence, bombings and shootings, the more I believed I was helping to try to sort out the killers who had taken it upon themselves to undermine the social fabric of the Province. If IRA members were prepared to kill and maim innocent civilians, then they had to bear the consequences.

CHAPTER NINE

DURING THE NEXT nine weeks we would be called upon to only execute another two IRA prisoners, both caught by an SAS unit on the border as they tried to cross into the north. They would be handed over to us at different map references. Each killing followed the same pattern. There would be no alteration in the orders given to Don whenever he was called to headquarters in Lisburn and told that another shipment was to be picked up and disposed of in the usual way.

As a result, we felt that for the great majority of the time at Long Kesh we led an idle life and the killings became a tiresome bore that we had little enthusiasm to continue with. We kept fit, we worked out, we drank tea and went to pubs and discos but, at heart, we were bored with our life. We also felt the work we were being ordered to do, usually once every fortnight or so, should not have been a job for the SAS.

We would have much preferred to be involved in

proper soldiering, as the other SAS units were, living in the field, maintaining surveillance, passing on intelligence information and, whenever necessary, ambushing infiltrators. Then we would have really enjoyed our two-week breaks after a month in the field.

Most of the executions went as planned. A couple went awry.

On one occasion we arrived at the SAS rendezvous on the border. Benny had been given the 'border special' to carry out this particular execution. After seeing the red flashing light, he walked towards the SAS man and his prisoner. At the moment of handover, the prisoner sprinted away from Benny and the SAS bloke.

I heard a shout and looked up. I had been standing guard behind the car on that occasion and saw the man running towards me. I heard the thump of the 'border special' but the man kept running. Seconds later I heard another thump and the man collapsed just as he was running past the car. I ran towards him as he writhed and moaned on the ground. Benny raced up and put another round into him, silencing him instantly.

'Shit,' said Benny. 'I shouldn't have let that happen. I had no idea he was going to do a runner.'

'Quick,' said Don, 'open the boot, put him in and let's get the fuck out of here.'

Minutes later we were driving north towards Blackskull Lane, fearful that we might be stopped by a patrolling army squad or the RUC.

Don said, 'If we get stopped by an army unit, leave me to do the talking. I will give them the codename, "Nemesis", and tell them to contact their commanding officer. If they demand to open the boot, I will then explain who we are and what we are doing. If they demand we go along with them then that's what we will do. As long as we stick with the army everything will be fine.'

He went on: 'If we get stopped by a couple of cops I will talk first and see if I can persuade them to let us go on our way. If they insist on opening the boot then we will have to take them out. We cannot afford to be caught. We could end up doing a long time inside. Just keep your fingers crossed.'

Thank God nothing happened. I would have found it difficult to shoot two cops in cold blood for no reason.

On our return to Long Kesh we had our first major discussion about the extraordinary tasks we were being ordered to carry out. None of us had thought for one moment when joining the SAS that we would be ordered to act as an execution squad, and yet that was all we had done since arriving in Northern Ireland.

Over coffee that night, I asked Don what would have happened if we had come across a unit of eight RUC cops at a road block. 'We surely wouldn't have tried to take on all of them, would we?' I asked in disbelief.

Don replied, 'If that had happened we would have been in deep shit.'

We all looked at each other, waiting for him to continue and wondering what he meant. We had all believed that the codeword 'Nemesis' had been given to us as protection, a password that would ensure there would be no problems with either the army or the police. Now it seemed as though the codeword would have proved useless with the police.

Don went on: 'No way could you expect that number of cops to keep their mouths shut about our operations. No matter how we tried to explain our way out of the predicament, I don't think the authorities could have come to our aid. In fact, I'm sure they would never do so.

'Those cops would have passed our codeword to their superior officers and they would have contacted

Lisburn headquarters. But I believe that Lisburn would have denied everything, denied knowing anything about the codeword, denied our very existence.'

We all looked at Don in astonishment.

'Listen to me,' he went on. 'Let me explain. Eight or ten cops could never keep their mouths shut and, within days or weeks, it would be common knowledge that SAS units were being used to kidnap and execute IRA blokes at random. That would cause the most almighty row. The authorities, or rather the politicians, would turn their backs on us, tell the police that we were a rogue unit that had gone AWOL (absent without leave) and that they had been trying to capture us themselves. We would have been turned over to the police, taken to court, charged with murder and banged up.'

'Shit,' I thought.

However, Don hadn't finished yet. 'Worse than that,' he went on, 'we would have been told by some army smart-arse that if we opened our mouths in open court, and let the cat out of the bag, then we would never see daylight again.'

I suddenly felt cold.

I had believed, perhaps naively, that we were obeying orders; that whatever happened the army would stand by us. We were carrying out the dirtiest part of a bloody awful campaign against the IRA and yet, if the shit hit the fan, we would be sacrificed, left to spend fifteen or twenty years inside for doing nothing except obeying orders from the Lisburn headquarters.

I looked at the other three and imagined they were thinking the same. We had all joined the SAS because this was Britain's élite force, the toughest fucking troops in the British Army. We had all been put through hell to make the grade and earn the winged dagger. We had been so proud when we had been issued with the SAS badge, with those famous words written underneath 'Who dares wins'.

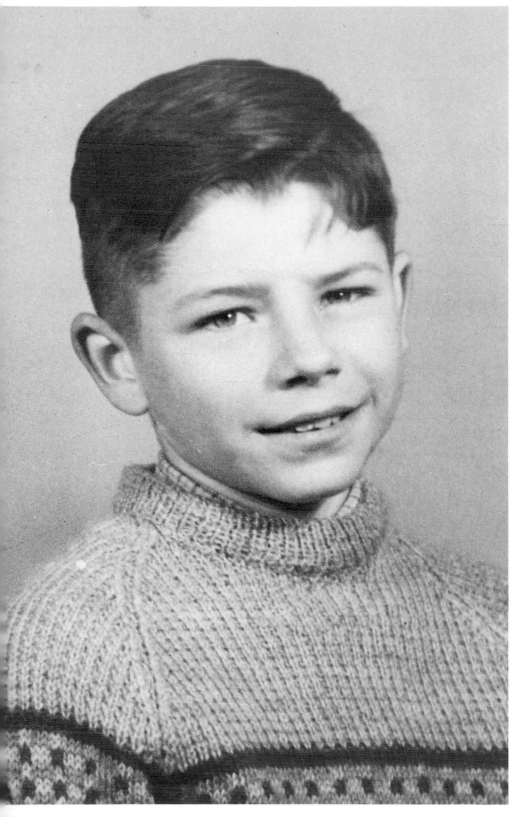

The author, Paul Bruce, aged 10.

Top: Brigadier Frank Kitson, MC, Commander of the 39th Infantry Regiment, 1970-1972. An acknowledged expert in counter insurgency. Because of his ruthless approach towards IRA gunmen he remained top of the IRA's hit list even when he left Ulster.

Right: General Sir Harry Tuzo appointed GOC and Director of Operations, Northern Ireland, 1971.

Opposite top left: William Whitelaw, appointed Secretary of State for Northern Ireland in 1972 after the British Government suspended the Northern Ireland Parliament, bringing to an end fifty years of Unionist rule in the Province. He took control of all security matters.

Opposite top right: Jack Lynch, Taoiseach (Head of Government of Ireland), 1966-1973. He failed to persuade Britain to bring in United Nations troops to police the border with Northern Ireland.

Opposite below right: Edward Heath, British Prime Minister, 1970-1974. He feared the Northern Ireland crisis could have developed into a full-scale civil war.

Top: A Belfast demonstration at the beginning of the troubles, 1970.

Below: A lone British soldier looks on helplessly after Catholic rioters hijack a double-decker bus and set it ablaze.

Top: Thousands of Protestants march through Belfast in 1972 celebrating the Battle of the Boyne, 1690.

Left: A bomb explodes in Belfast city centre killing and maiming workers and passers-by.

Above: A stand-off in Belfast. Demonstrators face British troops, 1972.

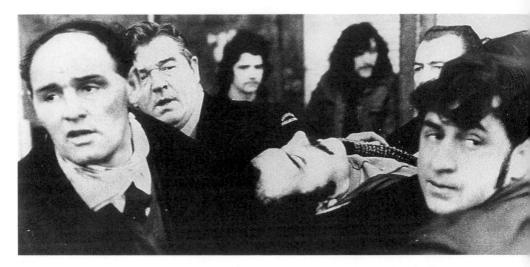

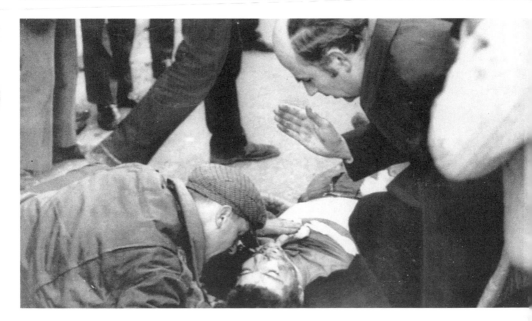

Bloody Sunday, January 30, 1972. Troops from the Parachute Regiment opened fire durin a peaceful Catholic rally in Londonderry. Thirteen innocent people were shot dead.

op: The remains of the Parachute Regiment's Headquarters in Aldershot after the IRA
ad bombed the building in response to Bloody Sunday.

elow: Hooded IRA gunmen stand guard in Londonderry.

Top: The headquarters of 39th Infantry Regiment, Lisburn, 1971.
Below: Victims of IRA bombs in Belfast, 1972.

Now the full horror hit us. We were expected to go out on a limb, carry out the shittiest work of any army unit in Northern Ireland and risk being charged with murder, found guilty and banged up for twenty years. Was that the privilege of being a member of the SAS?

The only crumb of comfort Don could offer us that night was the belief that he didn't think we would be employed for much longer doing this particular job. 'It's obviously not working. It's obvious from every-thing we read in the papers that, far from being on the edge of defeat, the IRA have hundreds of active service blokes happy and willing to fight and die for the cause.'

We knew he was right and hoped the authorities in Lisburn would realise the part we were playing was all but useless in stopping the IRA recruits from rallying to the tricolour.

In November, Prime Minister Edward Heath had all but accepted that the IRA had moved on from being a tiny band of dedicated activists to become a major force when he stated that 'a war situation' existed in the United Kingdom.

Throughout November and December 1971 the IRA stepped up their campaign of bombings and shootings. Since we had arrived in the Province the security situation had deteriorated alarmingly and now it appeared that the Protestant paramilitary organisations were becoming actively involved.

At first, the Ulster Protestants had been prepared to let the authorities, i.e. the police, backed by the British Army, contain the situation. But then they had seen the situation go from bad to worse and the IRA become stronger every week.

On Saturday 4 December, the loyalists hit back. An organisation calling themselves The League of Empire Loyalists exploded the biggest-ever bomb planted in Belfast since the troubles began. They were determined to show the IRA that they could hit them when and where they wanted. The bomb ripped apart one of Belfast's most famous Catholic pubs – McGurk's Bar – at the junction of Queen Street and Great George Street in the Catholic New Lodge area. Sixteen people were killed and thirteen seriously injured when the 50-lb bomb exploded.

We noted everything that was going on in Ulster but would always be dragged back to our little world of dirty deeds. Most executions went according to plan, but once again JR was to screw up. On this occasion everything went as clockwork until it came to the point when JR, who had been delegated to carry out the execution that night, once again could not control his nerves. As he went to shoot the man in the back of the head, he missed, hitting him in the neck, the round exiting from the man's mouth.

In those circumstances JR should, of course, have immediately put another round into the man's head or heart to finish him off as quickly as possible. The man was screaming with pain and fear but JR froze, unable to pull the trigger again. At the time I was standing next to JR, so, to put the poor bastard out of his agony and to shut him up, I pulled out my pistol and shot him through the head, killing him instantly.

'What the fuck are you playing at?' I said to JR when the poor bloke had been finished off.

'I don't know,' he said. 'I couldn't do anything... I just froze.'

Back at Long Kesh Don turned to JR and said, 'Right. It seems we can't trust you to handle a situation, so from now on you'll just be the fucking driver. OK?'

JR mumbled a reply but, from that day on, he would become the gofor of the unit, relegated to driving, making the tea and coffee and running any errands we wanted. He never complained. In some ways he seemed relieved that he would never again have to face the stress and tension that he obviously found difficult to cope with.

There were odd occasions which later made us laugh at our predicament, although it seemed a little sick. Driving back to Blackskull Lane in the dead of night, with a prisoner in the car, we had a puncture in the front nearside tyre. Everyone had to get out and lend a hand while Benny guarded the prisoner. It seemed extraordinary that we needed to stop for ten minutes to change a wheel and that the poor, wretched IRA man had no idea that he had just been given an extra ten minutes of life. We wondered what on earth we would have done if someone had come along and asked if we needed any help while we tried to pretend that the IRA man was one of us.

On another occasion the Cortina slid on an icy patch and the car buffeted along the nearside grassy bank, ripping off the bumper and damaging the front end and the doors on the nearside. The timing could not have been better for the very next day it had been arranged that we would change our Q-car from a dark blue to a dark green Cortina. Jokingly, we blamed JR for the driving error but it wasn't his fault.

By Christmas 1971 all four of us had steady girl-friends who we had been dating since mid-November. The IRA had announced a 48-hour Christmas ceasefire and Don had been informed that we would not be required over the holiday period. We determined to enjoy ourselves and let our hair down.

Early in December Lizzie's parents had invited me to spend Christmas with them, which really gave me a buzz. It would be wonderful to enjoy a happy, relaxed Christmas atmosphere with roast turkey, plenty of booze and, more important for me, a few days of uninterrupted Lizzie. We had become lovers in November and were becoming more and more involved with each other.

Lizzie knew her parents would sleep soundly every night because they really enjoyed a good drink with friends at the club and at home. Each night, at about 3.30 in the morning, Lizzie would come to my room and we would spend the rest of the night making love. At 7.30 Lizzie would tiptoe back to her room, hoping her parents would let her sleep in until ten in the morning. With little sleep, too much booze and tons of good, homely food I arrived back at Long Kesh feeling unfit and shattered but remarkably happy.

Over the next few days we were determined to get fit again with long, hard runs and plenty of weight training in the gym. I think we all needed it.

In December we had read a long newspaper article, illustrated with pictures, which had obviously had the full backing of the Ministry of Defence public relations outfit, showing how the 42nd Commando, Royal Marines were guarding the border, allegedly preventing IRA activists from crossing into the north.

The pictures showed Wessex and Sioux helicopters in action, along with Panhard armoured cars and armoured Land-Rovers, as well as Marines in full combat gear. Allegedly, the troops patrolled for 118 hours a week and had been successful in stemming the numbers infiltrating the Province. It seemed certain, so the article claimed, that the presence of the Marines had proved a deterrent to those IRA sympathisers, usually teenage boys, who wanted to travel to the north to fight and die for a 'free Ireland'.

We knew differently. Despite the presence of 42nd Commando, we were still required to drive down to the border every so often to pick up a prisoner, take him back to Blackskull and shoot him. It seemed to us that one section of the border had been deliberately kept clear of Marines so that the IRA, believing they had found a gap in our defences, would send through men who were known to the authorities in the north and who could not, therefore, simply drive across as some raw IRA recruits did. The senior IRA men had to risk the dangers of a night crossing of the border in order to return to the north. It would be at that exact spot that the SAS would be waiting. The Marines were making the SAS task easier because we did not have to keep watch on so large a section of the border.

Sunday 30 January 1972 was a day I will never forget. We were sitting in our Portakabin in Long Kesh, idly watching TV, when a news flash announced that shooting had taken place in the Bogside in Londonderry and there were unconfirmed reports that a number of people had been hit.

That day, 10,000 people, mainly Catholic supporters, accompanied by some Protestants and clergymen from both faiths, had been taking part in a peaceful march organised by the Civil Rights Association. The marchers were approaching Free 'Derry Corner when troops on duty barred their route and made them turn back.

The Civil Rights leaders decided to stop the march and set up a microphone for the speakers to address the vast throng of people. Bernadette Devlin, the young firebrand nationalist MP, who had become the youngest MP in the House of Commons when voted into Westminster in 1969 at the age of 21, had barely begun to speak when the sound of gunfire reverberated across the area.

Film footage showed members of the Paratroop Regiment firing at the marchers as they fled in panic from the scene. The Paras were shown running after the marchers, kneeling, taking aim and firing; while other Paras stood at corners firing at will.

When the firing stopped and the mayhem had calmed down, thirteen innocent people lay dead, all shot by rounds fired by the Paras. Bloody Sunday would forever be remembered by the Catholic minority.

Despite protests from the Parachute Regiment that they had only returned fire after coming under sniper fire, no evidence was ever produced that anyone else, other than the Paras, had opened fire. The British Government set up a judicial inquiry; the Irish Government declared a day of mourning; in London, Belfast and Dublin tens of thousands of workers stayed away from work and left factories, offices, shops, schools and universities in protest at the killings.

In Dublin the Union Jack was burned outside the British Embassy and the Paratroopers were accused of 'wilful murder'. Anti-British protests grew, with seven attacks on British firms based in Dublin; a bomb was thrown at the British Embassy in Dublin; violence and rioting broke out in Catholic areas across Northern Ireland; and children as young as seven began throwing nail bombs and stones at British Army vehicles.

On Wednesday 2 February, more than 20,000 people attended the funerals of the thirteen marchers who had been gunned down.

In our tiny Portakabin we would discuss the whole appalling episode on frequent occasions during the next few weeks. As I watched repeated screenings of the killings, I could not bring myself to believe I was witnessing disciplined British troops behaving in such an ill-disciplined way. The more we watched reruns of the film, the more dismayed we became with the behaviour of the Paras.

We were even more amazed when no action whatsoever was taken to discipline those soldiers who had seemingly run amok, firing indiscriminately at innocent people. They would never be charged with any offence. And yet we realised that if we were caught carrying out the executions of known IRA killers, we would probably be arrested, charged and left to languish in jail for twenty years. It seemed that everything I had ever believed in about Britain and the British Army was disintegrating before my eyes. I began to feel sick.

CHAPTER TEN

DURING THE FIRST three months of 1972,
Lizzie and I saw each other two or three times
a week and her parents would invite me to stay
most weekends.

It seemed that the more I saw of Lizzie, the more
I needed to see her. Every Thursday we would go to
the disco together and spend most of the time on the
dance floor wrapped in each other's arms. The lads
came to recognise that we were so close that they
called Lizzie my 'missus'.

I didn't mind at all. Lizzie would be kind, gentle
and considerate to me. She could make me laugh
when much of the time I felt more like breaking down
in tears. Yet I could tell Lizzie nothing of what we
were doing.

On occasions when we took her dog Bella, a young
Basset hound, for a long country walk, I would be
tempted to tell her everything about my job and yet I
knew I could tell her nothing. I could not even hint

what we were doing. Indeed, she would never know that I was a member of the SAS. I had told her that I was a vehicle mechanic with the REME, which, in part, was true. If the occasion had ever arisen, I would have known exactly what to do, what to look for if called upon to check a car in an emergency. One weekend I did prove my REME background by changing the clutch on her car.

We did have great fun together. Once the worst of the winter weather had passed, we would spend many weekends out on the moors north of Belfast or driving around the coast. She, too, loved birds and wildlife and I enjoyed pointing out the different species to her.

On occasions we went rock climbing along the coast at the very tip of Northern Ireland, searching for Leach's petrels, which, until then, had only bred on St Kilda off the north-west coast of Scotland. I had read, however, that they had been sighted in Northern Ireland and I wanted to check whether any had, in fact, begun to nest in Ireland.

We did see some petrels. They would find themselves a particular ledge, on an obscure part of the cliff, and would visit that ledge for perhaps three or four years, inspecting the area to check whether it would be suitable. During that year Lizzie and I saw a number of them, but none had started to nest. About three years later I would read that the petrels had indeed begun breeding in Northern Ireland.

I would go climbing up the face of the cliffs and Lizzie would stay below, shouting at me to take care. 'I hate you taking such risks,' she would say on occasions. 'There is no need for you to take any risks. They're only birds.'

'It's fantastic,' I would reply. 'I love checking out such birds because they are so rare.'

'Well, thank goodness you don't do anything scary with the army. I don't mind you being in the REME; they always stay safely in barracks.'

'Yes, I know, darling,' I lied, giving her a kiss.

In my heart I was happy that she had no idea what work I had become engaged in doing. On those occasions I felt a warmth in my heart that I did keep my nerve, that I had never told her the truth. I vowed I never would.

On one occasion we were nearly run down by a herd of young steers. The sun was shining, the birds were building their nests and we decided to take a short cut across a field to check out some hooded crows' nests. We had noticed the steers at the other side of the field but I thought they were happily chewing the cud, minding their own business.

When we were about halfway across, with another 60 yards to go, a couple of steers looked up and began to walk towards us. The rest of the herd, perhaps as many as 50, followed and then they all began walking quite fast towards us. I had always been under the impression that, if confronted by a herd of steers, the only way to avoid being chased was to stand absolutely still.

I said to Lizzie, 'Stand still, don't move a muscle and everything will be OK.'

She held my hand and, together, we stood still. Far from this making the steers come to a halt, they suddenly all began to run towards where we were standing with Lizzie's dog. At first I couldn't decide what to do, but decided to put my theory to the test and hope they would stop.

'Paul, they're not going to stop, they're coming straight for us,' Lizzie screamed as she held my hand in a tight grip, watching the steers running towards us.

I could see the look of fear on her face and when I looked back at the herd they were less than twenty yards from us and running harder than ever. Bella, it seemed, had more sense than we did for she had seen the advancing cattle and had already run for cover.

I suddenly realised that Lizzie might not be able to make the hedge in time, so I picked her up in a fireman's lift, threw her over my shoulder and began running like hell.

'My shoes,' Lizzie screamed as I picked her up. 'I've lost my shoes. They're stuck in the mud.'

'Forget them,' I yelled back as I ran with her towards the hedge, occasionally glancing over my shoulder at the steers bearing down on us.

I was convinced the herd would catch us. As we reached the barbed-wire fence, I simply threw Lizzie over and then dived over myself. The charging herd kept running and I prayed that the fence would hold. We were both lying on the ground, trying to scramble to our feet. As they reached the wire, however, they put on their brakes and the fence held. My heart was thumping. I had never been so scared in my life.

When we realised that we were indeed safe and that the herd had decided to move off, we both burst into laughter. It may have been through a sense of relief, but I laughed because I had been so bloody stupid as to think a herd of cattle would simply stop and stare if I decided to stand still. I would never put that theory to the test ever again. I had learned a lesson.

I waited until the herd had drifted off to the other side of the field and walked back to the centre to find Lizzie's shoes buried deep in the mud by the trampling hooves of the cattle. Lizzie stayed on the other side of the fence, thank goodness, for, as soon as the steers saw me trespassing in their field again, they began to move towards me once more. This time I just turned and ran.

When we arrived back home, looking dishevelled and muddy, Lizzie's mother asked what on earth had happened. We told her, making sure we didn't make it sound as though we had been at any risk. Lizzie asked, 'What's for lunch?'

Her mother replied, 'Roast beef, your favourite.' Lizzie just crumpled with laughter.

On another occasion, when out walking with Bella, we had just returned from a walk in the country and popped down to the corner shop for some sweets, when we noticed about twenty dogs outside the shop. Bella was on the lead and didn't seem in the least interested in the other dogs.

Lizzie suddenly realised that Bella had come into season. Like all Basset hounds, of course, Bella, could not run fast, only trundle along, so Lizzie half-ran, half-walked the hundred yards back to her home while I tried to keep the randy dogs at bay. Once we were safely inside the house, of course, the dogs continued milling around, barking. After a while Lizzie asked me if I would go outside with buckets of cold water. I must have thrown half a dozen buckets of water at them but it didn't make the slightest difference.

During the months that I spent with Lizzie I was to witness the unacceptable face of Protestant bigotry. Until I was exposed to the Protestant viewpoint, I had assumed that the problems of Northern Ireland had been caused solely because the southerners, the Catholics, the republicans wanted to take over the north to bring about one Ireland, united under the tri-colour and the Catholic religion. Furthermore, they seemed prepared to shoot, bomb and terrorise the northern community, killing innocent men, women and children until their demands were met by the British Government.

At the Union Club most weekends I would listen to respectable, middle-class Protestants, both men and women, all intelligent people, discuss the problems facing the Province. They may not have realised what they were saying to one another but I noted that they spoke with utter contempt about all Catholics, not just those involved in terrorism.

'I would never employ a Catholic' . . . 'I would never let a son of mine marry a Catholic' . . . 'I cannot imagine why the Catholics don't leave us alone' . . . 'I don't see why we should permit any Catholics to live in the Province' . . . 'No Catholics should ever be employed in the army or the police.'

These remarks were repeated over and over again during the months I lived among the Protestant community. The more I heard about the way in which the Protestants treated the Catholics – not much better, it seemed, than as sub-humans – the more appalled I became. I began to understand some of the reasons why the Catholic population believed they did have a just cause. Not for one moment could I condone the methods they used but I began to realise why they had taken up arms after so many years of oppression.

The more time I spent among the Protestants, the ordinary, God-fearing folk of Ulster, the more I understood why the Catholics were prepared to risk so much. I was not among paramilitary Protestant loyalists, prepared to kill and maim Catholics. These people were intelligent and, they believed, fair-minded. I often thought that I myself would have become an active member of the IRA if I had been born into a Catholic family in the north, being treated like a second-class citizen, being barred from employment, from housing, from any organisation dominated by Protestants.

The more executions that Don, JR, Benny and I were ordered to carry out, the more revulsion I felt towards the tasks we were asked to perform and the people, whoever they were, who had decreed that such a policy should be introduced and implemented. It became more difficult to have a pint of beer in the Union Club, or accept a pint from a Protestant hand, when I felt that they would cheer me as a hero if they knew I was engaged in executing Catholics captured on the border.

None of this, however, did I ever mention to Lizzie; none of this did I ever even hint at to those Protestants with whom I drank and rubbed shoulders; and I vowed never to discuss politics with Lizzie, her family or their friends. I was a sergeant serving in the SAS; I wasn't paid to think.

The more exposed I became to Protestant thinking, the more I tried to forget what I was engaged in doing, and Lizzie did help me to forget.

Lizzie would become my lifeline with reality, the one person who could make me forget the jobs that still cropped up once a week or so. When we were together we would spend hours making love.

We would always disco at Sydenham on the Thursday evening and spend an hour or more making love in the car – nearly always two or three bouts of feverish, passionate sex. Lizzie would collect me on Friday afternoon and we would make love before her parents returned home in the evening. Most Friday and Saturday nights – from midnight till seven in the morning – we would make love as often as I could, forgetting everything else.

She would threaten to make me take cold showers but she never did. I believe she loved the attention and the mammoth sessions of sex, while to me those sessions were magic. On the nights I slept in the Long Kesh Portakabin, I would spend hours tossing and turning, thinking and worrying before finally sleeping at perhaps four or five a.m. With Lizzie I would fall asleep satiated and relaxed without a thought of the horrors I wanted to leave behind. When I was making love to Lizzie I could forget everything: my life, my fears, my job, the executions, the poor bastards I was having to kill, the whole sordid, sorry, bloody mess. Sometimes I felt it had all become too much and I was beginning to hate life in the army. Worse, I was beginning to despise myself for doing it; for not having the guts to walk out of the army. Yet I knew

I couldn't do that. I hoped and expected that we would soon be moved back to Hereford; to make way for another unit; and then I could escape back to sanity.

Meanwhile, I knew that Lizzie would be there and that I could survive with her help and her love, although she had no idea what drove me, what made me act in the way I did. She had become my safety valve.

Occasionally, Don would arrange for the four of us to be invited to Palace Barracks, Hollywood, not far from Belfast Lough, where other SAS units stayed when resting from their border patrols. They told us of life in the fields on the border. They were happy to share their experiences with us. They had adopted the Vietcong idea of not simply living rough under hedgerows and shrubs, but actually making large, underground burrows and living in far greater comfort, with greater protection from the elements.

The Vietcong, of course, went on to construct mini-villages underground, with hospitals, arms dumps and living quarters. The simple burrows our mates dug had taken some weeks to build but two blokes at a time could sit or sleep in some degree of comfort. They would also take turns eating their food inside. Much of it was the same type carried by American Marines, in cans that would automatically heat the contents when opened.

They told us that each and every week they arrested eight or nine IRA blokes, all infiltrators, but only the real villains, about one every couple of weeks, would be handed over to us. The rest were handed over to the RUC, Special Branch or other intelligence services, for questioning.

I felt how lucky they were to be doing a proper soldiering job, one we had all been trained to carry out, that they could be proud of doing as professionals. As we drove back to Long Kesh, I believe we all felt that we had drawn the short straw and we all wanted out.

In this operation, however, the SAS were taking a back seat compared to the poor soldiers carrying out the everyday duties of patrolling the streets of Belfast and Londonderry. From the beginning of January 1972, the bombings and shootings escalated as the Provisional IRA became more daring, more professional and more determined.

The IRA had begun ambushing army patrols on the border, planting large Claymore mines, up to 100 lbs of gelignite a time, which they would detonate by remote control when an army Land-Rover or armoured personnel carrier drove by. They would sit in a field nearby, keeping watch, and, on most occasions, would explode the mine with precision, causing death and many injuries.

Then the IRA gained access to anti-personnel mines which they would lay on the border at places where they believed British troops would patrol. At the beginning of February, 21 AP mines were discovered in two days. They had to be careful, however, of where and when they planted the AP mines because of the number of IRA personnel crossing the border each week.

St Valentine's Day 1972 brought death and destruction to the centre of Belfast when six huge bombs blasted six separate business premises across the city.

Four days later a total of nineteen major bombs exploded in towns and cities across the Province. The IRA were stepping up the pressure and it seemed that the RUC and the British Army were powerless to stop them.

On Tuesday 22 February, the IRA finally got their revenge for Bloody Sunday. Seven people were killed and seventeen injured when a bomb ripped out the front of the officers' mess at the headquarters of the

16th Parachute Brigade in Aldershot. The IRA had proved they could successfully move their area of operations out of Northern Ireland and into any corner of the mainland they wished.

Ever since Bloody Sunday the intelligence services had warned of the probability of a revenge attack on the Paras. Despite the warning and increased vigilance at all Para HQs, the IRA had been able to mount a serious attack with impunity. They had also made the Parachute Regiment look remarkably unprofessional.

However, the political capital the IRA hoped to make from the bomb blast would be heavily diffused because all the people killed or wounded were civilians, kitchen staff and others employed in the building. Not one Parachute officer, NCO or private soldier was killed or wounded in the attack.

The IRA must have known that the bombings would bring about major retaliation from the Protestant paramilitary organisations who were becoming increasingly restless.

At 4.30 on the afternoon of Saturday 4 March, two people were killed and 136 wounded when a bomb tore apart the Catholic-owned Abercorn Restaurant in Castle Lane, Belfast, while a cabaret was in progress. Film footage of the scene of destruction, the horrific injuries to the wounded and the screams of those who survived proved too much for TV chiefs and hardly any clips were shown on the nation's TV screens.

Appalling tit-for-tat bombings, that were to become a mark of sectarian violence, now began in earnest. On Monday 20 March, one of the worst IRA atrocities shocked the entire community, both Catholic and Protestant. Six people were killed and 146 injured when a bomb exploded at twelve noon in the centre of Belfast, in busy Lower Donegall Street.

The callousness of those planting the bomb could

not be imagined. Minutes before the blast, telephone calls had been made to newspaper offices, reporting that bombs were about to explode in churches and offices in the area. Warned by police, office workers began pouring out on to the streets in a bid to escape the blasts. Minutes later the massive bomb exploded. Never before had the IRA deliberately set out to draw hundreds of innocent people, both Catholic and Protestant, to the scene of a bomb they had planted and timed to explode to cause the maximum of casualties. The scenes on the streets were horrendous.

Four days later the British Government suspended Stormont for twelve months, one of the principal demands the IRA had been making ever since the troubles began. One of Britain's most senior politicians, William Whitelaw, was appointed Secretary of State for Northern Ireland. He immediately flew to Belfast to take over direct control of all security matters, bringing to an end 50 years of Unionist rule in the Province.

The IRA issued a statement claiming that the suspension of Stormont had brought real hope for peace and, allegedly, debated whether to end their campaign of violence. It was not to be. A few days later the Provisional IRA's Chief of Staff, Sean MacStiofain, repudiated the idea of any peace initiatives or even negotiations, issuing a statement which, in part, read: 'If we become hesitant the fight of this generation is lost. We want freedom. Any other attitude is a betrayal of the internees, the political prisoners and the 'Derry dead.'

Seven days later, on 7 April 1972, Whitelaw freed 72 internees. Their freedom was celebrated far into the night throughout Catholic areas in Belfast and Londonderry, with bonfires and parties. For the IRA that wasn't enough. There were still another 842 men held, 611 internees as well as 161 detained for questioning.

For two weeks a lull in the bombings and shootings brought a little hope to the traumatised people of the Province but it would not last. On Thursday 13 April, 30 explosions, directed mainly at civilian targets, reverberated across Belfast, bringing chaos and mayhem.

Two days later Joe McCann, a well-known and leading member of the Official IRA, had run away when challenged by a Paratrooper on patrol in the Market area of Belfast. The Paratrooper opened fire, killing McCann with one round. IRA chiefs were furious, accusing the British Army of assassinating one of their most senior officers. Within 24 hours three British soldiers had been shot dead while on patrol, the IRA declared the Turf Lodge area of Belfast a 'no-go' area and shootings, stoning and riots broke out afresh in Belfast and Londonderry.

Throughout February, March and April our thankless task continued. As before, we were given orders to rendezvous at one or another map reference on the border and we would collect another prisoner, another victim to be executed. We noticed, however, that a change had come over the prisoners. They seemed comatose, drugged, barely aware of what was happening and with no fighting spirit about them. Indeed, some seemed so semi-conscious and relaxed that they didn't even bother to talk, behaving as if totally unaware of what was happening.

This made our task much easier for not one of them wanted to argue, make a run for it, put up a struggle or even say anything as we drove them on the 30-minute journey to Blackskull Lane. When we asked them to leave the car, it seemed that they were resigned to their fate, as though not caring if they lived or died, but happy to do as we asked without question.

Their total compliance made me feel far more guilty than before. Killing a man with anger and vengeance in his heart, who showed arrogance and a distaste for our abilities, had, somehow, made the killing more acceptable. Now the executions seemed to be without reason, as though we were shooting innocent, helpless victims.

On one occasion we drove back to Long Kesh having, once more, carried out our grisly duty, the car silent, all of us feeling that little bit lower than the time before, wondering when it would all stop and we could return home to sanity. As we drove towards our Portakabin inside the camp we thought we heard the sound of gunfire coming from the grassy area of the disused airfield. We stopped and saw two torches about 100 yards away. Then we heard two more gunshots and we all went for our pistols.

We switched off the car lights and threw ourselves out of the car on to the ground. When we realised that they were not firing directly at us, we crept towards them, in a line about ten yards apart, still with our pistols at the ready, our fingers on the trigger. We had no idea what to expect but we had just come from Blackskull and our minds were on edge.

Then we saw two men, illuminated from behind by the arc lights overlooking Long Kesh. The men were wearing SD caps . . . they were British officers.

'What the fuck are you doing?' shouted Don at the two officers.

The officers appeared startled and, as we walked closer, we realised they had been having a few drinks. 'Sorry, chaps,' one said. 'Sorry if we alarmed you but we decided to do a spot of night-time rabbit shooting.'

Don replied, 'Well, all I can tell you is that you are fucking lucky to be still alive. In another few seconds you could have been dead.'

We walked back to the car, wondering what the hell was happening. We had just been ordered to execute some poor bastard and these two British officers were fooling around, taking potshots at rabbits.

CHAPTER ELEVEN

ONE RAINY MORNING in early April, Don returned to our Long Kesh Portakabin after a briefing from his senior officers at Lisburn headquarters. He looked downcast. We feared the worst.

'I've got some bad news,' Don said. 'I'm sorry to disappoint you, lads, but it doesn't look as though we're going home just yet.'

Only a few days earlier we had been down to the border to collect another prisoner and, as usual, had driven the man to Blackskull and the grave he would share with his compatriots. The weather had been cold and wet and we were all hoping that we wouldn't have to continue doing this bloody awful task for very much longer. We felt we had done our share of dirty work and deserved a break.

'Go on,' said Benny, 'let's hear the worst.'

'We've been given a new location for our customers.'

I looked at him, not wanting to comprehend what

he had just told us. Did this mean that we would be in Ireland for another six months, another year perhaps, having to collect and execute more and more total strangers? For some time I had been growing increasingly concerned about our role but was managing to keep going in the hope that we would soon return to Hereford.

I felt hurt and angry. I felt we were being used in a most terrible way to do the dirty work of others. I could not for a minute believe that the job we were doing was the work the SAS should have been assigned to carry out. I kept wondering who on earth issued these orders, directing soldiers to arrest, abduct and kill young men who were fighting for what they saw as their just cause.

At that moment I felt anger that we were being used by the authorities in a way in which they did not have the right to use us. In those few minutes before my anger subsided I could have gone off to Lisburn and shot the rotten bastards giving those orders in the same way I had been called on to execute the poor IRA blokes coming over the border. But I knew I couldn't do anything like that. I had signed up for 22 years. I was a soldier and my job in life would always be to obey orders. I knew I could never do anything that would bring disgrace to the SAS.

As I fought to control my fury I kept repeating, over and over again, that I wasn't paid to think: I was only paid to obey orders.

I knew that part of SAS training included a course in abduction and assassination techniques. I had never done that course but I expected that, one day, I would be called upon to do so. In my mind, there-fore, I kept telling myself that the executions we were carrying out were perhaps a normal part of SAS life.

Confused and seeking assurance about the job we were doing, I asked Don, 'Is it usual for the SAS to be knocking off people like this?'

'Yes,' he replied. 'It's part of our job but not in these numbers. I've never done anything like this before and I've never heard of any other SAS units carrying out so many executions. Abductions and assassinations do take place from time to time and we are trained to do that.'

I understood the reasoning behind the abductions and executions of these IRA men. I understood that they were intended to cause alarm and despondency within IRA ranks as well as causing disruption to their operations. The authorities in Lisburn who supported this policy must have believed that the mysterious disappearance of so many of their key men would cause major problems for the IRA, not just logistically, but also for IRA efforts to recruit others prepared to run the gauntlet of the border.

It seemed obvious to all of us, however, that the policy simply wasn't working. In our original briefing at Lisburn, those in command had informed us that the IRA were down to only 60 or 70 senior men. We had already executed a dozen or more and we knew from our SAS colleagues patrolling the border that eight or nine a week were still coming over. Now, it seemed, Lisburn had decided to step up our workrate by ordering more executions.

'I know what you're all thinking,' Don said, 'and I feel much the same. But a job's a job so we had better get on with it. We'll have a cup of coffee and then get to it.'

We drove north-west out of Belfast towards Londonderry with our new map reference. We climbed past rows of picturesque bungalows nestling in the hills overlooking the city where the ambitious middle classes sought to buy prestigious property, and out into open country. Deliberately, we kept away from the main roads, preferring the anonymity of small country lanes with their drystone walls, low hedgerows and wire fencing.

After about 30 minutes we saw ahead of us Tardree Forest, mountain slopes dense with pine trees, many of them mature 20-foot high trees. It seemed obvious that the forest was being properly managed, with trees at different stages of growth while, in other parts, they were being chopped down, logged and stacked. Along the lane were numbers of large notices in red, saying 'Keep Out'.

We turned off the lane up a gravel track and drove for about 200 yards until we came into the forest proper. We continued to drive down a narrow track with mature pines on either side that all but obscured the daylight. After about 70 yards we turned left into an open clearing perhaps the size of a football field, where all the trees had been chopped down and taken away. Around the edges were some logs waiting for collection. From the road it had been impossible to see the clearing. This was the precise map reference of the new mass grave: 925182.

Stationary on the left, halfway down the clearing, we saw another yellow JCB digger. A man who was sitting in the driving seat clambered down as we drove up and parked.

'Afternoon,' he said in a broad Belfast accent. Of average build and about five feet eight inches tall, he was an unshaven, scruffy-looking bloke, probably in his forties. He wore an olive-green woollen hat, jeans and a combat jacket.

'All right lads?' he asked breezily. We only nodded. Trying to start a conversation, he said, 'I hear you're doing a good job.'

'Someone's got a big mouth,' I thought to myself. It was the only time during the six months we had been in the Province that anyone had ever suggested to us that they were aware of the operation we were carrying out. I decided to say nothing and let Don do the talking.

Don replied diplomatically, 'Well, that remains to

be seen.' He went on: 'I hope you realise the delicacy of what we are doing and you keep all this strictly to yourself.'

The forester replied, 'Don't you worry. Of course I'll keep it to myself. I won't breathe a word.' After a pause he went on, 'I know my head's on the block with this one you know. Mum's the word. Come with me anyway, I've got something to show you.'

We walked over towards the end of the clearing where we could see a mound of earth about 40 yards long. On the other side of the mound he showed us a recently excavated trench, also 40 yards long, dug to a depth of perhaps seven feet and about three feet across. My heart sank. It would have been possible to dispose of a hundred bodies, or more, in that trench.

'Don't worry about a thing,' the forester went on. 'I'll be here early every morning and if there is anything for me to get rid of you can be sure that I'll cover it so no one could find it. No one will ever be the wiser.'

'We'll be off then,' said Don and the four of us walked back in silence to our car, wondering when we would ever escape from this God-forsaken place.

That night we had a good meal at the cookhouse and went to the disco. As always, Lizzie was there to brighten the evening but all I wanted to do was have a bloody good drink. So did Don, Benny and JR. We knocked back pints of beer nonstop for four hours, ordering rounds while the last pints were still half-full.

That would be the only night I could remember Lizzie complaining. 'I may as well go home,' she whispered in my ear, 'I don't think I'm wanted tonight,' and she squeezed my arm and gave me a kiss.

She had interpreted my feelings correctly and I would have loved to explain everything to her so that she would understand why I needed a bellyful of beer. I knew I couldn't, and never would, say a word to her about the job we were doing in Northern Ireland. I felt good that she was so innocent of all that was happening. She didn't deserve to have to shoulder any of the shit we were putting up with; it had nothing to do with her.

Later, after I had managed to leave the pints of beer for a dance, I suggested to Lizzie that she should go home.

'What's the matter?' she asked. 'Is it me? Have I done something to annoy you?'

'No,' I told her honestly. 'It's not you, I promise. But you have to understand, tonight we all need a drink more than anything else.' I went on, 'Why don't you go home and get an early night. I'll see you tomorrow,' and I tried to give her a weak smile. I was becoming drunk and I knew it and I was glad. All I wanted to do was to forget.

That night Benny nearly became involved in a brawl with a couple of REME soldiers who had managed to upset him. Don and I heard the commotion, went over and dragged him back to the bar. 'He's had a hard day, give him a break,' we said to the REME blokes.

None of us knew how JR managed to drive the Cortina the seven miles from Sydenham Docks to Long Kesh that night, but somehow he did, although he had drunk a skinful and should never have attempted the drive. If we had been more sober we would have found someone to drive us back but we were too far gone to care a damn.

One day early the following week, Don returned to Long Kesh after his Lisburn briefing with the news that we would be carrying out another job that night and then heading for the new graveyard in the forest.

It rained throughout the evening and, with the windscreen wipers hardly able to cope with the lashing rain, JR drove really slowly along the border lanes. We found our map reference, picked up the prisoner, who appeared lifeless and half-comatose, and drove north to the forest.

We hauled the IRA man out of the car and he walked quite happily in the rain towards the mound of earth behind which we knew the trench stretched for 40 yards or more. As he climbed the mound, oblivious to what was about to happen, I shot him in the back of the head and he fell forwards into the darkness of the trench. I heard a splash as his body hit the water that had gathered in the bottom of the trench but I did not want to see how he had fallen. I bent down, picked up the single case and walked back to the car.

This would become the pattern of our lives during the next few weeks – disposing of a victim on average once every ten days or so but, on one occasion, being asked to deal with two men in a week. Sometimes we would not be called upon for three weeks.

It had been decided that Don and I would do the actual killings, that JR would stay in the car and Benny would act as guard and back-up. It worked better like this. Everyone knew his job. More important, there were no cock ups. The whole operation always seemed more fraught when things went wrong; it became easier to cope with what we were doing when nothing went wrong to remind us more starkly of the awful, gruesome task we were being ordered to carry out.

Towards the end of April I knew that I had to get away. I had tried to carry out the executions without becoming involved; deliberately stopping myself thinking about them; trying to push to the back of my mind the awful memories that seemed to be gathering like a black storm about to envelop me. So, out of the blue, I phoned Maria at the post office in Tidworth.

I don't know why I felt the need to phone her.

Lizzie was wonderful and understanding and she had been kind and generous to me but I had never felt as close to her as I had to Maria. Perhaps my feelings were changing towards her because she was part of the Province, part of my life that I had ended up hating.

'Hi, it's Paul.'

It took more than a few seconds for her to realise who was calling her after a break of nearly a year.

'Who?' she had to ask twice.

I wondered in those few seconds whether I should just put down the phone and forget it. I could be certain that a girl like Maria would have another boyfriend and I wondered if she had become engaged, or, God forbid, even married since we had last seen each other.

Tentatively she said, 'Is it you Paul?'

'You've got it in one,' I replied.

'Where are you?' she asked. 'What do you want? It's ages since we spoke.'

'Well,' I said, gathering courage, 'I'm in Ireland and I've got a seventy-two hour pass. I was wondering, if you're doing nothing, whether we could see each other.'

My heart was thumping as I waited for her reply. 'Yes, yes,' she said, sounding confused.

'Good,' I said.

Maria cut in, saying, 'Paul, I'd love to. We've got a lot of catching up to do.'

A sense of relief came over me. 'Great,' I said. 'I'll see you at the weekend, this weekend about eight o'clock Friday night. Is that OK?'

'Yes, of course it is. That'll be fine,' she said with the same enthusiasm in her voice that I remembered so well. 'See you on Friday then. I've got to go. Bye.'

'Bye,' I replied but she had already put down the telephone.

The instant I saw Maria that weekend the months

we had been separated disappeared in a moment. She was smiling and happy, looking better than I'd ever seen her. I felt she had grown up in those ten months, or was it a year? She seemed more assured of herself and I liked that.

I had flown from Aldersgrove in Belfast to Gatwick, hired a car and arrived at Maria's home early, just after 7.30 p.m. After saying 'hello' to her parents, we went for a drink at one of our favourite pubs on the main Tidworth–Salisbury Road.

Automatically, I ordered a pint of beer for myself and half a lager for Maria. 'Cheers,' I said and almost downed my pint in one.

'You're thirsty?' she said, for it had been unusual for me to drink so much so quickly.

'Yeah,' I lied, 'I just feel like a couple of pints under my belt to help me relax.'

Before Maria had barely taken a sip of her drink, I had bought myself another pint.

'What's wrong?' she asked out of the blue.

'Nothing,' I lied again. 'Why?'

'I can tell, that's all,' she replied. 'Now, why don't you just tell me all about it.'

'No, there's nothing,' I said with a false smile. 'Everything's fine.'

I hadn't expected this reaction and it worried me because Maria had immediately understood that I wasn't my old self. I had changed and she had noted that immediately. I had to snap out of my black mood of depression, forget about Northern Ireland or, I judged, the weekend would be a disaster and, as soon as I saw Maria, I knew in my heart that I needed her.

So I turned the conversation, asking Maria what she had been doing, suggesting that she had probably had a string of boyfriends since I had walked away from our relationship. I refused to believe her protestations of innocence.

'Go on, tell me,' I teased her.

I knew that she never would and she never did. All she would tell me was that she had dated one or two blokes but there had been nothing serious. I wanted to believe her, so I did. In any case, I told myself, if she hadn't wanted to see me she could easily have said 'no'.

By the end of the weekend I felt like my old self. It seemed wonderful to breathe the English country air, to listen to the birds, to listen to nothing but English accents. I felt at home and the feeling was comforting and exhilarating at the same time.

Before I drove back to Gatwick for my flight to Belfast, Maria put her arms around my neck and said, 'I have missed you. Don't leave it so long in future, eh?'

'I won't,' I promised and I meant it.

We arranged times for me to phone her and I tried my damnedest to make sure I did so. However, I had explained that, on occasions, if I missed a call it meant I was away from the barracks, out on duty. She didn't need to ask any further questions. She knew the secret lives SAS men lead from time to time.

Within a matter of days after returning to duty, Northern Ireland experienced its worst-ever weekend of sectarian violence. It erupted after a car bomb exploded outside Kelly's Tavern in the Springfield Road, Belfast, seriously injuring 63 people.

Within hours, gun battles raged between the Catholics on the Ballymurphy housing estate and the Protestants on the Springmartin estate opposite. Rifle and machine gun fire could be heard coming from both estates for several hours. The army was called in and drove their armoured vehicles into the road dividing the two warring parties, to form a barrier, and left them there until the firing ceased.

As soon as the army arrived on the spot, both sides temporarily forgot their gun battle and started firing at the army vehicles, hoping to find a chink in the armour. It seemed that both sides were beginning to blame the British Army for everything. Six civilians and one British soldier died in the battle that night.

The following day Harry West, a well-respected, former Northern Ireland minister, issued a statement claiming that the Province was now on the verge of civil war. He went on to challenge British Government ministers to visit Northern Ireland to see for themselves the extent to which the situation had deteriorated. No one took up the challenge.

Since June 1970, when five Protestants were killed on the Crumlin Road and in East Belfast, there appeared to have been an undeclared truce between the two communities. The gun battle that weekend saw the first significant expression of open Protestant violence for two years.

During the weeks before this there had been an emergence of Protestant gunmen on the streets, the erection of barricades, the emergence of Protestant 'no-go' areas, strongly worded statements from members of the Ulster Defence Association, hijacking of lorries and vehicles for barricades and the appearance of youths and young men in paramilitary clothes.

Never before that weekend in May had the British Army come under simultaneous gunfire from both Protestant and Catholic gunmen, a chilling scenario which had haunted senior British officers ever since the army first arrived in Northern Ireland. Intelligence reports that weekend warned British Government ministers that the spectre of an all-out sectarian war on the streets of Belfast had become a real prospect.

The Protestant muscle-flexing culminated that weekend in several hundred Protestant vigilantes, clad in military-style uniforms, turning the loyalist Woodvale area of Belfast into a one-day 'no-go' area, demonstrating that they could adopt the same tactics as the Catholic minority. They would also borrow IRA tactics by using the press to publicise their demands.

Standing in well-drawn ranks for the benefit of photographers, their hands stuck ominously in the pockets of their combat jackets, as though holding pistols, they were reminiscent of photographs showing IRA men riding shotgun on the backs of hijacked vehicles in 'Free 'Derry'. The vigilante organisers, the Ulster Defence Association, wanted to give the world the impression that the time had come for the Protestant majority to take the law into their own hands.

Two days later, on 18 May, William Whitelaw told the House of Commons that the IRA were desperately trying to provoke a Protestant backlash. He appealed to the Protestant community to show restraint and to stay calm, claiming that the security forces would protect the bulk of the population.

Indeed, Whitelaw's words appeared to be prophetic. Within days of his speech Britain's crack forces – the SAS – would be set loose on the streets of Belfast. Their orders were secretly to kill and wound Catholics.

CHAPTER TWELVE

WITH NORTHERN IRELAND seemingly on the brink of civil war; with politicians warning that sectarian warfare had finally broken out on the streets of Belfast, we were stunned when Don returned from a Lisburn briefing one day during the middle of May to tell us our new mission.

'You're not going to believe this,' he said, 'but the top brass want us to change tactics; they've ordered us to stir up trouble on the streets of Belfast.'

'What?' we chorused in unison.

We couldn't believe what he was telling us. During the past few weeks the troubles had escalated incredibly, with bombings and shootings, as well as sectarian gun battles, occurring nearly every day.

We bombarded Don with questions, wondering what was meant by stirring up trouble in Belfast. We thought there was far too much trouble already.

Then Don explained. 'According to the brass at Lisburn, it seems that the job we've carried out here for the past eight months has not been very successful,' he said, 'and they want to adopt a different policy.'

As he said those words, a sense of great relief came over me. I had been almost praying for the day when we would no longer have to go out picking up and executing unknown victims.

Then Don added, 'Don't look so happy. It's worse.'

We stared at him, wondering what could possibly be any worse than the operations we had been involved in so far.

He went on: 'The idea is this. The brass want to encourage a no-holds-barred, real sectarian war between the Catholics and the Protestants so that the army can stand back and see the two sides tear each other apart. They reckon that within a matter of weeks both sides will want a truce and then the politicians can start to put the Province back together again, in peace.

We wondered how this would involve us.

'Our job', he went on, 'is to make sure the war starts between the two sides and keeps going. We will be going into Catholic areas of Belfast at night, shooting at anyone we see on the streets. The idea is to kill Catholics, to provoke an even greater backlash against the Protestants.'

'This can't be true,' I suggested in an agonised voice. 'This can't be for real.'

'It is true,' he said, 'and we start tonight.'

I looked at JR and Benny. They looked grim. I felt the same, unable to comprehend what the hell was really going on. Until this moment we had been informed that the victims we were executing were known IRA killers, captured on the border. We had been told they were dangerous men, determined to continue their campaign of bombings and shootings, killing innocent people.

Now we were being ordered to go out on the streets and kill totally innocent people, just young men we happened to come across walking down the

streets in Catholic areas. The orders seemed
unbelievable. They also appeared grotesque.

'Are you sure?' I asked Don, hoping that I hadn't
heard correctly what he had explained.

'Yes,' he said. 'I felt the same as you do when they
told me. I checked. It's for real all right.'

Don felt our mood of scepticism but he also knew
that he could not permit us to challenge the orders
he had been given to carry out. 'Listen,' he said. 'Its
no good arguing, no good asking questions. We've
been given our orders and we must obey them.
Remember, we're just the soldiers; our duty is to
carry out the orders we are given and we will carry
them out to the best of our ability. That's our job. So
we had better all shut up and get on with it.'

Don decided that we should venture into the
Catholic sections of Belfast, into the Falls and Ballymurphy areas, on reconnaissance exercises, checking
the streets and making ourselves fully aware of the
layout of the roads, especially checking possible
getaway routes.

We knew this new operation would be dangerous
because the IRA always kept look-outs, many armed,
to check any strange vehicles that ventured through
their areas. We knew that, given half a chance, they
would try to stop and check a strange car, especially
one containing four young men who they would
assume would be either Protestant loyalists or an SAS
unit on the prowl.

It was decided that JR would always drive and
Don told him to make sure he spent rest periods
studying a street map of Belfast so that he would
know precisely where he was at all times, day or
night.

Don also decided that he would ride shotgun in
the front passenger seat and that Benny and I, with
weapons at the ready, would remain in the back seat.

It was decided that JR would carry only the one

pistol he had always kept in his shoulder holster. We kept the 'border special' in the glove box, in case it ever became necessary to use it. Don, Benny and I would all carry Sterling sub-machine guns, firing 7.62 rounds, and capable of firing off a magazine of twenty in three seconds.

Each of us had two magazines, one on the weapon, the other taped to it, for speed. In that way, we could change magazines within two seconds. Taping magazines in this way had been banned by the army some years before but the SAS encouraged it. Using the taped method allowed you to change magazines three times quicker than the traditional way and that's all that mattered. The SAS weapons instructor had told us: 'Learn to change mags this way; it could save your life.'

We always carried a spare can of petrol in the boot of the car just in case we ran out while driving to and from the border. Now we needed the petrol can for a different reason. We realised that if the IRA or, just as important, the RUC, sussed our car, we must have no hesitation in burning it immediately. The can of petrol would make that quicker and easier.

We knew that there was very little love lost between the British Army and the RUC. The RUC always maintained that, if left to their own devices, they would have put an end to the troubles without any need for army intervention. They resented the fact that the British Government had disbanded their special forces, the infamous B-Specials, and they also resented British troops being sent to the Province.

We knew that if we were stopped by the army, our codeword, 'Nemesis', would immediately be passed to higher authorities, letting us off the hook. We feared that the RUC, on the other hand, might use our plight for their own political advantage, perhaps even arresting and charging us publicly before Lisburn HQ were aware that we had been picked up. That could end in a long jail sentence for the four of us.

That night we took off at dusk in our green Ford Cortina to check out the Catholic areas of Belfast. The light summer nights were fast approaching but we never wanted to make a hit after the pubs had closed at 10.30. We knew that when the young wild ones left the pubs around that time they were looking for trouble and an unknown, unmarked car with four men inside would have provided them with the perfect target.

We spent an hour making a 'recce' of the two main Catholic areas, checking where all the 'no-go' barricades had been erected, making sure the streets we intended to patrol had at least two avenues of escape. We all knew what would happen to us if we were ever picked up by the IRA. The notion was too horrifying to think about.

On our return, Don briefed us on the plan of action. 'We all have to know exactly what we will do if the worst happens and we're sussed by the IRA or, perhaps, the car breaks down or we're involved in a crash.'

He went on: 'If the car breaks down and there is no one around, we will simply burn the car and leg it. If, however, we're sussed and they're coming for us, then we must take control of the situation. No one must panic. If we have to fight our way out of the situation then we will do just that. Remember. If they catch us we're dead. Remember your training. Back at Hereford we were all trained to stick together in a fire fight for that is the best chance any unit has of surviving in such circumstances.'

Speaking slowly, he went on, 'If the worst happens and we have to abandon the car with a crowd coming for us, we will first fire over their heads. If that doesn't stop them we will let them have it, all of us, at once. Then we fuck off, but in a disciplined way, keeping five yards between each of us, as we were trained.'

He looked around. 'Any questions?'

We had none. We all knew what we would have to do.

Two days later we cleaned and oiled our SMGs and loaded the magazines, ready for our first 'milk run', the name we would always give to these operations.

At nine p.m. we set off as planned and made for the Falls area, arriving about 9.30. Don had told us before leaving that he would carry out the first shooting, but we still held our SMGs at the ready, between our legs, with the butt folded up and the barrel facing the floor of the car. It would have taken only a few seconds to bring up the gun, take aim through the window and fire.

The adrenalin was flowing. This would be the first live action Benny, JR and I had seen in our lives. We knew Don had seen action in various parts of the world but we were raw novices. We had not counted the executions as action for that had been awful and boring, even degrading. This would be different. We knew this could be dangerous.

That night the Lower Falls area seemed almost deserted, except for some children playing football and we had no intention of targeting them. Nor did we ever target any women or any men older than 50.

We noticed an army foot patrol dodging in and out of shop doorways, keeping their eyes peeled for any rooftop snipers. In the street half a dozen ten or twelve year olds were kicking a football about and taking not the slightest notice of the armed eight-man army patrol in their combat kit. It seemed such an extraordinary contrast – the innocent kids playing happily within yards of armed soldiers who feared an attack at any moment.

It seemed unbelievable that parents still allowed

their young children out on the streets at dusk when most of the violence took place. A stray round, a ricochet, cross-fire, a bomb – any of these could have ended their lives or seriously injured them any night and yet, most nights when we went out on the 'milk run', the kids would be on the streets, playing like any other kids anywhere.

We drove into the Ballymurphy area, on the edge of IRA heartland, and saw a number of men who could have been potential targets. We weren't sure, however, so we decided to drive to the Falls Road area.

We had only turned off the main road for a few minutes, and the street seemed almost deserted, when we saw a bloke walking towards us on the pavement on our near side, I noticed Don sit up.

As we drove slowly towards the man, Don raised his SMG, put the barrel to the open window and gave him a short burst of perhaps five or six rounds, firing when only a few feet from him. I saw the man collapse to the ground in a heap. I looked back. He hadn't moved.

The noise of the firing panicked JR and, unbelievably, he slammed his foot on the accelerator and roared away from the scene.

'Slow down,' Don shouted. 'For fuck's sake slow down. You'll only draw attention to us.'

JR obeyed, slowing the car to about 30 mph, but we could see his eyes searching the road ahead and behind for any possible trouble. There was none.

As we drove back, Don said, 'Now you can see how easy it is. He didn't even look at the car, let alone know what hit him. And if JR doesn't fucking panic we should have no trouble whatsoever.'

I had anticipated that there might be some danger yet there had been none. I felt uneasy that we were, once again, being ordered to carry out a mission which I felt was unfair; driving up to totally unsuspecting, probably innocent, vitims and blasting them away. We had heard the politicians going on about the appalling, cowardly actions of the IRA in killing innocent people with bombs or bullets. Now we were doing precisely the same.

That night as I lay in bed thinking of our new mission, I couldn't help asking myself why we had to stoop to the IRA's cowardly ways of operating. I knew I would find killing what could be innocent victims in cold blood very, very difficult when my turn came.

The following day we checked the newspaper to see whether our shooting in Ballymurphy had been recorded by the police and passed to the press. We were virtually certain the man must have died but there were no reports of a man being shot from a passing car.

The next day we again checked the papers and read a report saying that a young man, who lived in the Lower Falls Road district, had been shot down in cold blood by four men in a passing car. We knew instinctively that he was the man we had shot.

Reading the report of our 'hit' in the paper made me realise how vulnerable to questioning we would be if the RUC stopped us at any time and discovered weapons on us. I also realised that we would have some real explaining to do if they stopped us when we were carrying three SMGs, the 'border special' and JR's holster pistol. The police would know exactly what we had been doing without needing to ask a single question. Even simply reading about it in the paper made us realise that the RUC would now be touring around on duty just looking for four young men in a car, any car. That would be enough for them to become suspicious and to stop and question us.

We knew we had our codeword as a standby but we never put all our faith in that because we knew that if we became politically embarrassing we would be left to carry the can.

That weekend at the Union Club, I listened with interest when a loyalist club member told us of an IRA hit squad which, a few days before, had shot seven workers from Mackie's Engineering as they left work at the end of their shift. Understandably, the man was very angry that the IRA could carry out such attacks in broad daylight on innocent workers.

I stayed silent but wondered whether the attack had taken place in revenge for our killing of a Catholic man the night before.

Early the following week we again went out on a 'milk run'. Again we toured round trying to find a young man walking alone in a solid Catholic area and keeping an eye open for any RUC car patrols. A number of people gave us suspicious looks as we toured the area and we were convinced that our car had become known. We would need to change it.

We found that night's target walking alone towards us in a street off the Falls Road. Benny, sitting directly behind Don, would be the hitman. Don told JR to drive at under 30 miles an hour, but not to go too slowly because that would arouse immediate suspicion.

As we drew level with the man, he looked up. He seemed about 40, casually dressed, in shirt, trousers and jacket. A split second later Benny had fired half a dozen rounds into him, the empty cases bouncing back into the car and hitting JR on the head.

JR shouted, 'Fuck me', as the empty cases hit his head for, at first, he wasn't sure what the hell was going on and the empty cases were hot. When we realised what had happened, the three of us couldn't help roaring with laughter for JR believed that someone had taken a potshot at him.

Later, JR enjoyed the joke too. 'Next time I'm going to wear a fucking crash helmet,' he said. 'It's too dangerous in this car.'

Again, I had looked back as we drove away. I saw

only a crumpled body lying in the gutter. I stopped laughing.

Later that week we were again out on a 'milk run' and again we found a lone young man walking in a street off the Falls Road. It was my turn to carry out the assassination. As the man walked towards the car, dressed in jeans and a sweater, I knew I would have a window of opportunity of perhaps five seconds to make sure of a hit. This time he was on the opposite pavement but still only about ten yards away. He never looked up. With the SMG on rapid, I pulled the trigger, firing off only three shots. I never saw his face. By the time I had lowered the gun and looked back he was slowly collapsing to the ground. I didn't hear him utter a sound.

As we drove back to camp, I felt a sense of relief that I had not only carried out my first hit but that I would not be called upon to carry out another one for perhaps a week or two. Back at camp, though, I needed three cups of strong coffee to bring me back to my senses. I fell silent, not wanting to talk about it, already trying to forget the part I had played in the poor bastard's death.

On 1 June we read in the paper of increases in sectarian violence and sectarian murders. The paper stated that between 20 and 30 May two middle-aged Catholic men had been murdered while walking alone in the Ballymurphy and Falls Road areas of the city. We felt sure that we had been responsible for their deaths.

The newspapers were also full of the troubles and the politics behind the ever-changing situation. We read that Protestant loyalist groups were adopting a much higher profile, setting up road blocks in the Mount Pottinger and Woodstock Road areas of Belfast, both hard-line Protestant estates.

They were openly challenging both the RUC and the army who tried, without success, to persuade them to dismantle them. Sometimes the loyalists would erect barricades for a weekend, perhaps for only a night or sometimes for a week at a time, testing the authorities.

In the newspapers loyalist politicians argued, reasonably enough, that the Catholics of the Bogside and Creggan in Londonderry had been permitted to set up their own 'no-go' areas for months at a time without any interference whatsoever from police or army. Loyalists argued that this gave the IRA the opportunity to set up bomb-making factories with impunity and to train and arm young IRA recruits who could use their 'no-go' areas from which to go out and attack police, army and civilian targets.

We also noted that many reasonable Catholic families were unhappy with the near civil war conditions now prevailing in Belfast and Londonderry and some were determined to try to put an end to the conflict. The first major peace meeting held in the Creggan on Tuesday 23 May drew 2,000 people and all the speakers had called for an end to violence.

However, in the audience there were about 100 known IRA hardmen. They deliberately disrupted the meeting, drowning out the speakers by chanting, shouting and demanding that the meeting be broken up. Finally, the organisers could not continue and the meeting ended. Later the IRA issued a statement saying, 'We are not in favour of ending the violence.'

Five days later, on Sunday 28 May, 5,000 Catholics turned out in Londonderry to attend a peace gathering, in open defiance of the IRA leadership who had called for all Catholics to stay away. The meeting was a great success but the IRA weren't happy with the turn of events.

Behind the scenes the IRA had warned those organising the peace demonstration that they must never repeat such demands for fear of a backlash from hardline IRA supporters. The peace organisers were left in no doubt what might happen if they continued to challenge the men of violence.

On the same Sunday, 10,000 Protestant loyalists took to the streets of Belfast, marching in their uniforms in the largest show of strength ever presented since the troubles had begun three years earlier. Organised by the Ulster Defence Association and the Loyalist Association of Workers, it seemed that the Protestants were more determined than ever to take the law into their own hands.

The following day Don went off to Lisburn in the green Cortina and returned driving a dark brown Marina. We were taking no chances.

Twice in June we would be ordered back to the forest, north west of Belfast, to dispose of IRA men handed over to us by our SAS mates on the border. Twice I would pull the trigger as the drugged young men walked, without the least resistance, the twenty yards from where JR parked the car to the trench carefully prepared by the forester at the end of the clearing.

By now, it had become difficult for me to carry out these executions. Before each mission I would feel physically sick, fighting to keep down the meal I had just eaten, worried that I would vomit in front of my three mates. I knew JR and Benny would think I had simply been ill but I knew Don would know the real reason behind it.

I needed to keep a tight hold on my nerves, especially when we were driving with the victim in the car, sitting right next to me, his leg pressed against mine in the tight confines of the back seat. I would listen to his breathing, knowing that, within a matter of a few minutes, he would have taken his last breath. I was secretly happy that they were now being drugged before being handed over to us, because now they didn't move or speak. If they had spoken, I wondered whether I would still have the nerve to go through with the shooting.

After each execution I found it almost impossible to fall asleep, unable to sort out in my mind whether I was engaged in carrying out a job of which I should be justifiably proud, keeping killers off the streets of Northern Ireland, or whether I had really become nothing but a killer myself, a member of an assassination squad. That thought made my stomach turn.

During those months I would wake perhaps two or three times a week, having suffered yet another ghastly nightmare. I would be covered in sweat and shaking. Yet somehow I didn't cry out and my mates never realised the hell I was going through. If they had thought my nerve had gone, Don would have shipped me back to Hereford. He would not have wanted another liability on his hands, for we were already carrying JR.

The more agitated I became, the more my thoughts turned to Maria back in England. I yearned to be back on the mainland, away from Ireland and the killings, and to be with her. From time to time I still saw Lizzie but I had found that she could not give me the same support and understanding that I had found in the hours I spent with Maria.

I was worried. I felt that Lizzie's father had decided I would be an acceptable son in law. He didn't understand that I had no wish to stay in his beloved Northern Ireland. He had talked of putting our name down for a council house, suggesting that we would not have to wait very long, although we were not yet engaged, let alone planning to marry.

He couldn't understand, as Lizzie couldn't understand, that Ulster had become the last place on earth where I wanted to settle down. They had no idea of the life I had been living, no idea of the senseless, endless killings I had been ordered to carry out. I had come to hate the place and all the people who lived there – Protestants as well as Catholics. I came to see the sectarian hatred everywhere I looked, in every conversation I heard, even in Lizzie. And yet, in reality, Lizzie had never gone out of her way to blame the Catholics for pushing the Province to the edge of civil war; indeed, some of the discussions she became involved in suggested she felt an understanding, even sympathy, for the Catholic minority over the way the Protestants had treated them for generations.

I felt guilty about Lizzie every time I saw her because I now knew that I could never stay with her, even if we were to settle down together somewhere in England. I came to realise that if I settled down with Lizzie I would never be able to escape the horror of my life in Ulster. It would not be her fault at all but I knew that would be the reality of it and that would be unfair on her and her family.

The time had come for me to leave Lizzie but I found it difficult to find the strength to say so. Arguments began between us and the fun and the love we had shared for months evaporated. She knew it. Repeatedly she would ask me what was wrong and whether I still loved her and every time I lied because I didn't want to hurt her.

I knew I could never tell her the truth of my life in Northern Ireland and so I began to tell white lies, telling her that I was on duty for nights at a time when, in reality, I wouldn't be. It took perhaps a month or so before she realised that I was a changed man and that the relationship was heading for the rocks.

She didn't want that. She seemed genuinely in love with me and I believe she wanted us to marry but I knew I couldn't go through with it, for her sake as well as mine. She would cry and cry whenever we said goodnight and I would feel guilty whenever we made love. I felt guilty just sharing a meal with the family and prayed that the move back to Hereford would come quickly but there was no word of our future. It seemed, indeed, as though the authorities believed we were doing rather a good job causing fear and alarm among the Catholics of Belfast.

Whenever possible, I would telephone Maria at her post office in Tidworth, trying to find the best time when she could chat for more than a couple of minutes. I came to rely on those phone calls because they brought me closer to her. The calls formed a life-line, together with my dream of escaping from Ireland. The more I talked to her, the more I felt there was an end, not far away, a time when I would leave the Province and return to a life of normality in England.

I had also discovered another escape from reality – alcohol. I had never been a big drinker, always secure in my mind that I didn't need much alcohol to enjoy myself. My SAS training had also taught me that the more I drank the less fit I would become. As someone had said to me at training camp, 'When did you last see a really fit drunk?'

Now, whenever the pressures became too much for me, I would want to go out and have a real drink, perhaps four or five pints of beer, with Bacardi chasers. That always did the trick, enabling me to get some sleep at night rather than lying awake worrying and miserable.

However, we were about to be given a mission which would help to restore some pride in our professionalism. We were selected to trace, find and take out a violent IRA man who had beaten, tortured and killed an innocent British soldier.

CHAPTER THIRTEEN

NINETEEN-YEAR-OLD William Best, a young Catholic boy from the Creggan, who had been brought up in Londonderry, signed on with the Royal Irish Rangers, a British regiment drawn from both Catholic and Protestant sides of the Province.

Before joining the army in 1971, IRA activists had put pressure on him, seeking his active support in the republican cause, appealing through his religion and nationalism for him to join them and fight the British Army.

He had wanted none of it and went off to Belfast to join the army, the only way he knew to escape the pressure from the strong IRA contingent in Londonderry who seemed to wield all the power in the Catholic areas of the city.

After serving for twelve months with the Rangers, he decided to go home to see his parents and family in Londonderry. That decision would cost him his life.

On 25 May 1972, while out visiting friends in another part of Londonderry, an IRA squad picked him off the street as he walked back home.

He disappeared. His parents, his extended family and friends of the Best family scoured the streets searching for him after he failed to make contact or return home. They became worried because he had promised to return by ten p.m.

The police were notified but to no avail. He had disappeared without trace.

Two days later Private William Best's body was discovered lying in a pool of blood on waste ground in William Street, Londonderry, in full view of passersby. His head was covered by a hood; his hands tied with wire behind his back.

When his parents went to identify their son, he was unrecognisable. Private Best had been beaten and tortured for 48 hours by squads of IRA thugs who had been permitted to come and take out their anger and hatred on a defenceless young soldier, a member of a good Catholic family, one of their own, who had dared to join the British Army.

The torture and killing of Private Best would become a watershed in the IRA's campaign in Londonderry. Hundreds of women, most of them Catholics, turned out for his funeral, venting their rage on the IRA for daring to kill one of their own, an innocent youth of nineteen who had decided to leave the troubles behind him and seek a new life in the British Army, as many young Catholics had done before.

The killing caused such violent argument and dissension within the ranks of the Official IRA that, as a direct result, the Officials issued a statement repudiating violence and announcing an end to all violent action. From that time on the Official IRA turned instead to political aims, leaving the hard men of the Provisional IRA to take the centre ground, declaring themselves the only true saviours of the Catholic and nationalist causes.

At Lisburn headquarters, however, a decision was

taken that, come what may, the IRA thugs who had beaten, tortured and murdered young Best would be traced, hounded and killed in retribution for their evil deed.

One morning in mid-June, Don returned from a briefing at Lisburn with the news that intelligence sources had traced one of the men primarily responsible for the torture and murder of Private Best and we had been selected to deal with him. Don had been shown a photograph of the wanted man.

He had quit Londonderry and the Official IRA and moved to Belfast where he had been welcomed by the hard men of the Belfast Brigade of the Provisional IRA. Because of his record of torture and killing, the wanted man had been treated almost as a hero and made most welcome.

Intelligence officers had heard rumours that the man would be on the move again shortly, leaving his safe house in Belfast perhaps later that day. His destination was unknown and therefore he would have to be traced, lifted and dealt with that very day and in broad daylight. The safe house was on the edge of a strong Catholic area south of Belfast.

We immediately cleaned and oiled our weapons and the 'border special' and set off shortly after midday. We also took with us a couple of lengths of parachute cord. They would prove very useful.

We drove at some speed towards the area, not far from the Protestant part of Sandy Row. JR cruised past the Victorian terraced house, which had a dark green front door, and parked the car round the next corner, about 100 yards away. We synchronised watches.

Don sent Benny and me round the back of the house to guard the rear door, for Don intended to break down the front door himself, with JR as his back up. Benny and I walked along the row of terraced houses and dodged down the alleyway that ran from the street to the yards at the back. We had counted the houses and knew precisely which one the man would be resting in.

We checked the windows of the house and then took cover behind a brick wall at the end of the tiny yard, waiting for the seconds to tick away. On the stroke of one p.m. we went through the back gate, our pistols drawn. I went to the back door, hoping to hear what was happening inside while Benny watched the windows for any sign of life.

I heard the crash of splintered wood as Don took a running leap at the front door, crashing his shoulder into it and smashing the lock. Behind him JR, pistol at the ready, watched the windows. I tried the door and, unbelievably, it was open. I went straight into the kitchen as Benny gave cover.

As I moved through the kitchen I could hear Don halfway up the stairs. He had obviously checked the front room and, finding no one there, had decided that he had to get to the man before he could get to his gun. We knew he would be armed. We hoped he had only a .38 revolver and no machine gun.

I raced up the stairs behind Don, leaving Benny and JR below in case of any trouble from neighbours or IRA gunmen who might have returned to the house. I was only halfway up the single flight of stairs when a bedroom door above was thrown open and a man came hurtling out.

In his hand I saw a revolver and thanked God the man hadn't a Thompson SMG with him. He crashed into Don who went sprawling. Somehow, the man stayed on his feet and I hit him with a rugby tackle as he took off, trying to jump over me from the top of the stairs.

Together we crashed down the stairs and, thank God, as we fell, his revolver flew out of his hand. As we landed in a heap at the bottom I saw Benny grab our man and hit him twice across the head with the butt of his pistol. He didn't hit him too hard because we wanted him conscious and able to walk. By the time the man came to, Benny had him in an arm lock; he couldn't move.

After checking the other bedrooms, Don came down the stairs and told JR to collect the car and bring it to the front door. Benny and I had our man sitting on the floor with his hands tied tightly behind him with the parachute cord. Don looked at him. He said, 'It's him all right.'

'Who the fuck are you?' said our man.

'Shut up,' said Don. 'If you utter another word I'll blow your fucking brains out.'

'You don't frighten me,' our man replied.

'We soon will,' said Don, 'because you're the fucking rat who did for Private Willie Best, down in 'Derry.'

For a split second the man seemed stunned. 'Bullshit,' he said.

'So you know the name then,' said Don.

' 'Course I do, everyone knows that fucker's name,' he said.

Don picked him up roughly from the floor and told him to start walking towards the front door. The man tried to sit down, not wanting to leave what he believed was his safe haven.

'If you don't move I'll fucking shoot you here and now,' said Don, putting his pistol to the man's head. He moved.

Don and Benny put the man into the back of the car and I took the passenger seat.

'What's it like to beat someone senseless?' Don asked. 'Is that how you get your kicks?'

'I don't know what you're talking about,' he replied.

'Well you soon will,' Don said. 'We're going to do to you everything you did to that poor soldier. If you treat soldiers like that, I can tell you that we will find you and deal with you in exactly the same way.'

The man began to stutter, struggling to find the right words to convince us that he knew nothing about Private Best, denying he had ever lived in Londonderry.

'Shut up,' said Don. 'I know you're the guilty man because I've seen your picture. We got it from one of your IRA mates. They want you done in because you are a homocidal maniac, a fucking liability. Now do you understand?'

The man began to look worried.

'I'm going to tell you what we're going to do with you.'

'Fuck off,' said the man. 'Just fuck off.'

'Yeah, we will fuck off,' Don said, 'but only after we have shot you in the legs a few times, working slowly up the body till we put a couple of rounds into your balls. Then we'll ask you if you tortured and shot Willy Best. And if you deny it we'll start to put a few rounds in your arms until you do confess.'

The man began to shake and his voice dropped to a quiet, almost inaudible, murmer, his bravado at an end.

Later, as we drove towards the clearing in Tardree Forest, he tried to speak again, to protest his innocence.

'Shut up,' said Don. 'All I want is your confession that you shot Willy Best.'

The man fell silent again, his head bowed, looking at the floor of the car.

Thirty minutes later we arrived at the clearing and Don and Benny pulled him out of the car. Our grave digger was at work, moving logs with his JCB. JR went over and told him to disappear for half an hour.

We made our man walk the hundred yards to the trench. Don told him to kneel down on the mound of earth, looking down into the trench. 'You've got one last chance,' Don told him. 'If you don't confess to killing Willy Best I'm going to start shooting you in the legs.'

There was silence.

'I'll count to five,' Don said. 'It's up to you. One, two, three . . .'

'All right, all right . . . it was me,' he said. 'But I had to do it,' he said, beginning to sob. 'They made me do it.'

They would be the last words he ever uttered. Don pulled the trigger of the 'border special', shooting the man in the back of the head. He fell forward into the trench and disappeared from our view. We turned and walked away, happy that we had avenged Best's dreadful murder.

That night on television we saw Colonel Gaddafi of Libya saying in a recorded interview that he had decided to supply the IRA with whatever arms and ammunition they wanted. He told how he wanted to help the Irish in their struggle for liberation from the British Army.

'Well at least Gaddafi's honest,' I said. 'It's a pity the British Government couldn't be honest, then we wouldn't have to play all this cloak and dagger crap and we could get out there and fight the IRA properly. Then we would see how much fight they had in them.'

Throughout most of June we were sent out searching for victims to hit on the streets of Belfast but more often than not we would return to Long Kesh without finding a suitable target. We would never make a hit if there were too many possible witnesses around; we would never target someone if they were accompanied by a woman or a child; we would never make a hit if there were any children about; and we would only target those Catholics who would have been of military age.

From all we read in the newspapers perhaps our work had proved of some use in causing some strife and doubt in the ranks of the Provisional IRA. Ever since the Official IRA had announced their ceasefire in May, Secretary of State William Whitelaw had initiated a policy of conciliation, releasing members of the Official IRA from detention. By 6 June, Whitelaw had released 470 of the 936 who had been held without trial. Nearly all were Officials.

Of course, this policy caused greater strife between the Provos and the Officials. Intelligence sources discovered that unexplained deaths on the streets of Belfast were sometimes blamed on both factions, no one certain who was responsible for the random killings.

They also knew that the Provisionals had determined on a campaign of sectarian violence against the Protestants as well as keeping up the pressure on the British Army by persuading young people to riot constantly against British troops, while IRA snipers on rooftops tried to take advantage of finding soldiers in their gun sights. Barely a week would pass at this time without a soldier being killed by sniper fire.

The Provisionals also increased the tempo of violence, trying to bomb Belfast and Londonderry into a state of chaos, trying to ruin the economy of the Province. The Provos aimed to put as many businesses as possible out of action.

There was precious little the authorities could do to counter such destructive action. A meeting of the Joint Security Committee, consisting of all intelligence chiefs, senior army officers and police, and headed by William Whitelaw, did all in their power to stop the bombers, banning all unattended vehicles throughout the city centres seven days a week and implementing searches of everyone and everything moving in and out of the city centres.

Anyone visiting Londonderry in June 1972 would have believed they were in some Central European city immediately after the Second World War, what with all the bomb and fire damage and the check points. Anyone driving through Londonderry at that time would have to negotiate seven separate check points, two guarded by the IRA, three by the British Army and two more by the loyalists. All check points were guarded by armed men and all of them seemingly held absolute authority.

The IRA's bombing campaign put great pressure on the Northern Ireland people and they responded with remarkable courage, understanding and patience. They realised full well that the only way to defeat the bombers was with patience and diligence. Body searches would be carried out at every store and building; women's handbags and shopping baskets were searched at every entrance; men's briefcases inspected.

Day and night, cars, buses and trucks would be searched at check points and during random police and army alerts. The people responded with grit and determination as the mayhem and violence continued. Throughout Northern Ireland virtually every family had been touched by death or injury but their spirit of endurance had somehow survived throughout more than twenty years of troubles.

Believing that their campaign of violence and wanton destruction was winning the war, the Provisional IRA sought a secret meeting with William Whitelaw after proposing a ceasefire. Their demands, however, proved totally unacceptable to the British Government, although Whitelaw informed the IRA that he would return with an answer from the Cabinet a week later.

The Provisionals did not wait for a formal reply. With no announcement, they unleashed a new campaign of violence, bombings and shootings, killing six civilians, including a thirteen-year-old girl and a Roman Catholic priest on the first day. Later the same day bomb explosions rocked both Belfast and Londonderry.

The Heath Government decided to take a tougher line with the Provisionals. William Whitelaw personally ordered 600 troops to attack IRA gunmen in Andersonstown after three soldiers had been killed during a four-day attack by the IRA on the Lenadoon Avenue army post. The IRA fired 400 rounds at the post before the army went on to the offensive.

Whitelaw announced that the attack on the IRA gunmen was the start of a government offensive, a new policy of 'an eye for an eye' in which any IRA ferocity would be repaid by army ferocity. As a result, fierce gun battles raged for hours on end.

Outgunned by the army, the IRA resorted to bombings. In one hour on Friday 21 July, eleven people were killed and 130 injured when twenty huge bombs exploded across Belfast, the IRA selecting the most vulnerable targets by bombing bus shelters, the railway station and a hotel.

It would prove to be one of the most gruesome and violent IRA bombing sprees. It also proved highly embarrassing for William Whitelaw and the government for the bombs exploded only a matter of hours after Whitelaw had announced to the House of Commons in London that stringent new security measures had been introduced during the previous few days in both Belfast and Londonderry, which 'would thwart the bombers'.

The Lower Falls area of Belfast was the one area we kept well away from. As we drove down Grosvenor Road we could see the IRA hitmen on guard duty in the side streets, most wearing balaclavas and nearly all carrying American Armalite rifles or Thompson sub-machine guns. We also knew those streets would always have snipers on the rooftops, keeping watch. To have dared to drive into that area would have resulted in an instant fire fight. We might have escaped with our lives but we also knew that there would be every chance of innocent victims being hit in cross-fire or by ricochets.

More important, we had never been given orders to indulge in random fire fights or to put ourselves in a position where we could be shot, killed or kidnapped, for then the SAS involvement in undercover operations would have been blown. We would not have been popular at Lisburn or back at Hereford.

One night at the end of June we thought we had bought it.

We had driven around for nearly half an hour before we found a likely target, a man who appeared to be in his late thirties, walking towards us on the near side. He really looked like an IRA hitman – a squat, powerfully built man dressed in jeans and a dark blue donkey jacket.

'That's one,' Don said.

Seconds later, Don pulled the trigger of his SMG, letting go half a dozen rounds. He must have been only six feet from the victim when he opened fire. The man looked surprised, then open-mouthed as he was catapulted backwards by the force of the shots hitting him.

'Go,' said Don to JR, 'but slowly.'

Ten minutes later, as we were driving back to base, relaxing and looking forward to a coffee, we rounded a corner to be confronted with a blazing barricade only 30 yards ahead of us. 'Christ!' said JR.

We all looked up and JR put his foot down hard on the accelerator, making straight for the barricade which covered the entire width of the road. We could see a car on its side, well alight, as well as tyres, mattresses and old sofas, blazing away, filling the road with flames and smoke.

I thought JR had panicked and that he was planning to crash straight through the blazing mass ahead of us. Suddenly, bricks and bottles began raining down on the car. The windscreen shattered but JR continued to accelerate.

Without warning, I found myself thrown headlong against the side of the car as JR slammed on the handbrake with all his strength and turned 180 degrees with a great squeal of rubber as the tyres bit into the road. A split second later we were facing the other direction and racing away as bricks and stones rained down on us.

I had really believed that JR was about to smash through the barricade. We must have been less than five yards away from it when he made the U-turn.

'Shit,' Don said. 'That was fucking brilliant. Where did you learn to do that?'

'Something I just learned,' JR said, a great beaming smile across his face. That one single act had helped him to win back some self-esteem. He felt good. We felt relieved. There was little doubt that he had performed brilliantly. I am certain that we would never have survived if he had tried to smash through the road block.

Don decided that we needed to get rid of the car immediately. As we drove through Lisburn trying to find a quiet place to dump and set fire to the car we received the sort of odd looks you might expect, driving along with no windscreen, just four men sitting back and trying to appear as relaxed and non-chalant as possible. As soon as we found a farm track away from the main road, we parked the car, doused it with petrol from the can in the boot and threw on a match.

The fire erupted with a 'whoomf' and we legged it across country. We hadn't gone more than 800 yards when the car erupted like a bomb, producing a fire ball. The flames shot 50 feet in the air as the jerry can of petrol, which we had only half-emptied, exploded.

Thank goodness that night was overcast for we had to walk back to Long Kesh, a distance of perhaps six miles, with the sub-machine guns under our arms. If we had been spotted by police they would instantly have realised that we were carrying guns under our jackets. As it happened, we hardly saw a soul until we arrived back at camp.

We had, however, learned a valuable lesson. Keeping a jerry can of petrol in the boot had not been such a great idea because it meant that we would always have to get out of the car to get the petrol. From now on we made do without a jerry can but filled two large bottles with petrol and kept them under the front seats instead.

When we finally returned to the Portakabin, Benny cut a piece of cardboard from a packet of cigarettes and, using the silver cigarette paper, made a mock Victoria Cross. Amid lots of clapping, cheers and piss-taking, we presented the medal to JR for 'outstanding valour under fire'. He took it in good spirit. We celebrated with a cup of coffee.

Deep down, however, we all realised that he had saved us from a very awkward situation.

Two weeks later we had another near disaster. We were driving our new Q-car, a dark blue Cortina, when, by accident, we drove into a hard-line IRA area while out searching for a victim one night.

We had intended turning left into a main road which should have led us away from the 'no-go' area but, somehow, we missed the turning and found ourselves facing an IRA barricade, with gunmen, wearing balaclavas, on guard. Some of the sandbags had even been painted in the green, white and orange colours of the republican flag. The barricade had obviously been in position for weeks, if not months, a semi-permanent bulwark, constructed mainly of sandbags.

'Shit,' said, JR.

'Jeeeezus,' we all whispered as we realised we were sitting ducks. Instinctively, I clicked off the safety catch of my SMG, pushing it to automatic. I heard Don and Benny do the same. I was convinced we would be in the middle of a fire fight within seconds.

Almost together, Don and I said quietly, 'Cool it, act nonchalant. Do nothing.'

Don added, 'Be prepared.'

On this occasion JR had no room to accelerate, slam on the handbrake and do a 180-degree turn, for the barricade was only a matter of ten yards in front of us. He took the only sensible way out, beginning a three-point turn, the manoeuvre everyone practises for their driving test. Behind the barricade we could see blokes watching us, not sure what to do.

As JR was backing to make the second part of the three-point turn I heard a shout, 'Get the fuckers.'

We saw them raise their machine guns and Armalites on to the top of the barricade. Before they could fire a shot both Don and I, who were sitting on the near side, let them have it, emptying a magazine each towards where the men were standing.

As we fired we were met with a hail of rounds but most went over the top of the Cortina. A couple hit the boot of the car and at least one crashed through the rear window, splintering glass everywhere but, thankfully, missing us. JR put his foot hard to the floor and the wheels spun and the tyres screeched as he tried to accelerate away as fast as possible.

As we drove away, Don and I banged home another magazine each and Benny joined in as we sprayed the barricade with bursts of fire, emptying the three magazines. Seconds later JR had reached the corner of the street. We were away.

'Shit,' Don said. 'That was close.'

We all agreed. Finally we had come face to face with the enemy we had been fighting in our own way for more than nine months. This sort of fighting had been hair-raising but it was what we had been trained to do. The adrenalin was pumping and it felt good.

We decided to ditch the car almost immediately. Checking that the gunmen weren't following, we stopped a few hundred yards down the road. There were quite a number of people around but, for some unknown reason, we decided it would be better to burn the car immediately, rather than risk driving on. Perhaps we weren't thinking straight, perhaps we were all itching for a real fire fight, but that night we didn't care a damn. We splashed the petrol inside the car, threw a match in and walked off as nonchalantly as possible, carrying our SMGs under our arms once more.

We had only just rounded the corner when we heard the car explode. With a smile we kept walking. Once more no one bothered us as we walked the two miles back to our old barracks at Sydenham Docks. Fortunately, the NCO in charge of the guard that night recognised us and gave us a vehicle and driver to take us back to Long Kesh. We all felt like a drink but resisted the impulse to go out again. In the gung-ho mood we were in that would not have been sensible. We had narrowly escaped from two incidents which could have ended in disaster, even death. There was no need to risk our luck a third time.

CHAPTER FOURTEEN

THROUGHOUT THE MONTH of July orders came thick and fast from Lisburn encouraging us to go into the streets more often, to select Catholic victims, knock some of them off and take potshots at others. The officers in command of our operations wanted to stir up as much trouble as possible. We were, however, under strict instructions not to get caught because of the fear that the whole world would then know for certain that the SAS had been involved in such dubious clandestine operations.

Despite the risks we were taking, Don still got a ticking off from the senior officers at Lisburn for burning too many Q-cars. 'You must take greater care of the vehicles,' he was told on more than one occasion. 'You can't keep burning them every few weeks. They cost a lot of money to replace.'

Don would tell us about these conversations when he returned from Lisburn briefings, angry that the top brass expected us to take so many risks when all they seemed interested in was saving money. Those remarks made us even less keen to carry out the instructions they insisted upon.

We continued with Operation Nemesis nevertheless, but we were now taking fewer risks than we had before. We took greater care to keep as far away as possible from the hard-line 'no-go' areas, selecting targets which didn't necessitate risking becoming embroiled with IRA or loyalist gunmen.

Whenever we took out a victim on our nocturnal drives through Belfast, we would always buy a local Belfast paper the following day to check whether the person had died or simply been injured. On occasions there would be no report for a couple of days but few men we shot did, in fact, die. Only one or two would survive.

The more mayhem we caused, the more people we killed in our random shootings, the more dangerous the operation became for the four of us for now everyone in Belfast, both Catholic and Protestant, knew that these killings were being carried out by four men in a car. We began to feel vulnerable, believing that anyone seeing us regularly driving around would begin to suspect that we might be the four men responsible for the shootings. Despite that feeling of vulnerability, however, we continued to venture out of Long Kesh, always four of us together in the car, seemingly inviting the paramilitaries or the police to stop us and ask questions.

We discussed changing tactics, whether, on occasions, only two or three of us should go out together at night. We decided against it. We were an SAS unit; we had all been through the mill together and so we determined to stay together. There was another point. If ever we came across real trouble, if ever we had to shoot our way out of a position, we were trained to operate as a four-man unit. Furthermore, we would have more chance of making our escape with four of us firing away.

During July we carried out the occasional random shooting on the streets of Belfast. From checks we made in the newspapers following each shooting it seemed that we were probably responsible for the deaths of two men, both Catholics living in Belfast.

Three other Catholics died on the streets of Belfast during that July, all also shot by gunmen driving past in cars, so we knew that another bunch of men were involved in the same operation, although we would never know whether they were another SAS unit at work, Protestant paramilitary units adopting the same tactics or, perhaps, the result of inter-necine warfare between the two factions of the IRA.

On two occasions during July we were also given orders to return to our old job of executing known IRA men picked up on the border, who the authorities wanted disposed of. As before, Don would be given the map reference where we would meet our SAS mates to collect the men, both of whom appeared drugged.

Neither man complained, neither man uttered a word throughout the journeys from the border to the forest. As before, they would be told to get out of the car and walk towards the mound of earth at the end of the clearing. As before, they would be despatched with a single round from the 'border special' as they walked, as though in a daze, towards the trench. At the moment of death the only noise in the forest would be the 'thump' of the silencer. There were no words, no cries, no screams, not a sound save for a faint noise as the bodies collapsed into the bottom of the trench that would be their grave.

The more we were ordered to carry out these sickening killings, the more restless and miserable I became. I could not believe that the role we were being asked to carry out could, in any way, have any major effect in bringing this guerilla war to an end. I could not help thinking that we were simply being used by the authorities as part of some unknown, untried policy. I had joined the SAS because I believed it was a privilege to belong to Britain's élite fighting force; not to be part of an undercover execution squad.

My nightmares returned and I found it increasingly difficult to sleep. My dreams were becoming more bizarre, more frightening and all of them featured beatings and torture, killings and executions. I felt that my dreams were telling me what I was beginning to feel was true; that I could not continue operating like this for very much longer. As the summer wore on, I felt sure all of us were having the same thoughts, harbouring the same doubts.

One night in late July we went out for a few pints and took a couple of bottles of whisky back to the billet. I hated the taste of whisky, and always had done, but that night I saw whisky as a way of forgetting everything. We sat and drank. More important, we began to talk.

I had been right. My three mates had all had doubts, and JR and Benny had been suffering nightmares too.

Even Don admitted to the same reservations. 'Never in my wildest dreams', he admitted, 'did I ever imagine that I would be involved in something like this, executing people in cold blood and shooting down innocent bastards on the streets of a British city.'

He confessed that he had never known the SAS to be involved in any operations like this or on such a long time scale. He told us of numerous occasions when the SAS would be called upon to take out individuals, but never to take out so many people in such cowardly circumstances.

JR admitted how relieved he was that he had not been asked to carry out another execution. 'I honestly

don't think I would have been able to do it,' he confessed. 'Every time I saw one of you blokes pull the
trigger I felt like throwing up. I would watch the poor
bastard walking from the car knowing that in a few
seconds he would be dead meat and I shivered at the
thought and looked away.'

Frustrated and angry at the tasks we had been
made to carry out for the last nine months, Benny
said, 'Why don't we just go out and put an end to all
this. Every week in the press there are people
demanding the Catholics interned in Long Kesh must
be freed. Well, why don't we set them free?'

'What do you mean?' I asked him.

'Why don't we go and get four "gympies" [general
purpose machine-guns] from the armoury, go into the
jail and wipe out the fucking lot of them. Then it'll be
over; then maybe those fuckers in Lisburn will be
satisfied that we've killed enough of them and we'll
be able to go back to Hereford.'

We all agreed, though not in reality. For two hours
we talked about our predicament but none of us had
any idea how the hell we could escape and get back
to Hereford and sanity.

'Do you think you could have a word with those
sods at Lisburn?' I asked Don.

He looked dejected and said nothing for a
moment. Then he said, 'We can't do that. We're SAS.
We obey orders, remember. Somehow we've got to
make the best of it until they ship us out.' Then his
voice sounded more optimistic. 'I'll tell you what I will
do,' he continued. 'I'll explain that we've been cooped
up here for nine months and we need a break – at
least some decent home leave.'

That helped to lighten the atmosphere. Drunk and
miserable but cheered by the thought of seeing Maria,
I slept peacefully that night.

Early on Sunday 30 July, 150 Saladin and Saracen
armoured cars, with a 50-ton Centurion tank fitted

with special bulldozer blades, rumbled through the streets of Londonderry towards the IRA strongholds in the Bogside and Creggan. No army personnel or police had been in those 'no-go' areas for more than twelve months.

Operation Motorman took the IRA and the loyalist paramilitaries by surprise. Catholic and Protestant 'no-go' areas in Belfast were also targeted in the operation as the decision had been taken at Cabinet level in London to put an end to the 'no-go' areas of the United Kingdom. Twenty thousand troops and 8,000 RUC officers were involved that day.

Northern Ireland Secretary William Whitelaw claimed, 'The army's aim was to remove the capacity of the Provisional IRA to cause suffering and hardship in the community.'

William Whitelaw's words seemed prescient, for later that day the IRA, furious that their 'no-go' areas had been breached, their authority challenged, went to the tiny village of Claudy, nine miles from Londonderry, a village that had seen no violence, and, without any warning, exploded three car bombs, killing six people including a girl aged twelve. Thirty-two innocent people were injured.

A couple of days before Operation Motorman, Don had been informed that our services would not be required for a few days and we were each given a seven-day pass and a return air ticket to Gatwick. Don did not know what was about to happen but the news that we had seven days back at home pleased all of us.

He had walked into the billet looking downcast and miserable. We all expected the worst – another bloody execution. 'I'm afraid the news I've got for you is going to break your hearts,' he said calmly.

'Now what the fuck do they want us to go and do – shoot the Pope?' I said sarcastically.

'No,' he said. 'It's worse than that. We've been

given seven days' leave and I have the air tickets right here.'

We picked up the lightweight tin ashtrays and anything else that came to hand – pillows, boots and socks – and threw them at him for winding us up.

I have since wondered how we would have coped with the situation if Lisburn hadn't given us a break at that time. On occasions I felt, as did the others, that we had reached breaking point. The entire Province seemed on edge. Not surprisingly, for a total of 467 people would die in terrorist action during 1972.

I phoned Maria and asked if she could possibly get seven days' holiday. 'I don't know. I'll have to phone you back,' she said, 'but I doubt it. We're terribly busy here.'

'Can't you find a way? Can't you go sick or something?' I almost pleaded.

Later she would tell me that she could hear the tension in my voice and realised that a week's holiday together could well rekindle, if not cement, our old relationship.

'Leave it to me,' she said. 'I'll work out something.'

'Fantastic,' I said, 'I'll phone you from Gatwick tomorrow.'

Forty-eight hours later Maria and I were signing the register in a small bed and breakfast hotel not far from the promenade at Bournemouth. As we signed 'Mr and Mrs Bruce' Maria looked at me but said nothing.

We had hardly kissed since we met. I had picked her up from her parents' home at Tidworth in the rental car I collected at Gatwick. It seemed strange. We hardly said a word when we drove off but she seemed happy when I surprised her by saying we were going to Bournemouth together for a week.

After driving in near silence for an hour I thought it would be a good idea to stop in a pub for a bite of lunch and a drink. I needed a pint and felt sure Maria needed a drink to help her to relax. It worked. As we left the pub, she took hold of my hand and gave me a peck on the cheek. 'Welcome home,' she said. For the rest of the journey we talked and unwound and I began to feel human once again.

That week seemed like bliss and it went by at the speed of light. We would rise late in the morning, laze together on the beautiful sandy beach or go for long walks. We would have a pub lunch and go to bed for an hour every afternoon. At night we ate in different pubs and restaurants, usually ending the evening in a pub before returning to the hotel to spend hours making love.

As the end of our week together approached, I became nervous and withdrawn. I knew the reason – I didn't want to return to bloody Belfast and reality. I lay awake at night looking at the ceiling, looking at the sleeping, peaceful Maria at my side and the thought of executing more strangers made my stomach turn till I felt I would be sick.

Maria noticed the change and asked me what was wrong but I felt I couldn't tell her the truth. She believed I was having second thoughts about becoming involved with her again. Nothing was further from the truth.

One night, having drunk too much, I knew I had to tell her why I was behaving in such a way; I had to tell her that it was nothing whatsoever to do with her or our relationship. Trying to sound calm and sensible, I told her: 'I have not had such a wonderful week as this since I went to Belfast nearly a year ago. I think you're great and I love being with you.'

I paused and she waited for me to continue. 'I'm sorry that I have been so morose and such lousy company over the last couple of days but it's only because this week is coming to an end and I have to go back to Belfast.'

'What's so awful about Belfast?' she asked. 'Is it that bad out there?'

'I can't tell you, you know that.'

'But what's it got to do with?' she asked again.

I tried to explain to her without revealing things I knew I shouldn't tell her but in a way that would make some sense. 'Listen,' I began quietly, 'I'll only tell you this once because I don't want to go into the explanation more than that. Ever since I went to Belfast I've never worn a uniform. We've been engaged in undercover work and the missions have been truly horrendous. It's been worse than anything you've ever seen in the movies. I can't tell you exactly what's been happening but quite often I have felt physically sick at what we've been having to do . . .'

I paused again and Maria encouraged me to continue.

'And now I can't face it anymore. Neither can the others. The last thing I want to do is return to Belfast but I have to. Now do you understand?'

'Sort of,' she answered softly and grabbed my hand and kissed it. 'You poor thing.'

'Now you understand why I can't tell you anything more.'

'Of course I do'.

'Right,' I said. 'That's that settled then. Now I've got to ask you two questions.'

'Yes,' she said.

'Do you still want to go out with me?'

'Yes, definitely,' she said.

'Good,' I replied.

'And the second?'.

'What do you want to drink?'

'You bastard,' she said. 'I'll have another lager but I don't know whether you should have one. You've had one too many already.'

As I walked to the bar and ordered the beers, I felt a huge weight had been lifted from my shoulders.

I still had to return to Belfast but somehow the whole idea didn't seem so bad. I could face it. 'Fuck the army,' I thought.

As the aircraft circled over Belfast the following night, I reached a decision. I would leave the army. The only way I would be able to cope with staying in Belfast would be the knowledge that, whatever happened, it was only temporary.

I knew that my option to leave the army was due to come up at the beginning of October. In 1966 I had signed on for 22 years with an option of quitting after six years, in October 1972. To exercise that option, however, it would be necessary for me to inform my parent unit, the REME, two weeks before the due date, otherwise I would automatically be agreeing to carry on for a further three years. Come what may, I decided to tell the REME of my decision before the middle of September.

It seemed extraordinary to me that I could make such a decision so quickly and so decisively. I had believed that I had joined the army for the full 22 years. I intended the army to be my entire life. I had achieved my greatest ambition, to be accepted into the SAS and I still felt privileged that I had made the grade and been 'badged'.

However, the reality of being ordered to carry out executions in the way stipulated by Lisburn had extinguished my ambition to make the army my life. I knew the orders had nothing to do with the SAS. I knew we were simply carrying out a policy ordained from on high, either by politicians or senior officers. We had been given the most appalling job of any British soldiers serving in Ireland. That was our bad luck but I determined it wouldn't be my bad luck for more than a couple of months. I was leaving, come what may.

I also knew in my heart that if I didn't get out then I would be unable to continue. And I didn't want to let down my mates.

Back in Belfast we all sensed that we were hating every moment we stayed in the place. Even Don, who had experienced far more than we had with the SAS, felt the same way. He too wanted out of Belfast as quickly as possible.

Although Motorman had sorted out some immediate problems and restored the cities to some sense of normality, the numbers of army patrols in the Catholic and Protestant areas had increased to such an extent that we could no longer consider cruising around the streets, armed to the teeth, randomly shooting at passersby.

The days following Motorman had been relatively quiet, with neither the IRA nor Protestant loyalists risking taking to the streets with bombs or guns for fear of being stopped and arrested by the army and police patrols which seemed to be on every street corner.

On Monday 7 August, however, the Northern Ireland troubles claimed their five hundredth victim when a UDR member was shot dead as he returned home on leave.

With such a marked decrease in terrorist activity, William Whitelaw continued his policy of conciliation. During the past month the Secretary of State had released a number of Official IRA detainees for the Officials had not broken the ceasefire they had declared at the end of May. Now they were being rewarded.

Twelve months after the policy of internment had been introduced — a policy devised to bring an end to the bombing and shooting — the number detained without trial had been reduced from a maxiuum of nearly one thousand to under 250. And yet, during that year, the violence on the streets of Belfast and Londonderry had more than tripled.

Instead of cruising the streets during those weeks, we would spend most evenings, and half the days, in pubs outside Belfast, drinking to forget what we had been through. Sometimes we wouldn't even bother to go out to a pub but would visit the local off-licence and buy a load of canned beer and a bottle or two of whisky. We no longer considered trying to keep fit by going on runs or long marches or even by going to the gym.

In many ways we had become rebels – angry, miserable and thoroughly pissed off with the way we had been treated. It seemed that every hour of every day one of us would simply say, 'Fuck 'em, fuck the bastards, fuck the army.'

I bought a calendar and would strike off each day to my red-letter day, 7 October 1972. Benny and JR were really jealous of the fact that I would be out, free, in just a matter of weeks. They had signed on for 22 years, but with a nine-year option, which meant that they had to stay in for at least another three years.

Don had already done nine years. Although he hated what we had been doing in Ireland, there would be no question of him quitting. He was determined to stay for the full 22 years. 'Some you win, some you lose,' he would say. 'At least there is one good thing about the work we've done here. Never in the rest of my army career will I have to do anything as shitty again.'

He would tell us, especially after a few beers, how unlucky we had been in being landed with the tasks we had been set. He had never before heard of any SAS unit being used as a regular execution squad. There had been the odd occasion, certainly, but not as a frequent and sustained policy over so many months. He had sometimes wondered where the hell the orders were coming from. He knew damned well they would not be coming from the SAS.

'Shit,' Don said when he returned one morning from making his daily early morning phone call to

Lisburn. 'It looks as though we might have some work to do. They've called me in.'

Throughout the 90 minutes Don was away the three of us feared the worst. We wondered whether it would be back to cruising the streets of Belfast or a return to the border for another poor bastard.

'They want us to go back to cruising again,' he said with disgust in his voice on his return. 'It appears that the army have done everything for now', he said 'and they want us to stir the shit again.'

'When?' I asked, knowing full well that they would want us out that night.

'Tonight.'

'Fuck,' said Benny. 'Shit and fuck.'

For the first time ever we decided to toss a coin to see which of us would have the task of shooting that night. Benny lost.

We took off as usual in the Ford Cortina, with our SMGs at the ready and the 'border special' in the glove box. We rode around for perhaps 30 minutes, not wanting to find a target. We were on the verge of calling it a day when the perfect target loomed into view, a young man walking alone in a Catholic area.

'Go on, Benny,' said Don.

'Do I have to?' Benny asked.

' 'Course you do. Orders,' said Don.

As the man approached the car, not even bothering to look at us, Benny pulled up his SMG and fired a burst of just three rounds. The man went down, hit in the legs below the knee.

I looked back at the man lying in agony on the ground. 'Good shot,' I said to Benny. 'You got him in the legs.'

'Yes, I know,' Benny said, and winked at me.

When we returned to Long Kesh we went out immediately and picked up some booze. All of us were happy that the poor bastard had lived. We had obeyed orders: we had shot someone in a Catholic ghetto; but we knew we had also saved his life. Not one of us said anything openly but throughout the time we would remain in Belfast we would not kill another man again on the streets of the city.

A few days later, on 24 August, Don was again summoned to Lisburn and received orders to go out cruising the streets once more.

Again we tossed a coin. This time I lost. I knew what I would do that night but I said nothing. We had been driving only a short while when we found someone in the Short Strand, not far from Belfast market.

Deliberately, I put my SMG on 'rapid fire', not automatic, meaning that I could fire single rounds. As the man approached I waited until the very last second before shooting him once in the left shoulder and once in the left thigh. He spun round. I could see the shock in his face before he fell to the ground. I knew he would live.

In the newspaper the following day we read that a young Catholic man had been shot and wounded in the Short Strand by four men in a car. He could not identify the men. He was in hospital recovering from his injuries which were described as 'not serious'. I read the paragraph in the paper three or four times, smiling each time, knowing I had cheated Lisburn and saved a man's life.

CHAPTER FIFTEEN

WITHIN TWO WEEKS it would be the turn of Don and me to face almost certain death in Belfast. It seemed ironic that we should both come so close to death so soon after we had made the decision that we would not be killing any more Catholics on the streets of Belfast.

Don had been advised by Lisburn that the three informers, Yvonne, Mick and John, had been in touch again and that they knew where we could trace one of the other IRA men responsible for the torture and death of young Willy Best.

On this occasion we needed no second invitation. It had been arranged through Lisburn that we would meet Mick and John at a pub on the Crumlin Road, three miles from the city centre.

We went armed with only our 9 mm Brownings, the weapons we always carried whenever we left barracks, because we had no reason to believe there would be any shooting. We arrived at the pub on an overcast September evening about nine p.m. just before dusk. As we drove into the car park, I noticed a rusty, white Vauxhall Viva van parked near the pub with a man in the driving seat. I took no notice. JR parked about ten yards away from the van.

As Don and I got out of the car on the side nearest the van we saw two men pop up from the other side of the Vauxhall Viva. They were raising guns to fire at us.

'SAS scum,' I heard one of the men shout. We knew we had only seconds to respond, to shoot them before they killed us. By shouting at us they had not only alerted us to their intentions but also provided us with an extra split second in which to respond. It was certain they knew our identity and were intent on murder. In that instant I realised it would be them or us.

Don and I were standing targets, unable to find cover before the shots would start. We went for our pistols simultaneously, automatically ripping the 'millies' from our shoulder holsters, at the same time listening for the shots we knew would be aimed to kill. Before I had my 'millie' in my hand I heard the first shots. I felt nothing and realised we stood a chance. All of these thoughts went through my mind in a second or less.

I heard two more pistol shots but realised they were coming from one man only. I fired as I brought my pistol up, hitting the gunman holding the revolver somewhere in the lower body. As the round hit home his weapon flew from his hand and he went down, falling behind the van.

I looked at the other man and could see that he was having trouble with his Thompson sub-machine gun. He was pulling frantically at the cocking lever, desperately trying to cock the weapon so that he could fire a burst at us. He didn't get off a single round. Don shot him directly through the chest and he fell backwards.

We didn't bother to wait to see what had happened or whether the gunmen were dead or alive. We knew there was at least one other man, in the van's driving seat. We had no idea whether there were others waiting in the wings. 'Let's go,' said Don, without a hint of panic in his voice.

JR had the engine of our car revving as Don and I leapt in and we drove off fast towards Belfast.

'That was a fucking set-up,' said Don. 'And the only people who knew we would be here were the people we were meant to meet, Mick and John.'

'Do we know where they're shacked up?' I asked.

'No,' said Don, 'but we know where Yvonne lives and she should know.'

Fifteen minutes later we drew up outside Yvonne's flat, leaving JR in the car while the three of us went inside.

With barely a sound, we walked up the stairs to her second floor flat and tapped on the door. I stood to one side, my 'millie' in my hand, just in case a reception committee was waiting. Yvonne opened the door and, as she did so, Don smashed it open hard, the impact knocking her to the floor. He was taking no chances.

Don picked her up roughly, taking hold of her by the scruff of the neck, and pushed her into the kitchen.

I went into the bedroom, the sitting room and the bathroom to check if anyone else was around while Benny stood guard outside the door. There was no one.

'Where are your two friends then, Yvonne?' Don asked when she had gathered her breath.

'I don't know,' she said. 'I don't know. What's all this about?'

'Come on,' said Don. 'You can't expect me to believe that. You're the boss of this little ring of informers. You must know where we can find them.'

Nothing was said of the fact that we had only just narrowly escaped with our lives. Nothing was said of the ambush. We didn't know what she knew and what she didn't know and we weren't about to tell her.

'Listen,' said Don, 'we just want to have a talk to them. We want them to do a little bit of work for us, that's all.'

'Well, why did you come pushing in here, sending me flying?' she asked.

'We thought they might be here, that's all,' he said.

Don was in no mood to be messed about. 'Listen, and listen hard,' he said, taking out his pistol. 'I'm only going to ask you this question once. Tell me where they are. I want to know and I want to know now.'

Shaking and near to tears, Yvonne gave us an address where, she said, she believed they would be holed-up, a house on the Ballymurphy estate, a staunch Catholic ghetto, much of it under the control of the IRA.

'Right. Now sit down.'

Don signalled for me to come for a chat outside the room while Benny stood guard over Yvonne. 'If she as much as moves, shoot her,' Don said to Benny. Then he said to me, 'You stay here and I'll go with JR and Benny to find the other two bastards.'

He stood silent, thinking for a moment. 'She will have to disappear. We can't risk her turning in any others. We'll come back later when we've dealt with the other two. You know what you've got to do. If Mick and John show up here while we're gone you'll have to take them out as best you can. At least they won't be able to take you by surprise. They probably think we're all dead by now. We'll be back for you later.'

I walked back into the room and looked at

Yvonne. She had sat down and seemed more relaxed, although far from happy. She looked a mess – her hair all rumpled and dressed in a pair of old jeans and a cardigan. She offered to make a cup of coffee. 'I need one,' she said, still shaking.

As she sat on the sofa opposite me I wondered how I was going to kill her. For a while, she sat staring into her coffee mug as though oblivious to me and everything that had happened in the past ten minutes. I wondered what she was thinking. Suddenly I noticed tears rolling down her face but I said nothing. Her shoulders began to shake and I could see she was sobbing uncontrollably. The coffee began to spill over the sides of the mug and she put it on the floor.

'You're going to kill me, aren't you?' she said, looking up at me, her face raw with tears and tension.

'Why do you say that?' I asked.

'Because you've got to,' she said mumbling through her tears . . . 'It makes sense . . . I know why you want the other two . . . You're finished with them . . . they could cause trouble for you and your mates.'

'What do you mean?' I asked, never taking my eyes off her.

'They tried to kill you, didn't they?' she said, not really asking a question. In those few words Yvonne revealed that she already knew about the ambush that had so nearly cost us our lives. 'That's why you came here looking for them.'

I said nothing. Yvonne calmed down and went on with her story. 'They told me they were going to take you out, all of you. They asked me to join in but I refused. I wanted nothing to do with it.'

I wondered whether she was telling the truth. I knew she had more brains than Mick and John but I thought she was talking like this to save her own skin. I just looked at her sitting in the chair, defenceless and fearful.

Then she began to go to pieces. Tears filled her eyes and she began to sob again. 'I didn't know what to do,' she sobbed. 'If I warned you then they would have done for me, you know that. Please, please, you have to believe me. I promise you that I had nothing to do with the ambush or telling Lisburn we wanted to see you. That was their idea, I promise you.'

She looked at me, her eyes pleading to be believed, begging me to have pity on her. I didn't know what the hell to do. I had never killed a woman and I didn't want to start now, yet my head told me that she had known all about the ambush. She was as guilty as the other two. If they were going to die then she, too, had to die.

I took out my 'millie' and held it in my hand, deliberately not pointing it at her. 'Listen,' I said. 'I know that we will find your two mates. Even if we don't, another unit will find them. And if we don't find them then the IRA will. And you know that they wouldn't just kill them; they would first of all spend a few days finding out what information they gave us. And you must know how the IRA get information out of traitors. Before killing them, the IRA would beat the shit out of them.'

'I know, I know,' she sobbed, her whole body shaking with fear.

I looked at her. She seemed so pathetic, so vulnerable. I didn't want to kill her. I had had enough of killing defenceless people and this was a woman. I knew I couldn't kill a woman, not in cold blood; I knew I couldn't execute her as I had done all the others. Without realising what I was saying, I told her: 'You've got one chance and only one. If you fuck off down south and never show your face in Belfast again you might save your own skin. If you ever appear here again we'll get you.'

She crawled across the room and clutched me around the knees, shaking and sobbing, trying to speak, the words incoherent. 'I'll go, I'll go,' she stammered.

I didn't want her to act like this towards me. I just wanted her to go, quickly. 'You've got two minutes to collect your gear and go. If the others come back and find you here I don't know what will happen. Two minutes.'

Yvonne got to her feet and walked into the bedroom. I watched her as she walked away from me. I didn't bother to follow. She half closed the door and that movement brought me to my senses. Suddenly, I realised what a bloody fool I had become. I had let my feelings control me, feeling sorry for this traitor just because she was a woman, like my mother, my sisters. I thought, 'What the fuck am I playing at?' and jumped up and rushed into the bedroom after her, certain that she would have a gun there. In my mind's eye I could see her standing there, the gun pointing at me, waiting for me to walk in. Then she would let me have it.

As I threw open the door, my 'millie' in my hand, I saw Yvonne, her back towards me, rummaging through a hold-all on the bed. I convinced myself she was searching for her gun.

'Get away, get away,' I yelled at her and she turned, startled. I looked at her hands. They were empty. No gun.

I went over to the hold-all and searched through it trying to find a weapon but there was none. I was being stupid, I told myself. I had panicked for no reason. And yet there was a reason, a good reason. I asked myself whether I was risking my life, and the lives of others, in letting her walk out of the flat alive.

I thought of all the poor bastards I had executed and suddenly realised that it wasn't only because Yvonne was a woman that I was acting like this but because I was fed up, ashamed, disgusted at what I had done during the past year. I knew I couldn't kill her. I no longer had the stomach for it.

I watched her stuff a few things in the hold-all, her back to me as she leaned over the bed. My pistol was still in my hand. It would be so easy; just aim and fire. It would be over in a split second. I knew that's what I should do.

But I couldn't. I began to shake and I thought of the very first time outside the shop when I had stood shaking, not knowing if I had the guts or the confidence to pull the trigger on the two men who I could remember at that moment as if it had been yesterday. 'You can't take anything,' I said to her calmly. 'Just go, fuck off now, before I change my mind.'

She looked at me, wondering whether I meant what I was telling her. I looked into her tear-soaked, red, puffy eyes. As she looked at me I knew I could not kill her, although my head told me that I should.

'I'm going,' she said, 'Thank God for you, thank God.'

She walked down the stairs wiping her eyes and I walked behind her and watched her disappear though the door, turn left and walk off down the street, turning twice to check whether I had followed her.

After she had left I closed the door and walked back upstairs to her flat to await the others. I wondered if I had done the right thing or whether I had been stupid and sentimental just because she had been a woman. I knew that if she had been a man I would have killed.

In the hour I waited I knew my army career was over. I had taken more than I could cope with; I was at the end of my tether and I didn't know what to do. I looked at my hands and they were shaking; the more I tried to hold them steady, the more they shook.

About an hour later I saw the lights of a car and

heaved a sigh of relief when it stopped outside and I recognised Don sitting in the front passenger seat, his face illuminated by the street light.

I ran down the stairs two at a time, wanting to get away from the stench of death that seemed to have infiltrated that flat, the feeling that my life in Belfast had revolved around nothing but death and killing, executing people who had no means to fight back. As I slammed the car door and we took off, I said simply, 'She's gone. We'll hear nothing of her again.'

I was pleased no one asked me what had happened.

'Did you find them?' I asked later.

'Yep,' said Don. 'We took them for a ride to the forest. They won't be any more trouble either.'

When we returned to our Long Kesh Portakabin we made a cup of coffee and sat and talked. We all knew we had been bloody lucky to escape with our lives. I looked at the faces of my mates and they seemed drained of any feeling or emotion. Like me, they too had had enough of killing. I could see that in their eyes.

I broke the silence. 'That's it for me,' I said. 'I'm not doing any more. I couldn't care a fuck what Lisburn orders. I'm finished.'

Benny looked down at the ground and nodded agreement. JR looked at Don and me and said not a word. Don took a deep breath and spoke quietly, 'I never thought I would ever say this. But I don't care now. Whatever Lisburn says I'll just say "yes", but it's over for me too. I never thought I would ever say something like that.'

I lay awake throughout that night, not trying to sleep but staring at the darkness and thinking of the awful things I had had to do. I tried to rationalise everything; tried to tell myself that I had been saving the lives of innocent people by doing away with the gunmen. Then my mind would come back to the young men we had shot on the streets of Belfast. We hadn't known whether they were innocent victims or as guilty as hell.

That idea made me think even more. Perhaps the army intelligence brass had fucked it all up. Perhaps the young men turned over to us on the border were innocent. I had just taken the word of the brass and carried out orders.

That night I asked myself a hundred times why I had obeyed those orders instead of standing up to the bastards and asking in whose name these executions were ordered; asking by what right these men could simply be gunned down and thrown into a trench; asking why professionals of the SAS had been used to do such dirty work.

I knew that we were engaged in a war with the IRA, I knew the stupid saying 'all's fair in love and war', but fighting the IRA like this – picking up people and secretly executing them – was stooping to the lowest level.

Three times I drifted off to sleep and three times I awoke, sweating and shaking, unable to evade my awful dreams. As dawn broke all I wanted to do was to get the hell out of Belfast, quit the army and go back to a life of some sanity. I wondered if Maria would still be there or whether I had changed so much that I would be unable to cope with a relationship.

The following morning no one wanted to get out of bed. I didn't know what sort of night my mates had experienced but we all looked deathly as we struggled to shave and wash, like automatons, going about our daily business not caring a damn for anything.

After trying to eat some breakfast and having drunk a few cups of tea, I announced, about eleven a.m.: 'I'm going to get fucking, roaring drunk. Anyone coming?'

'Too fucking right,' said Benny. JR got up from his

bed and Don said, 'Come on, let's go. Let's get out of this poxy place.'

The following three weeks were nothing but a round of drinking, pub crawls and more drinking. The more I drank, however, the more I had to drink because I would become morose, my head full of the gruesome sights I had been part of for nearly a year.

I had phoned the REME major in charge of the workshop at Sydenham Docks, asking for an interview. When I went to see him, I told him my name, rank and number and said that I was taking up my six-year option to quit the army in October.

He tried to persuade me to stay on, to do another three years. He talked for half an hour, telling me what a wonderful life was available for someone like me, a member of the élite SAS. He told me of the places I would probably be sent after Ireland, places in the sun.

I listened to all he said and just looked at him because the poor man had not the slightest idea about the operations I had been carrying out. Pleased with his sales pitch, the major asked, 'Well, what do you think?' There was satisfaction in his voice. 'Have I been able to persuade you to change your mind?'

'I don't think so, sir,' I said quietly. 'I don't think so.'

'Ah, well,' he continued. 'I think you are making a grave mistake. It seems such a pity for the army to lose such a valued soldier who has proved himself so capable. And you have such a good record.' He paused, then went on, 'There is one other option. If you leave now and decide to rejoin in six months you know, don't you, that you won't have to do basic training again. Think on it. Don't be too hasty.'

'Thank you, sir,' I said.

'Well, good luck then, Bruce.'

'Thank you, sir,' I repeated.

'You'll be hearing from REME records,' he said.

I signed the piece of paper showing that I was taking up the option to quit and walked out of the office. As I walked down the steps a feeling of elation, of freedom, swept over me. I took huge gulps of air. I felt as if I was walking out of jail, a free man.

During those last two weeks, when we weren't drinking to forget, I would go off alone, birdwatching. The coast of Northern Ireland was alive with different species, birds that I would never see in a lifetime of living in London. I would spend perhaps six hours a day with my binoculars, perched on some rock watching them, thinking of what had happened and what would happen now that I was leaving the army.

One afternoon the weather turned, within an hour, from a beautiful, sunny day to rolling clouds and dramatic, lashing rain that struck my face like needles. I put my head down and began walking fast along the coast road, seeking some shelter.

Suddenly, I heard a scream and looked over the wall. The waves from the Irish Sea were rolling in, crashing against the groynes, the jetties built out from the shore to control erosion and break up the waves.

Standing on one of the groynes, about 25 yards from the sea wall, were three young girls, screaming and petrified, the waves crashing around their legs. They were too afraid to move because the top of the groyne was covered in green algae and very, very slippery.

They saw me looking at them. 'Help, help' I could hear as the wind and crashing waves all but swept away their cries.

I leapt over the wall and landed on the concrete shelf leading to the sea. Something inside me told me that I just had to save them. I clambered on to the groyne and edged myself slowly along the slippery concrete, at the same time yelling to the girls to stand still and not move. The rain lashed my face and the waves rolled in, covering my knees.

When I reached the girls they were soaked to the skin from the rain, the sea spray and the waves. I realised that the only way to save them would be to take them all at one go. I knew that leaving one or two behind would risk them being swept off the groyne.

I told the eldest one, who seemed about twelve years old, to put her arms around my neck and hold on. Then I picked up the other two, putting one under each arm. They were about eight and nine years old.

I looked up to see if there was anyone else around who could help for I feared that if I lost my footing we would all fall into the waves and God knows what would have happened then. I saw a couple walking along the footpath on the other side of the sea wall but they merely looked at us and walked on, oblivious to our plight.

'Hold on, hold on,' I kept telling the girls as I shuffled sideways along the eighteen-inch wide groyne, fearful of slipping. I just knew that I had to succeed; that I had to make it back. I felt that I would be unable to save all three girls if we were swept into the sea.

I don't know how long it took, perhaps only a few minutes, but it seemed like an age. I could feel the girls desperately holding on, the one round my neck all but strangling me, the others crying and screaming with fright as each wave crashed around our legs.

With every foot we edged towards safety, the two girls under my arms began to weigh heavily and at one stage I wondered if I would have to put them down to rest for a second or so. But I couldn't risk it. I would never forgive myself if I let them go.

We reached the concrete and I put the girls down, urging them to scramble on all fours to the safety of the sea wall. Then I picked them up, one by one, and put them over the wall.

'Thanks, mister,' said the oldest girl. The others seemed too petrified to say anything.

'Now get home quick,' I said and they ran off.

Dripping wet, I arrived back at the camp an hour or so later. 'Where the fuck have you been?' Don said. 'Been for a swim?'

'Sort of,' I replied but I told them nothing more.

While I was out the lads had been told that their tour of duty in Northern Ireland was over and they would be reporting back to Hereford after two weeks' leave.

The day we left Ireland, Saturday 7 October, the *Irish Times* reported a speech made the previous evening by Ivan Cooper, the Member of Parliament for Mid-'Derry, in which he maintained that William Whitelaw, the Secretary of State for Northern Ireland, had a duty to explain 'the extent and nature of the British Army plain clothes activity in Northern Ireland, in particular that of the SAS'.

Cooper said, 'A large number of people in the north are now connecting many of the assassinations which have occurred in Belfast with the plain clothes section of the British Army, in other words the SAS.

'It is surely hypocritical of the British Government to appeal for public co-operation in trying to discover those responsible for sectarian assassinations while its own troops are involved in these cloak and dagger activities.'

There was no response from the British Government nor from the Secretary of State's office in Northern Ireland.

We passed the newspaper around, each reading it slowly, no one saying anything about the report. There was nothing to say. We, more than anyone, knew the truth.

I read those words and realised how much I had come to loathe the work I had been involved in for almost twelve months. The anger I felt for those who had devised the policy, given the authorisation, planned the abductions and ordered the executions, would come later.

At that moment I hated myself for having gone through with it for so long; hated myself for not having had the guts to refuse to carry out the executions. We had all been keen, loyal, professional soldiers who had reached the peak of our ambition by passing the tough SAS training programme and had felt nothing but pride on receiving our SAS badges and berets. In twelve months we had been reduced to hating the work, the army and those bastards in Lisburn who had remained aloof in their headquarters while ordering us to carry out despicable, cowardly acts, killing perhaps 40 people, more than twenty of them with a single bullet in the back of the head.

I felt demoralised, defeated and sick. Now all I wanted was to get the hell out of fucking Belfast. Nothing had been said about handing in my kit and I had no intention of asking anyone. That could wait for later, forever, as far as I was concerned. All I wanted to do was escape from Northern Ireland and leave behind the shit I had been through.

I phoned Maria and told her my plans. 'Phone me when you know what time you will be arriving in London', she said, 'and I'll come and meet you at the station.'

'Fantastic,' I said, hoping that she would be able to save me from the trauma I was beginning to feel. 'That would be great.'

Before she put down the phone, Maria said, 'I love you.'

At Liverpool Dock the four of us said our farewells. As I shook their hands I hoped that I would never see any of them again for that would bring back the memories I must now work to forget. We were still suffering hangovers from the piss-up the night before when we had become drunk and maudlin, sad and angry, and very close to tears of desperation. We never did meet again.

On the journey to London I sat and drank coffee and looked out of the window. I thought of a future which I hoped would be with Maria. I had no idea what I would do. I had some money saved and knew I could get a job somewhere, sometime. The career to which I thought I had dedicated my life was over for good. I was 24.

As soon as I stepped off the train with my kitbag and hold-all I saw Maria standing alone at the end of the platform, waiting for me. She seemed so happy, with a broad smile on her face, her eyes dark and searching. I dropped my bags and put my arms around her, holding her, not wanting to kiss her but just to hold her.

EPILOGUE

I MARRIED MARIA and we had two wonderful children but I was unable to cope with my memories of Northern Ireland.

All I kept from my SAS career were the badges and the General Service Medal which every other squaddie, NCO and officer receive for serving in the Province.

I tried, and failed, to hold down various jobs as my life, my every waking thought, became dominated by memories of my gruesome career with the SAS.

Alcohol took over my life. Only when I would drink myself stupid could I forget the scenes that never seemed to leave my mind – visions of executions and the killing of innocent people.

For twelve years Maria managed to put up with my heavy drinking. She knew why I drank, although I never told her what I had actually done in Northern Ireland. I didn't think it fair to ask her to share my shame and guilt.

However, I was getting worse and I knew I was

on the edge of a nervous breakdown. I feared I might start hitting her or worse still, the kids.

It was at that point that she left me and I was happy that she did. I never wanted to lose her but for her safety, and that of the children, it was better that we split. Divorce followed.

Somehow, years later, I stopped drinking but I could not control the memories and the nightmares which seemed to be getting worse, not better. I told my doctor that if he didn't help me I was fearful of killing someone.

On his advice I entered a rehabilitation and treatment centre for alcoholics and drug addicts and spent eighteen months as a resident, undergoing constant therapy. For the first time I became able to talk about my experiences in Northern Ireland; for the first time I became capable of facing the truth.

It had taken twenty years.